Flash™ MX Design for TV and Video

Flash™ MX Design for TV and Video

Janet Galore and Todd Kelsey

Wiley Publishing, Inc.

Flash™ MX Design for TV and Video

Published by
Wiley Publishing, Inc.
10475 Crosspoint Boulevard
Indianapolis, IN 46256
www.wiley.com

Copyright © 2003 by Wiley Publishing, Inc., Indianapolis, Indiana

Library of Congress Control Number: 2002110247

ISBN: 0-7645-3681-8

Manufactured in the United States of America

10 9 8 7 6 5 4 3 2 1

1K/QU/RQ/QS/IN

Published by Wiley Publishing, Inc., Indianapolis, Indiana
Published simultaneously in Canada

For Edward, my paladin. — J.

For Liz, my scientist. — T

Foreword

Since its introduction in 1997, Macromedia Flash has quickly become the standard for high-quality animation and interactivity on the Web. What used to be a tedious manual process for cel animators was revolutionized, and artists such as John Kricfalusi of *Ren and Stimpy* fame and animators at Disney Online quickly adopted Macromedia Flash as a standard. Animation in Macromedia Flash is extremely flexible with its reusable symbol library and native vector files, which scale to any resolution. What would traditionally take a team of animators and digital artists weeks to accomplish could be created in a matter of days by a single animator. Over the years, we have continued to improve upon the animation features, adding onion skinning, tweening, shape morphing, alpha transparency, and QuickTime output.

As the entertainment industry took notice of the creative raw talent that Web animators demonstrated with Macromedia Flash, a number of top Macromedia Flash animators were hired to create original content that could be broadcast both to new mediums such as the Web and also to television. Macromedia Flash has also been adopted by a number of traditional animation studios. Until now, many of the secrets to successfully taking Macromedia Flash content to broadcast have been under tight wraps. In this book, Janet Galore, Todd Kelsey, and the contributors show you how to take advantage of the flexible, streamlined production capabilities of Macromedia Flash to deliver low-cost, broadcast-quality content for television.

Hollywood beware!

Jeremy Clark
Macromedia Flash Product Designer
Macromedia

Preface

This book is about how to get Flash MX animation out to video, television, and other video-based mediums, such as DVD. We also consider the notion of *broadcast quality* and explore ways to achieve it, both technically and creatively.

Since Version 2, Macromedia Flash has had the capability to export to video. It wasn't long before people began to experiment with transferring their Web animation to videotape and many have been successful. Now the wave is building.

Flash has revolutionized animation on the Web, and now it's revolutionizing the traditional animation world. It's a tool that traditional animators are embracing to help them streamline their production process for many types of animation. So as we explore the theories and techniques of producing broadcast-quality Flash animation, we'll also get a behind-the-scenes look at cutting-edge creative and production work from both online and traditional animation studios.

Flash MX Design for TV and Video is a guide and reference that introduces the most important aspects of authoring for broadcast television in Flash MX, using current techniques and methods. After reading the book, you will have a good general understanding of how television animation is created, how to adapt that process to Flash, and the main step-by-step methods used to create television-quality Flash animation. You will also learn what pitfalls to avoid and where to find additional resources on Flash, animation, and television production.

There are two primary audiences for this book. The first is Web-based Flash animators who would like to produce animated work for television or video, and the second is traditional animators who are curious about Flash and who want to know the latest Flash production methods and techniques for broadcast.

With the exception of discussing some basic Flash theory, we consider the material we cover on Flash intermediate to advanced. Some topics, such as working with Adobe After Effects, are discussed as an overview or an introduction, as they are beyond the scope of this book but are nevertheless important to address. Other topics assume a solid working knowledge of Flash animation techniques, so we can focus on specific broadcast quality or video export issues.

Although the book is called *Flash MX Design for TV and Video*, most of the techniques we cover work for versions of Flash 5 and above. We address Flash MX–specific topics as they apply to generating broadcast-quality video.

The book is laid out in three parts: Part I, Perspective and Production, Part II, Applied Animation Techniques, and Part III, Postproduction: Working with Flash Video. These sections discuss the theory, techniques, and nitty-gritty of getting Flash out to video, respectively.

- **Part I, Perspective and Production** covers a production process for broadcast quality Flash, how to get your work to look good on a TV display, Flash capabilities and limitations for broadcast animation, visual storytelling in film and TV, and sound techniques.

- **Part II, Applied Animation Techniques** covers specific case studies from top creative animation studios who are using Flash and Flash mixed with a variety of other programs. We look at animating with digital puppets, traditional animation techniques, moveable camera techniques with Flash and Toon Boom Studio, using Flash to mix 2D and 3D in a music video, and how Flash performs when making a half-hour TV series.

- **Part III, Postproduction: Working with Flash Video** covers exporting video from Flash, titles, fades and credits, polishing and delivering Flash video, an introduction to After Effects, and cross-purposing for Web, TV, and DVD.

There are many examples of Flash in broadcast animation that we wish we could have included in this book. Some projects were just getting started as the book was being written, and some projects we weren't able to fit into the time we had. So consider this just a taste of what is happening now, and what is yet to come. Please check the book's official Web site at www.wiley.com/go/ftv to see late-breaking news, tips, downloads, and more examples. Please also check out the list of resources at the end of the book.

Not much has been written about how Flash can be used to generate broadcast quality video. We hope that you'll find this book a useful guide, and more importantly, a source of inspiration.

— Janet Galore and Todd Kelsey

Acknowledgments

From Janet:

First of all, my thanks go to Todd Kelsey, a man of much patience and good will. Without Todd, this book would not have happened. Thanks to all the contributors and their studios bold enough to share their secrets, who took time from their work because they believed this book was a good idea. Chad, Tom, Sandy, Ron, Mark, Bob, Trevor, Rob, Mauro, Christopher, Johan, Dan, Damian, John — your creativity, skill, and vision make this book worth reading. I've learned a lot from working with you.

Thank you, Mike Roney, for taking a chance on me and for doing more than your part to support my efforts. Thanks to Ken Brown, Beth Taylor, and Bob Cesca for skillful editing and attention to detail. Thanks to Steve Mack, who warned me to be careful for what I wished for. Thanks to Bob Cesca and Erik Utter for letting me pick your brains about technical details. Thanks to Eric Holma for trying to capture elusive video artifacts.

Thanks to Suzanne Grippaldi at Fox Sports Network. Thanks also to Domino Records, Faith & Hope Records, Singleton Ogilvy & Mather, Bardel Entertainment, Storytellers Productions, and Mondo Media.

On a personal note, thanks to John Atcheson for being so patient and tolerant and giving excellent advice, and to everyone at Ads.com for your encouragement and support. Thanks to Johan Liedgren and Noah Tannen for creating Honkworm and for getting me started with this whole business. Noah and Christopher, thank you for *FishBar* and your demented genius. Thanks to my family for their encouragement. And especially, thanks to Edward Galore for his helpful editing, unconditional support, friendship, and love.

From Todd:

Thanks to Janet Galore, a woman of admirable initiative, vision, and artistic conscience. Without Janet, this book would not have been the same. Thanks to Chad for hanging in there and dealing with all the e-mail traffic violations.

Mike Roney, Ken Brown, Beth Taylor — you rock.

Special thanks to Terry Gilliam and Peter Gabriel for inspiration, the folks at FutureSplash and Macromedia for the tool, and the conspirators of the Gerbil Liberation Front, who helped me get started along the path of Flash, including Jim Cooper, Ben Miranda, Andy Brase, Brian Skipworth, Nancy, Alicia, Fantasia, Mazy, and the other cats of Alunniland. Thanks also to the Detholz for helping Minivids get off the ground.

To Todd Beamer, thanks for storming the cockpit on 9/11. I didn't really know you, but now I do, and I look forward to seeing you on the other side, where I will thank you again. To Lisa Beamer and the kids, your courage is inspiration.

To Beba for *I Was Born In The Jungle.*

To Soraya, Kyungwhee, Ben, and Brian for momentum and fun.

To Howie, Bobby, Joey, and Corey for the inspiring persistence and achievement.

To mom and dad and bro for being.

Contents at a Glance

Part I

Perspective and Production

Chapter 1

Flash: Breaking Out of the Web

If you embrace the body of knowledge from traditional animation and throw in techniques from Web animation, you have the best of both worlds — streamlined production methods, shorter development cycles, lower cost, and high production values.

Over the past few years, what was once known as FutureSplash Animator has matured from a simple way to animate text on a Web page into a robust tool used by most online content developers around the world. Macromedia Flash has become the standard for animation on the Web.

Since Flash animators first figured out how to export their Flash projects to video for demo reels, more and more Flash animators have been creating work specifically designed to go out to video or TV.

The idea of using Flash for broadcast television and video unites the worlds of Web-based animation, traditional animation, and video postproduction. Talk to a postproduction house, and you may hear that delivering Flash animation to broadcast is simply a matter of getting the Flash animation out to a video format and then fixing any problems in postproduction. Talk to a Web Flash animator, and you'll probably hear that Flash can be used to create a demo reel of your online work, but what happens in postproduction is a mystery. And who has access to a high-end video-editing suite, anyway? However, more and more online and traditional animators are discovering that Flash can be a fundamental part of creating broadcast quality animation. These artists merge online and offline techniques to get amazing results.

FLASH ON TV (THE EARLY YEARS)

Flash has actually been used for several years to generate video for broadcast. Early pioneers include Flash-based cartoon shorts, such as Honkworm's *FishBar*, which ran on MTV's *Cartoon Sushi* in 1998 (1.1). It later spawned a series of shorts including

● 1.1   FishBar © Honkworm International.

FishBar: Violence of the Lambs (1.2), which was made an official selection of the 2001 Sundance Online Film Festival, and the series was syndicated on the Web by Mondo Media (1.3).

Flash is now being recognized as a legitimate authoring tool to create broadcast-quality animation. More and more studios are bringing Flash-based cartoons to television, either as standalone animations or as parts of larger works.

FLASH ON TV TODAY

Flexible, low-cost broadcast animation work is in high demand from TV networks and their advertisers, and Flash is a great way to streamline production and reduce costs, as well as to cross-purpose content. Effective production methods and techniques have evolved to help you get smoothly from your desktop to the TV set. Here are some examples of Flash on TV today.

TV COMMERCIALS

Flash is increasingly being used to create TV commercials. Companies all over the world are turning to Flash to provide a unique look and feel to their advertisements. An interesting example is a campaign of 130 spots Honkworm International and ad agency Wongdoody created for the promotion of Major League Baseball games on Fox Sports Network. The agency and the network had seen Honkworm's *FishBar* series on the Web, and were drawn to the art direction. They ended up using a similar art direction in the TV spots (1.4). See the case study in Chapter 7 for more details on this project.

Sixty40, a full-service ad agency based in Australia, (www.sixty40.com) has done a steady stream of Flash-based work, including Flash-based commercial spots that aired on television for Qantas Airlines (1.5–1.7). A case study of this project is in Chapter 9, "The Movable Camera: Flash and Toon Boom Studio."

CARTOON SHORTS

Flash-based cartoon shorts have made many television appearances, including *Thugs on Film*, by Mondo Media. *Thugs on Film* was originally animated for the Web, then adapted for broadcast with a television debut on BBC America in 2001 (1.8–1.10). Other properties developed by Mondo Media include

● 1.2   FishBar © Honkworm International.

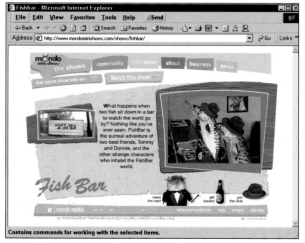

● 1.3   FishBar © Honkworm International. Mondo Mini Shows © Mondo Media. All rights reserved.

● 1.4   © Fox Sports Network

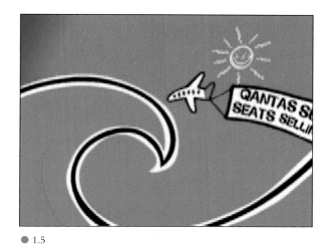

● 1.5

● 1.8

● 1.6

● 1.9

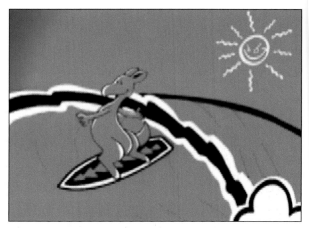

● 1.7

● 1.10

Happy Tree Friends, which has appeared on MTV (1.11), *Piki and Poko* (1.12), and *Like, News* (1.13).

MUSIC VIDEOS

Flash-based music videos are gaining popularity online, which has given rise to an increase of Flash-based music videos appearing on television. A good example is "The Second Line" video and game for the Liverpool band Clinic. The project was developed by unit9, an animation studio in London. They first created a Flash-based online game, then extended the game concept to make a music video for television distribution, which was shown on MTV in Germany (1.14–1.16).

Interview with John Evershed, President and CEO of Mondo Media

Janet Galore talked to John Evershed about taking Web properties to broadcast television.

JG: Mondo started out syndicating Web programming, but you have taken some properties to television, notably *Thugs on Film*. Did you conceive of TOF going to TV from the beginning?

JE: When we conceived of the company, we wanted to make entertainment that

can go anywhere. We made all our properties TV aspect ratio, and started looking for TV buyers right away. We don't design properties exclusively for TV — we just keep that possibility open.

JG: How big a part is TV playing in the future of Mondo Media?

JE: All entertainment companies need to sell content in as much and as many different mediums as possible. Mondo sells its properties internationally, in England, France, Germany, other European countries. TV is part of that plan.

JG: What about DVD?

JE: We're making a DVD of the *Happy Tree Friends* series. It's a good candidate for DVD because it has a strong Web following, and there are a lot of episodes that will keep people engaged over two hours.

JG: How do you decide what properties to sell to TV?

JE: We show our best Flash stuff to TV networks for consideration, shows that have a unique look and feel, like *Piki and Poko*, which has a very cool use of color that singles it out from a typical Flash look. The unusual look combined with the characters is very appealing.

TV SHOWS AND PILOTS

Flash-based full-length TV shows are now starting to be produced around the world. One of the first TV series to be animated in Flash is John Callahan's *QUADS!*. The series is co-produced by Media World Features and Canada's Nelvana Limited, and has appeared on Teletoon in Canada and SBS in Australia. It's based on the work of John Callahan, an artist whose controversial cartoons have appeared in magazines throughout North America. The animated series is a black comedy, developed in Flash by traditional animators. To see more information about *QUADS!* and a fun introduction, please visit the show's Web site at: www.animationworks.com.au/quads/intro.htm.

Another Flash cartoon series, *¡MUCHA LUCHA!*, is being produced by the Kids' WB! Network. *¡MUCHA LUCHA!* follows the story of three kids growing up in a culture of Mexican wrestling. Scheduled to debut in Fall of 2002, this will be the first Flash series to appear on a U.S. network.

Unfortunately, at the time of this writing, Kids' WB! is keeping the series under wraps and not much information is available. Please check the Flash MX Design for TV and Video Web site for new developments (www.wiley.com/go/ftv).

These two Flash series, shown on major networks, are just the first of many more to come. Meanwhile, many Web and traditional animation studios are using Flash to develop their own original programming for television.

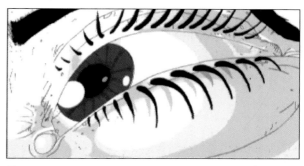
● 1.15 © Domino Record Co. Ltd.

● 1.14 © Domino Record Co. Ltd.

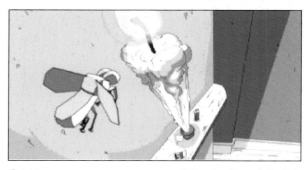
● 1.16 © Domino Record Co. Ltd.

Another series we have pitched to TV is Don Asmussen's *Like, News*. The art direction is very illustrative because Don's a cartoonist. The movement is puppet-like, and the show has a distinctive look.

We also think there's room on TV for timely animated parodies, and Flash can be a great tool for creating animation quickly, to respond to newsworthy events. For example, the *Like, News* "Al Quaeda Recruiting Video." For that we were working within the confines of Flash for the Web, but it's gotten two million show views in the last two months. Once you

have an audience that big, it translates to all sorts of syndication possibilities.

You see a lot of properties designed for the Web, and have been at the center of animated online entertainment. What are the challenges of taking Web properties to TV and film?

JE: The largest challenge is keeping up the energy level found in shorts. In a longer format, you need to blow out that world. What TV audiences want to see is that it's a world sustainable episode by episode.

JG: Do you think it's inherently difficult for Web properties to move to television?

JE: Look at *South Park*, which started out as a short, viral piece on the Web. The Internet was part of the equation in the beginning. There are tons of opportunities to start on the Web and migrate to wherever. Right now there's so much cynicism about the Web as an entertainment medium, and that cynicism is just garbage. Entertainment properties will propagate from the Web to other media — it just takes time.

● 1.17   © Camp Chaos. Camp Chaos™ is a trademark
of Camp Chaos Entertainment.

An example of a Web-based property animated in Flash successfully making the leap to television is the *Camp Chaos* TV series. It will be appearing on VH1, which has purchased eight episodes. Camp Chaos, the online entertainment company, is well-known for its Web cartoons, including *Angry Naked Pat*, *Napster Bad*, and *Monkey for President* (1.17–1.19).

Web animators are increasingly looking to television as an outlet, especially after the burst of the dot com bubble. Many Web entertainment creators are laying low, but just as many are now doing more work for TV.

Bob Cesca, president of online entertainment company Camp Chaos, says, "It used to be that the majority of hours we billed to clients was for animation delivered on the Web. Now, most of the Flash work we do is for television."

● 1.18   © Camp Chaos. Camp Chaos™ is a trademark
of Camp Chaos Entertainment.

● 1.19   © Camp Chaos. Camp Chaos™ is a trademark
of Camp Chaos Entertainment.

Think about comic books. The energy of a whole generation of kids was focused on this format of storytelling. But it took a couple of decades before that format started flowing into other media. Culturally that's where kids were, and that's where they still are. Even video games: That subculture is 10-20 years old, and just now stories from games are emerging onto the big screen (a la Laura Croft). In about 10 years, there will be a wave of game-based properties that

makes its way into long form. It's similar with the Internet. It's gonna take a while.

JG: The slow state of the Internet economy right now sure doesn't help things.

JE: True, but there's opportunity on the Web. There's a lot of creative freedom on the Net, and that's where new ideas will breed. Mondo Media has been around for 14 years, and we've seen a lot of ups and downs. We'll be here another 14 years. The networks aren't ignoring online entertainment – they're just

being more cautious. Our series *Happy Tree Friends* has aired on MTV, and has been licensed to broadcasters in Canada and Europe. And online, the series appears on ComedyCentral.com (among other sites we syndicate to). So there are opportunities to work with broadcast networks online as well as on TV.

We'll continue to sell into traditional media, to various TV partners. Another thing we have going for us is that we aren't in direct competition with the providers of kids' animation such as WB

Atomic Cartoons, a traditional and Flash animation studio in Vancouver, B.C., has developed a number of pilots for television, including *Dirty Lil' Baster* and *Dog in a Box with 2 Wheels* (co-developed by Honkworm International), among others (1.20 and 1.21).

Traditional animation companies like Atomic Cartoons are recognizing the value of Flash in the traditional animation process, as well as for individual animators. Rob Davies, co-founder of Atomic Cartoons, comments, "The beauty of Flash is that an independent animator can self-produce an animated film in his or her own basement without the involvement of a big production studio or a ton of capital investment. All an individual needs now is the Flash

● 1.20   © 2001 Atomic Cartoons

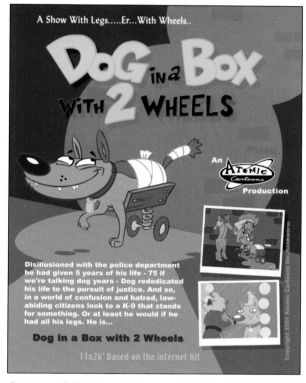

● 1.21   © 2001 Atomic Cartoons and Honkworm International

and Cartoon Network, since we're focused on an older, 18–34 year-old, demographic.

JG: Why do you think it's taken so long for Flash to be recognized as a way to create low-cost animation for TV?

JE: One reason is that the "Internet look" influenced opinions. People looked at the constraints put on Flash-based artwork and storytelling methods so it could play on the Net, and couldn't visualize how that would translate to TV, or how things could look in Flash if you didn't have those constraints.

JG: It seems that there's a prejudice on TV against properties coming from the Web.

JE: I think there is some cultural resistance. But people are starting to understand that Flash is a production tool, and in the hands of the right people it can look great. We've worked hard on creating properties that break out of the standard Flash look. Flash is a very good production tool for certain kinds of animation, but it's all about intellectual property – the quality of the content you create.

I still believe in the notion of a kid sitting in his or her bedroom, building an entertainment franchise. Joe Cartoon made his own franchise – others can, too. Look at the "Laid Off" piece by Odd Todd (www.oddtodd.com). That guy has an agent now. There's room for the individual creator to build a world. It's like being a stand-up comic — you need a willingness to practice and do things for nothing while you build your skills. Once you put something online, there's an explosive potential for something that will be seen by millions. If the story's good enough, it can go anywhere.

program, a little elbow grease, and their imagination to produce an Internet, film festival, or television-ready cartoon."

FEATURE LENGTH FILMS

We know of at least two Flash feature films currently in development. *Angry Naked Pat* is a popular Web series written by Brian Lynch, which Camp Chaos is developing into a feature-length film of the same name (1.22). With a run-time of about 80 minutes, the film will first appear in festival circuits. To see more about the series and the film, visit the Angry Naked Pat Movie site: www.angrynakedpat.com/animation/movie/index.php.

Another upcoming Flash-based film is Lil' Pimp. Created by Peter Gilstrap and Mark Brooks, the film is based on a Web series of the same name, which can

be viewed at the Media Trip Web site: (www.mediatrip.com/ent/shows/lilpimp/). The film is being distributed by Columbia Pictures in 2003, with Mark Brooks, Peter Gilstrap, William Shatner, Bernie Mac, and Jennifer Tilly contributing voices. To our knowledge, Lil' Pimp will be the first feature-length, Flash-based film.

DVD AND CROSS PURPOSING

Broadcast quality Flash has been making its way onto DVD as well, usually in conjunction with creative properties that have been developed with television in mind, but also with projects that were first released on the Web, such as a DVD release by Camp Chaos, "The Best of the Web #2" (1.23).

For those who want to deliver Flash-based content in a variety of directions, disc-based delivery methods such as DVD and CD-ROM offer interesting possibilities for cross purposing. "Gerbil Liberation Front"

● 1.22   © Camp Chaos Entertainment

● 1.23   © Camp Chaos Entertainment

(GLF), a Flash-based video project, is an example of an underground property moving into the mainstream by cross purposing on DVD, CD-ROM, Web, and e-mail (1.24, 1.25). The GLF video made an appearance in the *Macworld DVD Studio Pro Bible*, in the context of delivering a project across different media. We discuss DVD and cross-purposing options in Chapter 16, "Cross-Purposing Flash for Web, TV, and DVD."

ACCEPTANCE OF FLASH IN TRADITIONAL MEDIA

Looking at the examples, you may wonder why it's taken such a long time for Flash to break through into traditional media such as television and film. One reason is that there's been a divide between the traditional animation world and the online animation world, and not everyone in traditional media is willing to embrace Flash just yet. Fortunately, this situation is quickly changing.

The power of Flash has, in some ways, worked against it. Traditionally, animators study for years, perfecting their drawing skills one animation cel at a time. Before Flash, you couldn't be an animator without being a skilled artist, usually part of a big team of people. But Flash put the ability to animate in the hands of the individual. With the advent of Flash, newly minted Web animators could jump in and start animating without having to learn the principles of animation or develop their drawing skills. The result was a tremendous burst of creativity and animation that often fell short of being broadcast quality. Of course, this is not the case with all Web animation. Besides, Web animation does not have to

be "broadcast quality" to be successful, and many traditional techniques do not work well in the bandwidth and processor-constrained environment of the Web. However, for reasons just or unjust, Flash got a reputation in the traditional animation world (and in traditional media) as a tool that was capable of producing only sub-standard animation.

On the other hand, many folks, including the authors of this book, got into animation via Flash. Flash gives the masses a way to make objects come alive on-screen. And for some, it gives inspiration to learn how to draw, to learn how objects and living things move, and to learn how to tell a story visually. In short, Flash inspires people to become animators, which is a good thing.

In fact, some of the features of Flash that make it the perfect Web animation tool (such as libraries, inking and coloring tools, onion skinning, tweening, and scalability) are making Flash attractive to traditional animation studios. Studios using Flash in their production process are experiencing reduced development time, and a huge reduction in the cost of creating animation.

You can build libraries of art assets to reuse in Flash, and you don't need a separate drawing for every cel, so a small team of animators can get a lot done quickly. Libraries allow teams to share art and even behaviors; characters, backgrounds, and objects can be reused easily. Because everything is digital, you don't have to keep track of hundreds of thousands of acetate cels. And Flash is significantly less expensive per seat than other traditional 2D animation software, such as USAnimation, by as much as tenfold. To top it off, Flash has a unique look and feel that can be exploited or mixed with other visual styles.

● 1.24

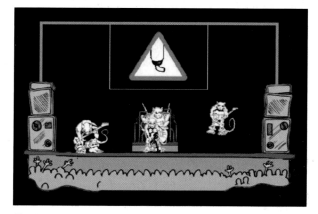

● 1.25

If you embrace the body of knowledge from traditional animation and throw in some techniques from Web animation, you have the best of both worlds—streamlined production methods, smaller teams, shorter development cycles, lower cost, and high production values.

PUSHING FLASH TO BROADCAST QUALITY

Throughout the book, we discuss the advantages and disadvantages of using Flash for broadcast animation. If you are new to Flash, understanding how Flash was designed to work, and why it works that way, is helpful in anticipating the efficiencies and pitfalls of taking Flash to TV or video.

Because it was born to create content for the Web, a key feature of Flash is that it's *object-oriented*; the building blocks of Flash are symbols and objects rather than frames or cels. Flash is all about economy of file size, which is very important when delivering on the Web, but is not an issue when delivering to video.

In traditional animation, you don't care that you have to repeat yourself. In fact, the more frames of animation you draw, the smoother the animation will be, if you know what you're doing. An economy of images or file size never outweighs the need for natural, believable movement generated by careful timing, keyframes, and in-betweening.

But with animation that's delivered over the Web, file size matters. A file that is too large means that the viewer may give up waiting around for the entire file to load and surf to another Web page. To address the file size and streaming problem, Flash stores art and assets in a library (1.26).

The symbols and other graphics from the Library are placed in keyframes, which load into the Flash animation as it's playing, instead of storing information about every single frame repeatedly. Motion between keyframes can be achieved through *motion tweening*. Motion tweening in Flash is basically the automated equivalent of a traditional animator drawing a character in a different spot in successive sheets of acetate to simulate motion. Flash becomes a powerful tool in the hands of an animator when working with multilayered, multicharacter animations, where you can control each character piece and layer separately, adjusting motion from frame to frame (1.27, 1.28).

At the same time, Flash is flexible. You can choose to ignore the Library and symbol features of Flash and draw directly into every frame without storing the art in the Library, which is fine if you export to a video format. However, this approach makes it virtually unplayable over the Web.

It turns out that a hybrid of these techniques works best for going to broadcast — taking advantage of the object-oriented nature of Flash without constraining yourself to minimizing file size.

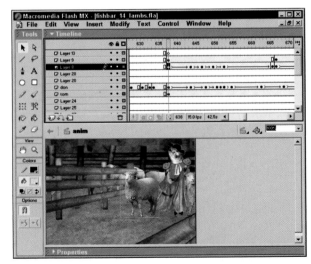

● 1.26

● 1.27

FLASH: GOOD, NOT SO GOOD

The Web-centric design of Flash has specific implications about how Flash behaves as a broadcast animation tool. Here we take a closer look at what Flash is good at, and not so good at.

Flash is good at

- **Low bitrates:** Flash has a relatively small file size due to reusing art and the object-oriented nature of symbols. When you download a Flash file from the Web, you don't download every frame, just the art and sound. Your computer does a lot of the work—keeping the frame rate in sync with the sound, doing the tweening, and so on.
- **Flexible animation methods:** Because you are working with symbols and libraries, you can easily do rough animation and work your way into the details, with the freedom to alter symbols and timing throughout the process. (Change a symbol in one place, and it changes everywhere you use the symbol.)
- **Compositing:** Layers in Flash can be used to composite art from other sources, such as bitmaps, video, or 3D.
- **Compatibility:** You can work with other illustration, animation, and video editing programs.
- **Saving money (animate once, multiple delivery vehicles):** Repurposing Flash for broadcast takes some adjustment, but you can count on reusing at least 50 percent if not 100 percent of what you produced with your art and animation budget for the Web, assuming that

delivery to TV has been considered all along in the midst of the production process. In short, the better you prepare, the more time and money you will save.

Flash is not good at

- **Handling high-resolution graphics and large sound files:** Flash has certain boundaries, which, if crossed, can lead to frequent crashing and many headaches. We show you how to avoid those problems in Chapter 4, "Flash Video Capabilities and Limitations," and throughout the book.
- **Complex techniques:** Flash is not good at native 3D, depth of field adjustments, or complex camera motion.
- **Teaching:** Flash is not good at teaching you how to animate or to draw. It gives you the ability to move objects around in a scene, but that's not the same thing as having the ability to tell a good story visually.

SO JUST WHAT IS BROADCAST QUALITY?

By definition, *broadcast quality* video conforms to specific signal standards set by the Federal Communications Commission (FCC) for on-air broadcast of commercial television. We give an overview of television broadcast formats and display issues in Chapter 3, "Working with Television Display." But people usually mean something more when they speak of video or animation as being broadcast quality.

Each person's definition tends to be slightly different. Throughout the book, we ask our contributors how they define broadcast quality, and the responses vary. When we use the term, we mean "something good enough that people would enjoy it on TV or the big screen."

This notion applies as much to the quality of the story and the artistic expression as it does to the production values. You can have the most beautiful color and sound, but the work can fall flat if the story puts you to sleep or the acting is unconvincing. Likewise, you can have a wonderful script and amazing art, but if it looks like it was made poorly, the story may not come through. Both content and production values are important, and this book covers how people are getting the best of both using Flash.

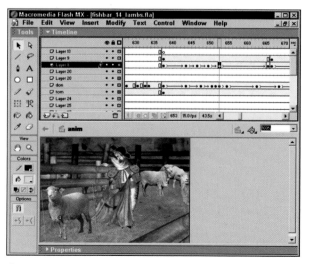

● 1.28   FishBar © Honkworm International

19

a bee flies in the scene, intrigued by
our creature.

20

22

23

Chapter 2

The Broadcast Flash Production Process

If you're prepared when you begin, the production can go very fast. The smoothness and speed of production is where you're going to save your money.

RON CROWN

In this chapter, we describe a broadcast production process used by many studios, and point out where Flash can simplify and streamline the work. Where appropriate, we note differences between traditional broadcast and Web animation processes, but we advocate a hybrid of online and offline techniques.

The use of Flash in broadcast animation varies from using Flash exclusively in a project, to simply using Flash in one step of the process, to using Flash in combination with a variety of other programs. Every studio has its own method, and even within one studio, different processes may be used for each new project, depending on the art direction, schedule, budget, team, and what cool new software has come out since the last project.

We outline a general process, based on our experience, the experience of traditional animators, and input from video production studios. The structure of this chapter follows the steps of the broadcast Flash production process, and, to a lesser extent, so does the book as a whole.

APPROACHES TO WORKFLOW

In this section, we take a look at a team structure and process we've adapted from traditional animation, video production, and Web animation.

THE BROADCAST FLASH TEAM

The organization of a team reflects the process the team uses to create an animation; as techniques vary, so does the structure of the team. Here are some of the major roles on a broadcast Flash animation team.

- **Producer:** In charge of budgeting, scheduling, day-to-day production details, licensing, and keeping the project moving smoothly.
- **Creative Director:** Has the overall vision for the project, and wrangles scriptwriters, musicians, clients, and the animation director. Often directs voice talent.
- **Animation Director:** Interprets the script, does storyboards, possibly keyframes and extreme poses, wrangles the animators, determines the timing of the animation, and often does final animation tweaks and editing. Often the creative director and animation director are the same person.
- **Artists:** Design characters, backgrounds, props, and realize the art direction as given by the creative director/animation director. Sometimes specialized production artists prepare art for the animators to use in Flash. Artists may also include special effects artists skilled in After Effects or 3D applications.
- **Animators:** Responsible for drawing and animating all the scenes based on the designs of the artists and director, they must be good actors and excellent artists themselves. More and more studios seek out traditionally trained animators who then learn Flash.
- **Writers:** Work with the directors to create the characters and story. Writers need to be familiar with the genre of the project. Writing

a three-minute short is a lot different than writing a series of half-hour TV shows.

- **Voice Talent:** Although many studios get away with amateur talent, to get good production values, hiring professional voice talent who can also act is critical. It's well worth the expense and auditioning of talent who can nail a scene in one or two takes. You also get more versatility in character types than if you do it in-house.
- **Sound Engineers:** Experienced professionals who do the audio recording, mixing, and sweetening. These people are trained to hear qualities in sound normal folks would never be aware of. The result is cleaner and more compelling sound.
- **Sound Effects Artist:** Often handled by the sound engineer or musician, having someone create custom sound effects helps bring the animation to life and adds to the story.
- **Musician/Composer:** The music may be what the animation is based on (as in a music video) or simple incidental music or a theme song at the beginning and end may be all that's needed. Either way, music raises the quality of an animation and can help tell the story.
- **Post-production technician:** This person is skilled on nonlinear video editing (NLE) systems, such as AVID, Media 100, Premiere, Final Cut Pro, or Vegas Video. He or she typically handles converting the Flash to a video format, editing, printing to video, and often also does sound sweetening.

Most studios get away with very few artists doing the animation. Traditional animation studios have more animators and more formal animation processes, because cel animation typically requires a lot more work and organization. Web-based Flash teams are streamlined, with a bare minimum of an artist/animator and sound designer. Many Flash studios don't do post-production. Instead, it is sent out for final rendering to tape. Sending it out is more expensive, but you get professional results and don't have the overhead of another person in-house.

PREPRODUCTION

Preproduction is the process of preparing to make an animation — getting all your ducks in a row. It involves strategic planning, such as locating and assigning resources, budgeting, working with the client on content and conceptual decisions, and preparing of materials. Many of the preproduction considerations for Flash-based video are borrowed from the traditional film and video process.

WHAT'S THE IDEA?

Early animations were often based on simple ideas and had enough gee-whiz factor to please the audience without being complicated or sophisticated. You might say the same thing about Web animation — putting a frog in a blender was enough to make Joe Cartoon a lot of money.

But as time goes by, people get used to a new medium and want better stories. Audiences start looking beyond the novelty of the medium. This happened long ago on television, and although a lot of shows

---

Interview with Johan Liedgren, Honkworm International.

Johan Liedgren (see Appendix E "Contributor Profiles") is the CEO and co-founder of an online entertainment studio called Honkworm International. Johan was interviewed by Janet Galore.

JG: At Honkworm, we used to have long philosophical discussions about the nature of storytelling for the Web. What are the most important things

to consider when writing a script for a series that can be on the Web and TV (assuming it would be a short)?

JL: It's always about the story — a good story told well. Long or short, humans crave stories, and we seek them out wherever we can — on the net, on television, eavesdropping on the bus, and so on. A good story, whether on TV or the Web, has a common set of elements and a structure that makes it a meaningful series of events to tell someone else. The protagonist needs to overcome some obstacle to

get to something desired and, in doing so, is taught something about life (and so are those listening).

JG: What's the difference between writing for the Web versus writing for TV?

JL: Writing stories for the Web is a craft unto itself, separate from sitcom and film writing. You can't take an existing television script and break it apart by scene into episodes, nor should you cram arthouse shorts onto a computer screen. As

on TV aren't great, the fact is that TV audiences have certain expectations about the quality of stories and content appearing on TV.

As you form the concept of your story, consider the following before diving into a script or storyboard:

- What's the story about? Write the "high concept" of the story in one sentence.
- Who are the characters, and what do they want? Are their goals and desires revealed by the story?
- Spend some time brainstorming first to define the *beats* of the animation and then work on the script. Beats can be thought of as the units of action in a scene — they are the building blocks of the narrative. Nailing down the characters and story is where the bulk of the heated debates occur among a creative team — and that's where they should occur, not during animation or post production.
- Who is the audience, and what does that imply about the nature of the characters, story, animation style, and art direction?
- Is the animation part of a series? If so, the characters and the arc of the story (how the story proceeds over time) need to have some substance. They need enough built-in structure and conflict to last over a series of episodes.
- Is the animation free form — an art piece? If it's not a traditional narrative, what are the elements of the animation that will hold it together? It's important to know the rules of storytelling before you break them.

- Who is the *buyer* or client, and what are their requirements? You may need to include specific elements in the script, certain ways to use existing characters, or a specific message that needs to be communicated.

[T I P]

Getting a network to buy a pilot is challenging. More often than not, the people with the money have already created the idea, and they want to hire you to make it come to life. But if you're pitching your own original programming, Trevor Bentley from Atomic Cartoons recommends, "Keep positive! It is a war of attrition. Keep your pitches short and to the point. They need to be clear, and if you use animation to sell the show, make it lively."

WRITING THE SCRIPT

People get into big arguments over scripts. Professional writers tell you such things as, "you need to establish all the primary conflicts in the first act and resolve them in the third act." Animators and artists usually dive into sketching out characters and storyboarding (a visual script of sorts) without a formal script and dialog. Whether it's written in words or drawn in pictures, the story is the heart of the animation.

If the project is destined for television (or even if it's not), we recommend spending the time and effort to write a formal script. Ironing out the story and dialog before you start production is one of the most

---

satisfying entertainment, Web or TV, it's about good storytelling. But on the Web, the audience is not willing to wait for the story to unfold over a long time. Web animation is not TV on your PC.

JG: What's the difference between TV and Web audiences?

JL: Look at the old television audience, those sitting down to kill one hour before going to bed. They are committed to be an audience and will zap around till it's bedtime. This is why longer stories will

work (the audience sticks around) and why TV stories can be a little more low-key. The Web audience manages several tasks at the same time. A Web story needs to hit hard, apart from being short, so you don't loose your audience to e-mail or stock quotes.

JG: How do *you* define broadcast quality?

JL: I don't. Anything worth watching on TV — a home video of a man filming himself jumping from the 70th floor of

a burning building to live another three seconds longer so he can say to his wife "I never really loved you," is watchable regardless of quality. However, it is clear that we are used to a certain quality of images and sound from watching TV the last 30 years. If you choose to show something that has a noticeably low quality, it had better be in the context of an art film, or perhaps a hard to make documentary — otherwise the audience will assume it's the clueless producer's fault.

important steps that you can take to improve the quality of your work. And, if you'll be pitching the concept to a TV network or other client, a solid script goes a long way to closing the deal and is usually required.

[T I P]

Make sure that it's clear who has final approval of the script, both internally and with the client. Those who have final approval should be involved early on, so you don't end up with major disagreements that lead to schedule slips.

For a series (Web or TV), consider writing a *bible*. This document goes into great detail on character descriptions, the world in which the story takes place (the setting), the main conflicts between the characters, samples of episode ideas, and the story arc that guides development of new episodes. The bible is like the engine that runs the whole series; it's got to have enough fuel to make the story interesting for a long time. A bible is also a handy reference to maintain consistency if you have a team of writers working on the series.

[N O T E]

An excellent reference on scriptwriting is *Alternative Scriptwriting: Writing Beyond the Rules,* by Ken Dancyger and Jeff Rush, published by Focal Press, 1995. This book runs through the traditional "rules" of storytelling and then shows you ways to have fun with them. John Kuramoto, Gary Leib, and Daniel Gray also have some great story and character tips in *The Art of Cartooning with Flash,* published by Sybex Inc., 2002.

Script Format and Timing Issues

If you're bothering to write a script, it's important to use proper script form. If you don't, you won't know how long your animation will run, and you won't be able to break the script down to give assignments to musicians, sound effects people, artists, and animators. You can find script templates for TV shows, commercials, films — you name it. The main thing is to use the industry standard for what your project is.

Professional script writing software, such as Final Draft (`www.finaldraft.com`), supports Screenplay, Stage Play, or Sit-Com standards. This type of software costs around $200 in the United States, but if you plan to write a lot and submit scripts and pilots to broadcast networks, purchasing it is probably worth it. A demo version is available for download. Final Draft includes automatic formatting for industry standard script elements, such as More and Continued (2.1). It also has customized interface elements, such as a Scene Navigator (2.2), which enables you to restructure your script interactively as you write, and additional tools to help you facilitate typical requirements such as Revisions, Scene Numbering, and Specialized Reports.

Alternatively, you can download a shareware Word template in the script format of your choice. One good choice is ScriptMaker, by Impact Pictures (`www3.sympatico.ca/mbelli/sm.htm`), for Word 2000 and later. Be sure to register and send in the fee if you use it for more than 30 days. ScriptMaker comes with an excellent help file.

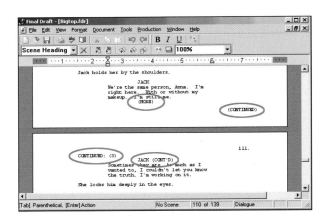

● 2.1

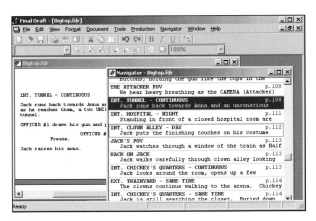

● 2.2

When working with scripts, if you use the right format and a standard writing style (not specifying every little detail and camera move, leaving some room for artistic interpretation), you can roughly gauge the timing at one minute per page (2.3).

● 2.3   FishBar © 1997–2002, Honkworm International, Inc.

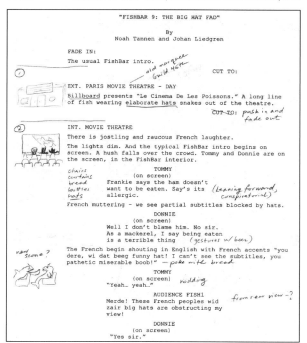

● 2.4   FishBar © 1997–2002, Honkworm International, Inc.

Using Storyboards

After you know what your story is, drawing it out in storyboards is critical to improving the production values of your animation. Storyboards (boards, for short) enable you to test drive the script and see how well it supports visual storytelling. Boards can reveal problems with the writing or story before you spend lots of time animating. Or you can find hidden brilliance — perhaps some hilarious tricks with timing you could pull, or if you just held a couple of extra beats on that character and made him roll his eyes first, the true import of the conversation would be clear.

Analyzing the Script

So how do you get from script to storyboard, if the script has come first? Here are Janet Galore's recommendations.

As soon as you have the final script in hand, read it over, visualizing or listening to different aspects, grasping the thing as a whole. Then read it aloud a couple of times and jot down notes in the margins — ideas for action and how to visually communicate what's going on (2.4).

Next, act it out, figuring out what scenes look short on paper but will actually be complex to animate or take a long time to show (for example, "The crab enters. Mayhem ensues."). Yes, really act it out. You can do an okay job at your desk, sitting down (though your co-workers will think you are losing your mind), but it's much better to get up and physically act it out in a big room. Pull in a volunteer or two to help if necessary. Then your co-workers will have confirmation you've lost it. Eventually at Honkworm people stopped staring at me when I'd jump up and practice prancing around like a drunk frog pretending to be a reindeer (which I was animating at the time). If you will be directing the voice over sessions, then this acting practice can help in that respect as well. It will not make you into an actor, but practicing will make you a better animator and director.

Finally, act it out again with a stopwatch and make final notes on timing, possible edits, alternate ideas, and trouble spots.

On a clean script, it's helpful to do a breakdown — drawing horizontal lines where the scene breaks occur; calling out where new character art is needed; identifying sets and backgrounds, props, sound effects, special effects, and so on. From this breakdown, you can create lists of art assets that need to be created.

If you skip the storyboards, you are missing out on giving yourself the opportunity to be clever. It's hard to be clever with no visual guide, animating on a deadline at 2 a.m. If you have a larger team of people working on a project, storyboards are essential to communicating the director's vision and to planning the animation.

The biggest reason to use storyboards is because without them, you'll wind up with the simplest solution to acting out a scene — not the best solution. And you'll waste a lot of time and money. Storyboards have proven critical to delivering projects on time and on budget (see Chapter 10, "Flash with 3D Applications: Making a Music Video").

Flash or pencil? It's up to you. Some studios draw storyboards directly in Flash. Most traditional studios working with Flash do the storyboards in pencil and then scan them and import them into Flash. We won't go into detail about the art of storyboarding here, but the main tasks to accomplish are

- Identifying the scenes and the actions/dialog in each scene
- Layout, composition, and camera direction for each scene

- Pacing — how fast or slow the action occurs
- Rhythm — making sure that there are variations in action, surprises, quiet parts, rhythm that reflects the rise in action of the story
- Looking for where scenes get bogged down (boring) and need to be shortened or resolved differently in the script, or similarly, in which scenes or shots might be confusing to the viewer
- Looking for where you can inject visual cleverness and meaning beyond what's in the script
- Confirming exactly what art and sound effects will be needed

Here are some examples of storyboards (and their eventual descendants) from Honkworm's *FishBar* (2.5-2.7). Storyboards don't have to be pretty; they just need to get the point across.

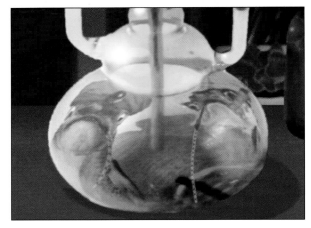

● 2.6   FishBar © 1997-2002, Honkworm International, Inc.

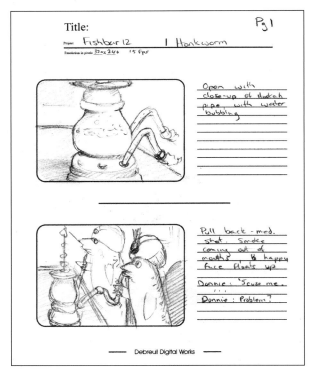

● 2.5   FishBar © 1997-2002, Honkworm International, Inc.

● 2.7   FishBar © 1997-2002, Honkworm International, Inc.

[T I P]

A classic book on storyboarding and directing is *Film Directing Shot by Shot: Visualizing from Concept to Screen*, by Steven D. Katz, published by Michael Wiese Productions, 1991. Though it deals with film technique, many of these ideas translate well to animation.

PRODUCTION

After all that planning — the script and storyboards are done, the team is hired, and the client is tapping their foot — you can finally get moving on producing the animation. The rest of the book goes into the production details, so in this discussion, we'll just give a simple overview of the steps involved.

Creating Art

Whatever the style, unless it's a very short one-off project, you'll want to create character sheets that show views of the character from each angle needed in the animation. Often a separate sheet of facial expressions is created as well as a sheet showing all the characters together and their relative sizes. Pose sheets are used to show the character in characteristic or extreme expressions (2.8 and 2.9). These sheets help to ensure that characters are drawn consistently throughout a show.

Whether the art is drawn directly into Flash or scanned in and converted to vectors, the various character sheets, pose sheets, and facial expression sheets become the building blocks of the animation.

These building blocks are usually stored in Flash libraries, ready for the animators to use.

At the same time the characters are being created, other artists and animators can get to work on the backgrounds, sets, props, and special effects. The producer or animation director usually keeps track of progress made on all art assets, and checks things off on an asset list. As with the characters, the art created at this stage can be imported directly into Flash libraries.

Of course, the process of creating the art and importing to Flash varies greatly with the art direction and tools used. The flexibility of Flash to accommodate art from various sources is surprising. A sample of animation styles you might see in Flash animation include

- Traditional keyframe animation, drawn directly in Flash, or with pencil and paper which is then scanned and imported into Flash, then inked and colored
- *Digital puppets* or photocollage style — characters and backgrounds that are created as vectors or bitmaps and then animated like puppets in Flash
- Some mix of animation composited with video (video backgrounds behind animated characters, or video characters in front of animated backgrounds)
- 3D animation, or a mix of 3D with 2D (such as 2D characters with 3D environments)
- Video converted to vectors or rotoscoped video

● 2.8   Atomic Betty © 2001, Atomic Cartoons, Inc.

● 2.9   Atomic Betty © 2001, Atomic Cartoons, Inc.

We discuss some of these art styles more in Chapters 7–11. Just remember that anything you can get into Flash can come out looking great on video, DVD, or TV.

Recording Sound and Voices

After the characters are designed and the voice talent has been hired, the dialog can be recorded. The sooner this is done, the better, because the animators can't move very far along without it. Some studios start out with a *scratch track* (placeholder soundtrack) of voices recorded in-house to use as a placeholder until the final recording is available.

[N O T E]

It's extremely rare for the animation to be created before the sound. Even Carl Stalling's perfectly synched musical scores for Warner Brothers were based off sketches, exposure sheets, and recorded "ticks" that kept the orchestra synched to the timing the animators were working with.

Some say sound makes or breaks an animation. We say this again later, but you should go for the highest-quality sound that you can afford and hire a sound engineer who knows what he or she is doing. Even if your sound design calls for a low-budget feel, it's better to get a high-quality recording and adjust it later. The combination of great voices, good acting, clever sound effects, a compelling score, and clean sound can measurably improve an animation. Likewise, sound that is lacking in quality reflects negatively on the visual storytelling.

Spending time to find the right voice talent and to rehearse is definitely worth it. If you don't have the right actor for the part, or if the actors are not familiar with the material, you'll be spending a lot more time in the recording booth than anyone wants to, and the final product will suffer.

[T I P]

Show the actors some storyboards and character designs while rehearsing. If an actor can see what huge buckteeth their horse character has, he or she can work that feature into their performance.

Along with dialog, animators sometimes use placeholder sound effects. Doing this helps with getting the action timed correctly during scenes with complex action and sound effects (for example, how an explosion looks or how a fight scene evolves). A great benefit of working in Flash is that it gives animators the freedom to be more flexible with timing than they could be with traditional cel animation.

Putting It Together — The Animatic

After the voice bed is laid down, you want to create an *animatic* (also known as a story reel or *boardamatic*). You can do this a lot of ways, but the gist is to put the storyboards together with the voice bed — like an animated slide show. Figure 2.10 is a screen shot of a storyboard imported into Flash, with the sound track. It's easy to adjust where the storyboards occur in the Timeline and to add more sketches or switch out scenes. This is the best way to get a true feel for the pacing and success of your work so far. At this step you have an opportunity to fix any problems with layout, scene changes, action sequences, and so on.

If the storyboards were done in Flash, the voice bed is simply imported and the timing is adjusted. If the storyboards were drawn in pencil, they are scanned

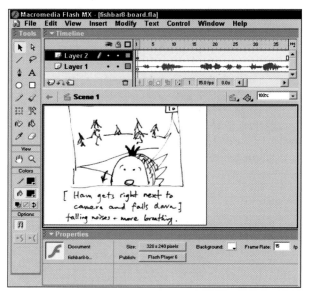

● 2.10

and placed at the appropriate place in the Timeline. If the animation is part of a series and you already have art for many characters, existing art is often used for the animatic. A convenient aspect of doing animatics in Flash is that the file size is small, so you can easily pass them around for input or approvals.

Dope Sheets

Dope sheets (also known as exposure sheets or X-sheets) are used in traditional hand-drawn animation. They help keep track of all the tens of thousands of cels that make up an animation. They also include a breakdown of the dialog as well as notes on the action, frame by frame. Dope sheets are a vital communication tool between the animation director, the animators, and the camera operator.

On a dope sheet, time runs vertically down the page by frame number. There are columns to write in the action, dialog track, and the layer numbers of the cels composing each frame (2.11). (Frames in traditional animation are composed of more than one layer of acetate, similar to the layers in Flash.)

There is also a column with "camera dial" numbers, so the camera operator can keep track of which frame he or she is shooting, and a column with frame-specific camera instructions. Every studio has a slightly different version of a dope sheet, but these elements are common to all.

When working in Flash, most animators don't use dope sheets to break down the dialog, because there's so much flexibility in timing. If you are off by a frame, no sweat — simply drag the keyframe over one frame. There's also no camera operator, and you don't have tens of thousands of cels that need to be kept in order by hand.

Nevertheless, understanding dope sheets is helpful if you work with other animation software, such as Toon Boom Studio, which uses the metaphor of a dope sheet (exposure sheet) in its interface. Any time you need to keep a strict eye on timing, the dope sheet is a tried and tested solution. Some studios working on Flash to broadcast projects with many animators do use dope sheets (see Chapter 11, "Creating a Television Series in Flash").

Visit the *Flash MX Design for TV* Web site (www. wiley.com/go/ftv) for an example of a dope sheet created in Excel that you can download.

Spend a lot of time getting the animatic right. Even though nothing is animated, the story should be clear, and the jokes should make sense. If not, you need to rearrange shots, take some out, and make some new ones. Watch it over and over and then have others watch and critique it. The shots that appear in the animatic determine all the art needed for the animation, so if a shot or scene is revised later, new art will probably need to be created. The same is true with dialog and timing — if you catch a place where things are dragging, it's much better to cut it out sooner than to spend a lot of time and money animating something that will be cut later. If a scene or transition isn't working, fix it now or forever hold your peace. Take the time to make it work, so you'll be happy with the results later on.

Refining the Animation

After the animatic is created, it can be used as a base for further refinement. Working from storyboards and dope sheets or other breakdowns, you can animate the scenes in stages.

Character art, backgrounds, sounds, and props are stored in the Library (see the "Library and Layer Organization" sidebar). Most Flash animators work on their own scene from start to finish, which is one of the major differences between Flash and traditional animation. In traditional animation, the animator draws out the keyframes, and someone else (the in-betweener) fills in the details, someone else does the inking, and someone else fills in the color,

● 2.11

so one person does not control what happens in a scene (unless it's the animation director). Changes to the plan are very expensive. In Flash, the timing and often the artwork in a scene is controlled by the animator working on that scene. If certain "Flash-friendly" animation techniques are used, changes to the scene can be made up to the last minute with little cost.

The primary method of animating characters in Flash is known widely as "digital puppetry." The idea is that characters are built with pieces from the library, which are re-used. These pieces are placed on the timeline and moved about to create the frames of animation, rather than redrawing each frame from scratch. If you use a "puppet" method to create and

animate the characters (see Chapter 7, "Working with Digital Puppets"), you can adjust the timing or the look of your art at any stage in the process. You have enormous freedom to change your mind along the way.

Library and Layer Organization

Managing assets in Flash can get challenging, especially with a team of people working on the same project. The object-oriented nature of Flash is great, but then you have to keep track of all those objects.

As you build the library, name things from general to specific, according to the pieces that make up your characters and scenes, for example, "Tommy-head-front" or "Frog-leg-left." Make alphabetizing work for you (2.12).

Keep assets organized and simply labeled if you are importing sequences of animation from another program. In that case, just use folders to organize art and layers and don't worry about naming. A new feature of Flash MX is that you can use folders to organize layers in the Timeline. Layer organization depends on how much animation you're actually doing in Flash. If you are importing animated sequences from outside Flash that contain many layers, you can now put those sequences into their own folders.

Usually characters are given their own layers, and if you have multilayered characters, folders really help to keep the Timeline organized. You can also collapse the layers in a folder to preserve screen real estate (2.13). No more scrolling forever. Other elements that can be grouped in folders include background layers, sound effects, and special effects. You can also group motion guide and masking layers in a folder with the layers they are controlling.

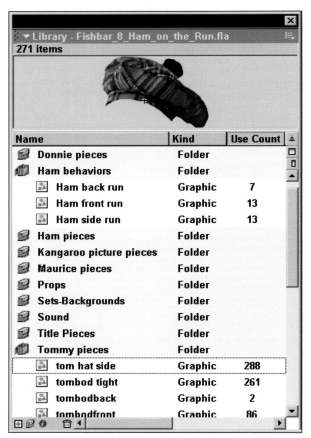

● 2.12

● 2.13

[W A R N I N G]

Digital puppets are great for the Web because they conserve file size, but if you're not careful, you'll find yourself compromising on the animation so you can re-use art. Don't fall into this trap. If you need a new angle, background, or facial expression, take the time to make it and put it in — the results are always worth it.

Refining the animation is a process of working from the general to the specific. We suggest

- Nail down the scenes, layout, and major transitions. Get the timing tight.
- Place the final backgrounds.
- Get the final character art in place for all the scenes.
- Animate the major poses and gestures.
- Work in between the main poses and get smaller gestures in.
- Put in "lip flaps" to roughly correspond to the dialog track.
- Do final lip sync.

Many studios mix animation techniques. In some scenes, digital puppets are used along with more traditional animation techniques, either straight through or pose-to-pose. Trevor Bentley from Atomic Cartoons points out, "Every show is different. We usually mix the different animation styles on any given show. It just depends on what the storyboard calls for. There's no big difference other than the time involved cleaning up traditional animation."

If you are using Flash to composite animation or video from other sources, you don't have as much flexibility with changing the artwork, but often you can still adjust the timing.

Finishing and Sweetening

When the animation is complete and as polished as possible, the Flash file is handed to the sound designer to make the final sound tweaks and add various sound effects that have not yet made their way into the animation (also known as sweetening).

This step makes a surprising difference. After spending weeks animating a piece, when you get it back and hear how much more punch it has from appropriately timed footsteps, raindrops, ambient noise, or explosions, you'll be amazed. For Web animations, obviously this step is done in Flash. If you are going out to video, the final audio sweetening may instead be done in whatever nonlinear editing program you're using. Either way works — as long as the audio imported into Flash is uncompressed at the highest quality (44 kHz, 16-bit stereo).

Optimize and Render to Video

The final step in Flash is to do quality checks across the whole animation, and through the Library, to check line quality, synching, and to clean up the project file. If the project might be repurposed later, or if it's part of a series, take the time to organize the project file; make sure the layers are not mislabled, delete unused elements in the library, and so on.

If the animation is to be published to the Web, there are many final optimizations that should be done to minimize file size. Thankfully, if you are going out to video, that step can be bypassed. Then the animation is exported to a video format, such as AVI or QuickTime, or perhaps rendered as a sequence of images, exporting the sound file separately. We discuss outputting to video in Chapter 12, "Exporting Video from Flash."

POSTPRODUCTION

After the Flash project has been rendered to video, it gets imported to your favorite non-linear video editing system for postproduction work. Postproduction for Flash video includes everything that usually goes on in the postproduction of live action video — color correction, timing tweaks, and sweetening, if necessary. Filters may be applied to keep the animation from flickering on a TV display. Special effects may be added with Adobe After Effects or other software, and if layers or scenes were created in Flash, these are brought together in Final Cut Pro, Premiere, Avid, Vegas Video, or some other non-linear editing system.

Creation of titles and credits may also be done at this point if they were not already completed in Flash. If the Flash animation was created at a lower framerate for the Web, the titles, fades, and credits should be re-rendered in post at a higher frame rate for a smoother feel.

Printing to videotape is the final step in the process. You can choose from a variety of video formats, which are discussed in Chapter 14, "Polishing and Delivering Flash Video." If you are going out to film, there's yet another step at a telecine bureau to transfer the video to film.

SUMMARY

Flash is flexible and extensible. By using a process culled from video and television production, traditional animation, and Flash animation, Flash can streamline production and blend with other applications to give broadcast-quality results.

As a reference and summary, we've included a diagram of the broadcast Flash production process that we've discussed (2.14).

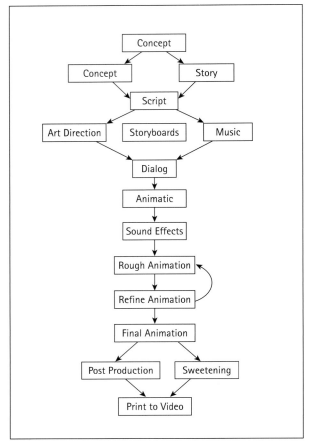

● 2.14

Chapter 3

Working with Television Display

Special thanks to Chad Fahs for primary development of this chapter.

Flash simulates reality with motion, and video simulates motion with reality.

Creating content for television requires an understanding of the medium's capabilities and limitations. How you think about video affects the way that you create and prepare content.

Viewing Flash in its native format (SWF) on a computer is pretty different from viewing the same content as video on a television screen. There are two primary differences: the way Flash or video uses graphics to represent motion, and the difference between viewing content on a computer display or a TV display.

When you go from Flash to video on a TV (or any other frame-based medium, for that matter), you are going from a format that is object-oriented and based on vector graphics to a format that is frame-oriented and based on pixels. Flash can take objects and actually move them around in a scene by using tweening. (Of course, Flash can also use keyframes.) Video and film use our persistence of vision to create the illusion of movement in a scene by flashing images rapidly in succession with small changes in each image (3.1). One way to think of this phenomena of movement is that Flash simulates *reality* with *motion*, and video simulates **motion** with *reality* (or a director's version of reality).

Flash is able to move things around in real-time because it deals primarily with objects that *can* be moved, such as vectors and symbols. Moving objects around takes up a lot less file size than showing sequences of images that change ever so slightly from image to image. It's a brilliant design, and one that

29

works great for the Web. Video comes from a long heritage starting with flipbooks, and it doesn't need to conserve file size or be cross-platform. It just needs to do a good job of showing pictures quickly and evenly.

The other difference between native Flash and video is how the content is displayed. When viewing a computer screen, you're looking at square pixels on a cathode-ray tube (CRT) or an active matrix display. The resolution is usually at least 800x600 pixels, refreshing (scanning) the whole screen from top to bottom at various rates, typically 75 times per second (or 75 Hz). If you look at video on a TV, the screen is not being refreshed from top to bottom as on the computer. You are looking at *alternating* lines being scanned at a lower resolution than on the typical computer monitor. These alternating scan lines are broken into *rectangular* pixels, and the lines of each successive image are updated with another image (on alternate lines) another $\frac{1}{60}$th (or $\frac{1}{50}$th) of a second later.

We'll get more into those details later, but what's the point we're getting at? Computer and TV displays are different. To make content that looks good on a TV, you need to have a good understanding of how to work with that display format, or else you'll get unpredictable results at best, and buzzing, twittering, low-res, bleeding, low production values at worst. In the end, your pitch to the cable network for a new cartoon series may get laughed out of the conference room if you're not careful.

UNDERSTANDING RASTER IMAGES

When you are working with an image or video editing application such as Photoshop, After Effects, or Flash, having an understanding of what kind of images you are using is very important. The most basic consideration is whether you are working with vector or raster images. In this section, we give you a crash course on raster images, which are important if you want to work with video.

We talked a bit about how video shows repeated images to create the illusion of motion. The native format for any video frame is a *raster* image. Most work in Photoshop is done with raster images, using digital photos, scanned art, or brush tools and effects.

The majority of the paint tools and effects in Photoshop are based on raster images.

The raster lines in a display are broken up into squares called *pixels* (picture element), and that's why any image composed of pixels is also a raster image. Pixels are the fundamental building blocks of a raster image, as opposed to vectors and symbols, which are the building blocks of Flash images. Raster images are also called bitmapped images. The first step in understanding television display is getting to know raster images, on the computer screen and on the television screen.

RASTER IMAGES VERSUS VECTOR IMAGES

Raster images are pixel-based, resolution dependent graphics. In contrast to vector images, raster images can't be resized according to a lossless algorithm. Vector images are based on paths and lines interpolated between given points — mathematical formulas that scale. Raster images can be very large in file size, at least in comparison to the more economical size of vector images, which simply contain enough information to determine how an image should be drawn. If you view an image at its original size, you may not be able to tell whether an image is vector or raster based (3.2). The difference can become clear if you take a close look. Although vector images can be resized without any loss in quality, raster images show significant degradation when blown up to a larger size. Viewing a raster image is like looking at a photo in a newspaper at a distance. As long as you don't use

a magnifying glass to read it, the picture appears normal. When you view it close-up, you begin to notice the dots that form the image (3.3). On the other hand, as you scale a vector image, pixels are added to preserve a smooth line, because the line is represented by a mathematical formula that draws lines between points (3.4).

Some applications, such as Flash and Photoshop, work with both raster and vector images. As we mentioned, Flash works primarily with vector images, although raster images, including JPEGs, PICTs, or PNGs, may be imported into Flash for use in an animation. Many times, illustrations are drawn or scanned into Photoshop and then exported for use in Flash. Flash also has the ability to vectorize raster images, which is one of its great features.

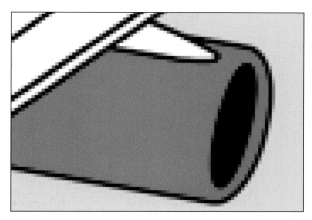

● 3.3

● 3.2

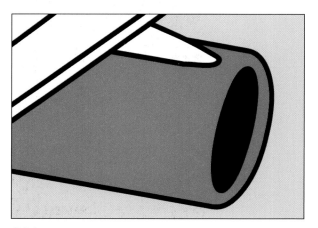

● 3.4

INDIVIDUAL FRAMES (STILL IMAGES)

Still images are defined by a few basic properties, no matter what type of image they represent. Although many of these properties also apply to images in a motion sequence, certain characteristics are unique to individual still graphics. This is especially true when it comes to file formats.

NUMBER OF PIXELS (RESOLUTION)

The size of an individual frame is measured in two dimensions — height and width. The number of pixels used to compose the height and width of an image determines the image's *resolution*. The more pixels per inch, the higher the resolution. The resolution of an image is a key factor in determining a picture's quality because having more pixels produces an increasingly lifelike effect, approaching the quality of film. In a lower-resolution image, the quality is usually blurry or pixelated (3.5), while a high-resolution image appears more like a photograph; it's crisper, with more definition (3.6).

NUMBER OF COLORS (BIT DEPTH)

Every graphic you create on a computer draws from a predefined set of distinct colors. When you have more bits of color information, you can create images that have a more lifelike appearance. The number of colors you can create and display is determined by the number of bits you can choose from to represent the colors (bit depth).

Technically speaking, *bit depth* is the number of bits used to store color information in each pixel of an image. Every pixel on a computer screen stores color information in bits and has at least 1 bit of information. The number of bits contained in a pixel relates to the number of possible colors, also known as the *color depth*. Here's how it works: A bit has two possible states (on or off); therefore, 1 bit produces two possible colors, 2-bit color allows for four possible colors, and so on (3.7).

Pixels that have a bit of two create a total of four possible color choices because it has 2 bits, and each bit has two states associated with it (2x2). Therefore, a 4-bit pixel can display a total of 16 possible colors because it contains 4 bits, two states for each bit (or 2x2x2x2). Remember that as your bit depth increases, so does your file size.

Today, most displays are capable of 24 bits, or millions of colors, using a format called RGB. RGB is based on a particular arrangement of 24-bit color. Each pixel has three color channels (red, green, and blue), with 8 bits of information per channel. The red, green, and blue color channels mix to form the color that the pixel displays.

Sometimes images are limited in number of colors due to their file formats. For example, the GIF format so prevalent on the Web is restricted to 8 bits of color information per pixel, and is therefore limited to a palette of 256 colors. The GIF format allows you to save images using lower bit depths as well, resulting in smaller color palettes and smaller file sizes, which is great for the Web.

For video, you generally want to work with images that have at least 24-bit color. There is also 32-bit color, which is 24-bit color with an extra eight bits reserved for determining the transparency of each pixel. This allows the image to have an *alpha channel*,

● 3.5

● 3.6

which is a fancy way to say that the image can have areas of transparency (for example, a transparent background).

FILE FORMAT

The overall quality of an image is sometimes determined by its file format. Many formats are available, so it is a good idea to carefully consider which one is right for a particular project:

- **TIFF:** Common format on both Mac and Windows machines. TIFF allows color depths that range from millions of colors to dithered black and white. The compression options for this format are limited to one type, although it is essentially lossless and great for maintaining the best possible quality for a photograph or other graphic. Still, TIFFs may not always be the appropriate format for your purposes because they create large file sizes that require additional storage space.

Bit Depth	Colors
1 bit	2
2 bit	4
3 bit	8
4 bit	16
5 bit	32
6 bit	64
7 bit	128
8 bit	256
16 bit	65,536
24 bit	16,777,215

1 Bit

2 Bit

3 Bit

4 Bit

5 Bit

● 3.7

- **JPEG:** Popular format for photographs that require a great deal of compression, yet still need to look good. With JPEGs, you can select the amount of compression, from 1 to 100, depending on the relative quality and file size you need. In addition, JPEGs can be created as grayscale or as color and, like TIFF, can support millions of colors. At their best, JPEGs look nearly identical to uncompressed images. However, when they are at their lowest quality setting, JPEGs can display significant pixelization and blockiness, which is a direct result of the lossy compression algorithm it employs. DCT, or Discrete Cosign Transform, is one of the techniques used to squeeze a complex image into a manageable JPEG file. Basically, it divides a picture into blocks and then applies compression to each of these sections according to a special algorithm. It's these "blocks" that sometimes cause visible distortion if they are not adequately refined, or if they appear in areas of complex shapes and patterns (diagonal lines, for example).
- **PICT:** Native to Macs, although they can be opened on PCs. PICT utilizes QuickTime codecs to assist in the compression of color and grayscale images, although it uses a generally lossless compression scheme. BMPs are the native uncompressed graphic image format for PCs. In general, they produce large file sizes on par with PICTs.
- **GIF:** Since the early days of the Internet, GIFs have been the favored file format for images transmitted in situations with limited bandwidth. Because they use only a select number of colors from a total of 256 possible choices (8-bit), GIFs are easily optimized for small file sizes. Of course, this narrow range of color limits the type of images you would want to display. For example, a photograph would look posterized with the limited color values available in the GIF format, and it is generally better to do photos in JPEG. However, GIFs are ideal for logos, clip art, and other simple graphics that do not require a wide selection of colors. They may also be used in self-contained animations (animated GIFs), which are great for rotating logos or other simple effects, because GIFs allow you to set a transparent background color.
- **Other formats:** Additional graphic formats include PNG and TGA files:

- PNG is actually the preferred format for images imported into Flash. PNGs can be 24-bit (millions of colors), with or without transparency.
- TGA, or Targa files, are a widely supported format and are often used when exporting image sequences from an NLE or 3D program for transport to another system or application. TGAs create high-quality images with millions of colors.

FRAME SEQUENCES (MOVING IMAGES)

In this chapter, we've touched upon concepts and principles that apply to individual, static images. Video is comprised of a sequence of images, or frames, and video achieves the effect of motion by rapidly displaying a *series* of *individual* images. When working with a sequence of images, then, there are new issues to consider, such as the *framerate* — and there are differences in the way that concepts such as compression relate to images when they are moving.

FRAMERATE (FPS)

Frames of video are complete images that move by at a predetermined rate. In general, NTSC video displays a new picture, or *frame*, 30 times every second. This is referred to as its framerate. Film has a framerate of 24 fps (frames per second), as compared to NTSC's 29.97 fps or PAL's 25 fps.

Typically, Flash content for the Web is delivered at 10, 12, or 15 fps. Even most video codecs for the Web use 15 fps due to bandwidth constraints.

Discrepancies in framerates cause some difficulty when attempting to convert one format to another. For example, transferring film to NTSC video requires a special technique known as *telecine*, which distributes two frames of film over three frames of video (also called 3:2 or 2:3 pull down) to compensate for different framerates (going from 24 fps to 29.97 fps). Converting content designed for the Web to video usually means that you have to convert framerates. Depending on your original framerate and the target framerate, doing so can either be simple or more complex. We'll cover this issue in Chapter 14, "Polishing and Delivering Flash Video."

FRAME SIZE (HEIGHT AND WEIGHT)

Again, make sure to consider the height and width of frames you are creating. As part of a sequence, there are usually fewer options for frame size because dimensions are often dictated by the particular video standard you are using, whether NTSC, PAL, or SECAM.

Like individual images, pixel dimensions designate the frame size. Frames with better resolution (more pixels) are higher quality and produce a more satisfying image. Television frames are composed of horizontal and vertical lines that determine its resolution. Later in this chapter, we discuss the importance of these lines.

NUMBER OF COLORS (BIT DEPTH)

As discussed earlier, every image on a computer has a set bit depth and maximum color resolution. This also holds true for video on a television set, however, an added dimension of color sampling occurs over time. This color sampling is derived from a ratio between the chrominance and luminance in a frame of video. 4:2:2 is a common ratio for broadcast video, which means four samples of luminance are taken for every two samples of color information. The higher the ratio numbers are, the better color and image reproduction you can expect. DV, or Digital Video, is generally measured at a ratio of 4:1:1. Therefore, less color information is in a frame of DV than is in a corresponding frame of a format such as Betacam SP, which uses a ratio of 4:2:2.

In addition to color sampling, you should consider the relative bit depth of video, as compared with still images. Both 8-bit and 10-bit versions are available, and the choice may significantly affect the output of your pictures. The majority of video (particularly consumer-level) is created at 8-bit, which samples 256 possible values for each pixel each second. However, 10-bit video samples 1,024 levels each second, producing a dramatic increase in the amount of information per frame. You'll notice the difference with 8-bit color when you are looking at fine gradations — the lack of information will often cause a *banding*, where you see distinct stripes when one color is blending into different shades, rather than a subtle, fine blend. Although you need special hardware cards to use 10-bit video, doing so can be worthwhile if you are creating graphics for high-resolution productions. This might include applications such as video that will be printed to file, and in this case the 10-bit video would be appropriate because it provides the capability of reproducing finer details.

FILE FORMAT

Computers can use a variety of file formats to store video information, such as Apple's QuickTime or the standard Windows AVI format. All formats incorporate a sequence of individual video frames within the file, which a computer displays at a chosen framerate to display the images:

- **QuickTime:** Video file format created by Apple that displays movie clips at scalable resolutions and framerates. Although the stand-alone QuickTime player is useful for viewing clips locally on your computer, a browser plug-in is also available for viewing QuickTime content through Web browsers such as Netscape or Internet Explorer. Web-based QuickTime content can include progressive downloads, where either a portion of the file or the entire file needs to download in order for the user to experience it, or it may be streaming QuickTime, where the audience sees the content in real-time as it streams from the Internet.
- **AVI:** Video file format created for PCs running the Windows operating system. Although this format is the native format for PCs, it can also be created and viewed on Macs. In many ways, AVI is similar to QuickTime. However, although many media creators prefer the flexibility and quality of QuickTime, AVI is so ubiquitous (thanks to the dominance of Microsoft) that it should not be overlooked. Later in the book, we discuss the pros and cons of AVI versus QT in Flash. A lot of people who work primarily with Macs still have a PC around to merge their Flash files into AVIs.
- **MPEG (Motion Picture Experts Group):** Video format used for CD-ROM, DVD, and the Web. Many people have encountered MPEG thanks to DVD videos, which use the higher-quality MPEG-2 format that produces broadcast

resolution images with stunning results. MPEG-1 is the precursor to this format, although it produces frame sizes at about half that of MPEG-2 and with lower-quality compression, due to its restricted bitrate. It has been used for larger video files on the Web, kiosks, and interactive content in Macromedia Director or on Video CDs. MPEG-4 is a new emerging standard that is starting to get used on the Web and other applications, such as wireless devices and broadband networks. MPEG-4 is intended to pack relatively good quality in extremely small file sizes to allow for efficient video streaming where bandwidth is a significant consideration (example: mobile devices such as video-capable cellphones). For more information on MPEG-4, visit the MPEG-4 Industry Forum (`www.m4if.org`) or the MPEG Web site (`http://mpeg.telecomitalialab.com`).

COMPRESSION CODECS

Video files on the computer require a large amount of storage space and a lot of bandwidth for proper playback. To confront these limitations, *codecs* (short for compressor-decompressor) are used to reduce file sizes and constrain bit rates. Uncompressed video can demand over 30MB per second, which is clearly unacceptable for most applications at this time, particularly in Web-based situations. The demanding nature is also a factor when *capturing* uncompressed video, a situation which ordinarily requires fast hardware and lots of storage to prevent dropped frames and create smooth playback.

Many of the newer codecs and formats (such as MPEG) use a combination of intraframe and interframe compression to squeeze video files. Intraframe compression refers to the compression within a single frame of video. These single frames are then used as keyframes, from which interframes are derived. Although *intraframes* are compressed apart from any other frame, *interframes* use surrounding frames as a reference to reduce the amount of information they need to display. This compression between frames of video stores only the details that have changed. For example, instead of storing all the details of someone's face and body for every frame, you can just compress the parts that move — their lips, for example.

Difficulties arise when a lot of unpredictable motion or artifacts are in your source video. If you use interframe compression, changes may be hard to predict if your video has excessive static or complex patterns that constantly change. Watch out for jerky camera motions, moving water, and low light situations that produce grain. In general, using a tripod and keeping your backgrounds simple can avoid many of these problems. Of course, if you are creating digital images solely on a computer, they should already be free of any irregular "noise" that may affect compression. Still, watching rapid shifts in colors or motion is important if you want to achieve optimal quality from your compression.

Sorenson

Sorenson is a QuickTime codec, developed primarily for disc and Web applications. This codec is the most popular choice for CD-ROM and the Internet because it produces an excellent compromise between good-quality video and small file sizes. Along with Cinepak, Sorenson relies on keyframe information (intraframes) and temporal compression (interframes) to produce these economical file sizes.

The native codec in Flash MX is Sorenson Spark, which differs somewhat from the standard Sorenson. The Spark codec is customized and integrated into Flash MX, designed specifically to compress video that will be used as a part of Flash projects. Sorenson also offers Sorenson Squeeze as an upgrade for Flash MX users. It comes with a suite of advanced compression tools, including a Pro version of the Sorenson Spark codec. For more information, see Chapter 4, "Flash Video Capabilites and Limitations," or visit www.macromedia.com/macromedia/proom/pr/2002/flash_mx_video.html or www.sorenson.com/content.php?pageID=35&id=16&nav=7.

Cinepak

Cinepak is an older QuickTime codec that was once the standard for CD-ROM delivery of video content. It was optimized to playback on 1x and 2x CD-ROM drives. The quality of Cinepak is questionable, particularly when we have better codecs available for use. More recently, Sorenson has replaced Cinepak as the default codec for video clips.

All the codecs we have mentioned here use *lossy* compression, meaning that information is thrown away to reduce the file size of a clip. The amount of information that is discarded depends on the specific codec and the amount of compression applied. Although file sizes are kept small, a drop in quality may be noticeable when compared to the original source material. *Lossless* codecs, on the other hand, reduce the file size for video without affecting the quality in any way. They can reassemble a file without getting rid of any bits of information. Most high-quality formats and codecs that are used today (DV or MPEG-2) are lossy, however, they are usually very good, and the sacrifice in quality is barely noticeable — at least when the source material is prepared properly.

[CROSS-REFERENCE]

For more information on video compression, check out Steve Mack's *Streaming Media Bible* from Wiley, Inc. Another good source can be found at www.nwfusion.com/research/streaming.html.

In a Flash to video project, a solid understanding of how video codecs work in the software you use can help you get the highest quality possible. Another aspect to consider is where and how the video will be broadcast.

BROADCAST STANDARDS

Depending on where you are located in the world or who your potential audience may be, broadcast standards are going to play a crucial role. Most likely, you are already aware of the particular television system that you are using (3.8). But at some point you may want to create content that can be delivered through a different broadcast standard, and it will help to consider the differences between the various systems, such as NTSC, PAL, or SECAM.

Note that, aside from such broadcast standards as NTSC and PAL, you can use other formats to transmit video information. One of the most common

Broadcast Format	Countries	Horizontal Lines	Frame Rate
NTSC	USA, Canada, Japan Korea, Mexico	525 lines	29.97 fps
PAL	Austarlia, China Most of Europe, South America	625 lines	25 fps
SECAM	France, Middle East, much of Africa	625 Lines	25 fps

● 3.8

formats in use today is DV, which involves both a file format, specified as DV-NTSC or DV-25, and a tape format, such as Mini-DV. Since its introduction into the consumer marketplace, DV, or digital video, has managed to exceed expectations (previously set by SVHS and Hi-8 formats) for a high-quality, low-cost acquisition medium.

DV (generally recorded onto Mini-DV tapes) is often used in the context of consumer devices, but there is a higher-quality version of DV called DVCAM, introduced by Sony, which is increasingly being used in broadcast situations as a lower-cost alternative to traditional analog tape formats, such as Betacam SP and the higher-priced digital broadcast tape formats.

NTSC

NTSC (National Television Standards Commission) has a standard aspect ratio of 4:3 and a pixel aspect ratio of 720x480 rectangular pixels. It uses 525 scan lines that refresh at 60 Hz (60 times per second), with a framerate of 29.97 fps. The nearly 30 fps framerate creates stable images without much flicker, and the amount of picture noise is noticeably better than other broadcast standards. NTSC is limited to use in the United States and its territories, along with Canada and Japan.

PAL

PAL (Phase Alternating Line) has a standard aspect ratio of 4:3 and a pixel aspect ratio of 720x576 rectangular pixels. It uses 625 scan lines, which operate at 50 Hz. The framerate is 25 fps. Because it contains more information per frame (greater resolution) and its framerate is nearly 24 fps, some professionals prefer this system when shooting video that is intended for transfer to film. However, the lower framerate can cause a noticeable flicker as compared with NTSC. In addition, the signal to noise ratio is lower and is not as good as NTSC. Still, PAL has a wider luminance signal than NTSC, which allows for a slightly sharper picture. In addition, the gamma ratio is higher, creating higher contrast levels than those available with NTSC.

SECAM

SECAM (Sequential Couleur Avec Memoire) is used in France, Russia, Tahiti, and a few countries in the Middle East. It has the same number of scan lines as PAL but transmits color information differently. The aspect ratio is a standard 4:3, with a pixel aspect ratio of 720x576 rectangular pixels. It uses 625 scan lines at 50 Hz, with a framerate of 25 fps, both identical to PAL. SECAM is primarily a broadcast format, and it is not often used for home video purposes. Even countries that use SECAM often rely on PAL in other situations because the two standards are so similar. For example, television programs are broadcast in the SECAM format, but PAL DVDs and videos are often played in the home. One benefit of SECAM over PAL is its slightly improved color accuracy.

HDTV

HDTV has an aspect ratio of 5.33:3 or 16x9 (16:9). In general, it uses 1,125 scan lines operating at 60 Hz, with a framerate of 30 fps. Aside from its greatly increased resolution and widescreen aspect ratio, HDTV has square pixels, which are much smaller than NTSC pixels. Other formats also exist within the specification for HDTV, with varying resolutions and framerates, including 1080 24p, 1080 23.976p, and 720p.

TELEVISION DISPLAY CHARACTERISTICS

Exporting a Flash movie to a video format on your computer is only part of the story. Aspects of how those electron guns shoot out an image to a TV screen affect how good or bad your Flash content looks in someone's living room. If you haven't designed for a TV display, you're at the mercy of how well your computer-generated digital content works in an analog world.

SCAN LINES AND INTERLACING

Every video signal is composed of horizontal and vertical lines that build each frame. The way these lines are transmitted and displayed on-screen can be understood if you are familiar with the concepts of scan lines and interlaced frames.

A frame of video may be either interlaced or progressive. When a frame is interlaced, the odd-number horizontal scan lines are drawn first and then the even-number lines (or vice versa). Therefore, every frame is divided in half, or into fields. Every interlaced frame is composed of two fields, with odd- or even-number lines (1, 3, 5 or 2, 4, 6, and so on). For example, interlaced video with a framerate of 30 fps contains 60 fields per second (3.9).

On the other hand, video frames that are completely drawn in one pass are called progressive frames. (This is how a computer monitor displays images.) Progressive frames have a more film-like appearance and look better when exported as stills, because all the video information for a frame is self-contained and is not spread across two fields.

The *scan rate* for an analog video signal refers to the amount of time it takes to draw lines of information on the screen. The horizontal scan rate is referenced in Hertz (or cycle per second), which directly relates to the number of lines painted onto the screen in one second's time. The horizontal scan rate of NTSC is 15,750 Hz, or 15,750 horizontal lines per second. The faster the scan rate, the less flicker you see on-screen.

[N O T E]

The horizontal scan rate should not be confused with the *refresh* rate for video, which refers to how many times the screen can be redrawn per second. As mentioned earlier, the refresh rate for NTSC is 60 Hz, or 60 fields per second.

If you display content from TV (or interlaced video) on a computer, because of the way analog TV scans interlaced images onto the screen, artifacts from interlacing can be noticeable. Figure 3.10 shows the effects of interlacing on a video image shown on a computer (progressive display). This figure helps illustrate that images displayed on interlaced video are inherently different from images created or displayed on a computer. Because we are discussing Flash content generated on a computer, we need to keep this in mind when going the other way, from the computer to interlaced video or TV.

If you televise content that was created on a computer with vector graphics, you may be setting yourself up for a lot of twittering and jittering lines. Lines that seem to vibrate can indicate that the edges of your images are too crisp or sharp. This problem can sometimes even create an audio buzz caused by *hot* edges and artifacts bleeding into the audio channel. Some horizontal lines can appear to flicker in and out on video because they are located along a particular scan line, which is only displayed every other field.

Of course, there are certain steps you can take to prevent these problems. One of the most useful solutions is to avoid horizontal lines that are less than two pixels wide. This can be avoided early on while you are creating your designs. In addition, your text should be large enough to avoid areas with these small lines. For example, choose a font size that is at least 18 points or larger. Also, it is advisable to use sans-serif fonts that do not contain complex edges and feet.

A good method for reducing jagged and jittering edges is by anti-aliasing or slightly blurring any graphics that go from black to white along a crisp edge, as in the before and after example (3.11, 3.12). Besides helping with interlacing artifacts, blurring sharp edges helps prevent artifacts created by the nature of the analog TV signal. The analog signal cannot easily jump from one pixel color to a very different color and has to ramp up from white to black or vice-versa. If it tries to jump from one to the other in the space of one pixel, it will freak out and *overshoot,* creating artifacts, twittering, or other problems.

● 3.10

● 3.9

[N O T E]

Newer HDTV sets and digital displays scan progressively (twice as fast, so a whole frame is scanned in ¹/₆₀th of a second) and do not have the same problems as regular NSTC, which scans alternate lines.

PIXEL FACTORS

Those little blocks, known as pixels, that form the basis of all our raster images have unique properties that can affect the way you produce and display video.

Pixel Aspect Ratios

Individual pixels have properties similar to the complete frames from which they are derived. When referring to pixels for video, it is acceptable to think of a pixel's height as the same size as the height of a horizontal scan line. By the same measurement, the width of a video pixel would be equal to the size of a vertical scan line. However, the width of a pixel in Photoshop doesn't translate directly to the TV screen. In fact, images created on a computer differ somewhat from those displayed on a television.

Square Versus Non-Square Pixels

NTSC has an aspect ratio of 4:3 (4 units wide by 3 units tall, or 1.33333:1) and a pixel resolution of

720x480. However, if you divide the horizontal resolution by the vertical resolution, it comes out to a ratio of 1.5:1. What's going on here? The answer is, NTSC has rectangular, or *non-square*, pixels (3.13), which are a little taller than they are wide. This differs from ordinary raster images created with square pixels in an application like Photoshop. Of course, the problem comes when we try to work with square pixel images that are intended for a non-square pixel display.

In square pixels, an aspect ratio of 4:3 for TV is 720x540. If you create projects at 720x540 and go out to video, you want to make sure that the program you are using preserves the correct aspect ratio (4:3)

● 3.12

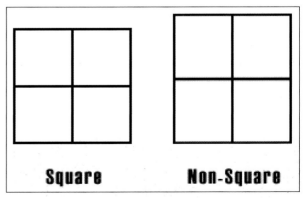

Square   Non-Square

● 3.13

● 3.11

while converting to rectangular pixels for output to video. This preparation can also be accomplished manually by resizing an unconstrained image created with square pixels from 720x540 pixels to 720x480 pixels (3.14).

FRAME FACTORS

As we mentioned earlier, frames are screens that present a complete video image. These frames are then placed in sequences to create the illusion of motion. Apart from the considerations we have already discussed, it is worthwhile to mention a few other factors that may impact the presentation of your frames. To begin with, you should understand the difference between composite and component video.

Composite video combines the *luminance* and *chrominance* information into one signal, so that it can pass through a single cable into your TV. Luminance is the portion of a video signal that carries brightness information, while chrominance is the portion of a video signal that represents hue and saturation.

Combining luminance and chrominance may simplify the transmission of video information, but it introduces potential problems because chroma and luma are sharing the same signal path. One problem is *dot crawl*, or lines of continually moving dots caused by poor separation of chrominance and luminance information. Component video, on the other hand, separates all the chrominance information into its three parts — red, green, and blue. Even though luminance information is also carried with these signals, component video represents the ideal for high quality TV display, eliminating many problems associated with composite signals, such as dot crawl.

Moiré patterns are another problem that can occur in television display, particularly with composite signals. These cross-hatch patterns of distortion appear in areas with fine detail, sometimes introducing rainbow-like colors that were never in the original image (3.15). This is why television newscasters never wear finely striped or checkered shirts.

Another factor to avoid is *cross-colors*, or overlapping patterns, that tend to confuse an analog video signal. This problem derives from fine patterns of similar color, which cause the chrominance and luminance elements of composite signals to leak into each other. The limited bandwidth of a composite signal causes luminance information to be interpreted as color. A *comb filter* can be applied to help separate the signals and compensate for minor variations in color. Comb filters are an essential part of a TV's composite input. They perform an important function, although they often degrade one part of a signal while improving another. If you are using Y/C, or S-Video inputs, then you won't have to worry about using a comb filter, because luminance and chrominance information is already separated.

Next to color and brightness information, the relative size of a frame is an important element to consider.

Aspect Ratios

The aspect ratio for a standard TV is 4:3, which has also become the preferred aspect ratio for most Web animation. HDTV has an aspect ratio of 5.33:3, or 16:9. What brought about this difference in aspect ratios? In the early days of film, many movies were shot and projected at an aspect ratio of approximately 4:3. When television was invented, it attempted to re-create the look of a movie screen for the home. Eventually, film producers decided that they should establish a unique look for movies, to set them apart from the every day features of television. Widescreen formats of all varieties were created, producing the "cinematic" look we've come to expect today (3.16). HDTV was developed to closely approximate a film look, both in its aspect ratio and in its ability to present high-resolution, progressive scan images. Ultimately, the choice of a 16:9 aspect ratio for

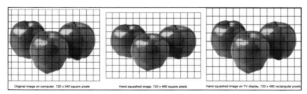

Original image on computer. 720 x 540 square pixels   Hand squashed image. 720 x 480 square pixels   Hand squashed image on TV display. 720 x 480 rectangular pixels

● 3.14

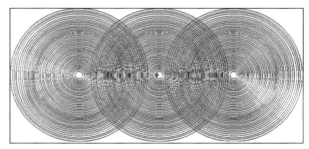

● 3.15

HDTV was a compromise between the various widescreen formats and technical requirements.

Anamorphic and Widescreen Video

Until recently, standard TV images have always been presented with an aspect ratio of 4:3. With the arrival of HDTV systems and 16:9 displays, widescreen video has finally become a practical option.

Widescreen video is more of a generic term that refers to either *anamorphic* video based on a standard definition signal, or HDTV content created for 16:9 displays. (Anamorphic video is video that is compressed and appears in original 16:9 format on widescreen televisions but would appear squeezed on regular 4:3 televisions.) Of course, there is also a characteristic "letterbox" look associated with widescreen video, and this look can be achieved by either cropping the top and bottom of standard video, or scaling 16:9 video down to fit onto a 4:3 frame.

Although standard 4:3 video may be confined to a fixed ratio, the actual frame can be stretched for a 16:9 display. Under normal circumstances, presenting a 4:3 image on a 16:9 screen would create a greatly distorted picture. However, it is possible to create images for a 4:3 signal with the intention of stretching it for a 16:9 display. You can do this by creating your content at the desired aspect ratio (for example, 864x486 pixels) then resizing it back to the size of a standard frame (720x480 pixels). When it is viewed on a 16:9 display, it automatically stretches to fill the space and is once again returned to its original aspect ratio. This is the basic concept for anamorphic video.

CRITICAL PRODUCTION ISSUES

As first and final considerations for any project, production issues address general concerns that may affect the performance of your project. These are issues that have the potential to significantly affect the quality and reception of your video program.

TITLE AND ACTION SAFE ZONES

For the most part, images that you create on a computer can be viewed exactly as you intend them until they are exported for playback on a TV, when you may notice minor differences, particularly as it pertains to the edges of your frames. Although the framing for all your movies may be correct on your computer monitor, they are going to look different when subjected to the limitations of a traditional TV screen, which actually displays less of an image than is present in the original signal. The amount that a display cuts off an image is referred to as the overscan. On some TVs, the cropping of your edges may be quite dramatic, while on others it is only slightly noticeable. In any case, it is important to design within established boundaries, which define areas that are safe for most action in your frame (action safe) and areas that are safe for any text or titles you may add (title safe).

Action safe for NTSC/PAL and other analog signals is generally agreed to be 90 percent of the screen (approximately 5 percent from each side), and title

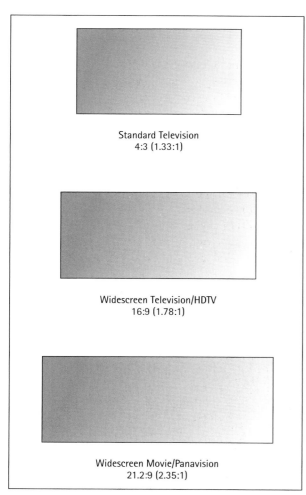

Standard Television
4:3 (1.33:1)

Widescreen Television/HDTV
16:9 (1.78:1)

Widescreen Movie/Panavision
21.2:9 (2.35:1)

● 3.16

safe is generally agreed to be 80 percent of the screen (about 10 percent off each side). These measurements are conservative, and some specifications for digital TVs that don't overscan as much are less conservative, because they operate differently and do not alter your original signal to the same degree.

Applications that are used for the creation or editing of video may include a built-in guide to assist in determining the title and action safe areas of a screen. For example, After Effects includes a guide that can be accessed at the bottom of a Composition window (3.17). By clicking on the guide icon, an image delineating the safe zones is overlayed on your video (3.18).

This guide feature is extremely useful when positioning critical elements, such as text, in your composition. It's suggested that you make use of this feature as often as possible to avoid potential problems. Imagine presenting a client with an animation in which part of their logo is cut off at the edge of the television screen. A little planning ahead of time can help you to avoid such a situation.

Working with Guide Layers in Flash

Using guide layers with Flash is essentially identical to working with guides in After Effects or other applications. The only difference is that you need to manually create or import a guide layer and then add it to your movie. After the file that is destined to be a guide layer has been imported, in can be converted into a guide layer by right-clicking the layer and choosing the Guide option (3.19, 3.20). Guide layers are not exported as part of your movie, so you don't have to worry about the guides appearing in the final render.

[N O T E]

You can download action and title safe Flash guides for popular video dimensions at the Flash MX Design for TV Web site, www.wiley.com/go/ftv.

TELEVISION SAFE COLOR

When working with colors in an image editing application, such as Photoshop, you are manipulating

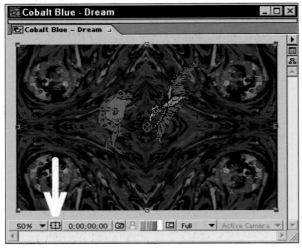

● 3.17

● 3.18

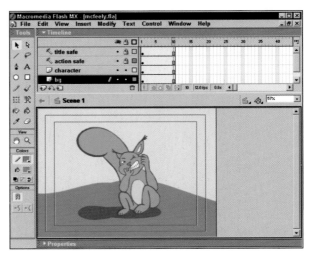

● 3.19

pure color values (RGB 0-255) that have been defined for high-resolution displays like computer monitors. Televisions, on the other hand, can only display a limited range of colors. This relatively narrow range of color causes complications when the display is fed a signal with values outside of its normal range. The results are easily spotted by the blown-out, blooming, or bleeding areas of color. In addition, each video standard has its own working range of colors, or *gamut*, from which these colors are drawn.

In Figure 3.21, the diagrams show the color gamuts for NTSC (A); PAL/SECAM (or European Broadcasting Union, EBU) (B) are indicated by triangles, showing their limited ranges within the larger RGB color space (C). You can see that there are many colors that are out of the legal color gamut for NTSC or PAL.

To avoid problems with television displays, keep all RGB color values between 16 and 235. Pure black has an RGB value of 16-16-16, versus the normal 0-0-0 value. Pure white color for NTSC television should be defined as 235-235-235, instead of the usual 255-255-255.

If you are working with stills, you can use the Levels control in Photoshop to adjust the color levels accordingly.

Photoshop

Working with television-safe colors is not difficult if you plan ahead. For example, when working with

Frame size 720x540

Action Safe 648x486   Title Safe 576x432

Images generated by efg's Computer Lab,
www.efg2.com/lab/

Photoshop, you can restrict the type of colors that you use in your projects in a couple of ways.

The first method involves setting up the color profile for your project. By doing this, you can concentrate on creating your images and not worry about choosing the correct color values:

1. Open Photoshop and create an image at the correct dimensions for your project. Start by creating a document that is 720x540 pixels (3.22), which is resized to 720x480 when you are ready to export.
2. Choose Edit→Color Settings (3.23) and then select on the Advanced Mode check box.

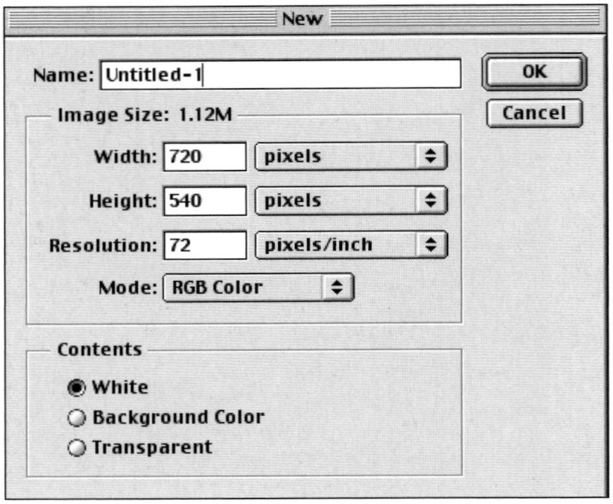

3.22

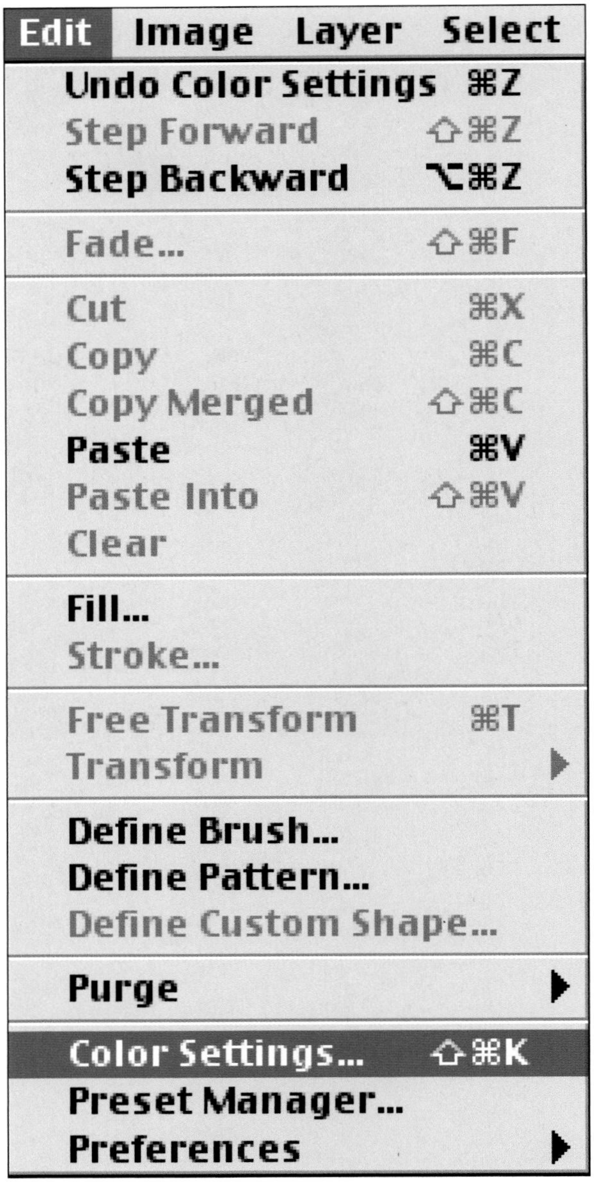

3.23

3. Under Working Spaces, select SMPTE-C for the RGB value then click OK (3.24).
4. Next, choose View➔Gamut Warning (3.25). With this option, any colors that are not safe for video should be grayed-out in the Color Picker.

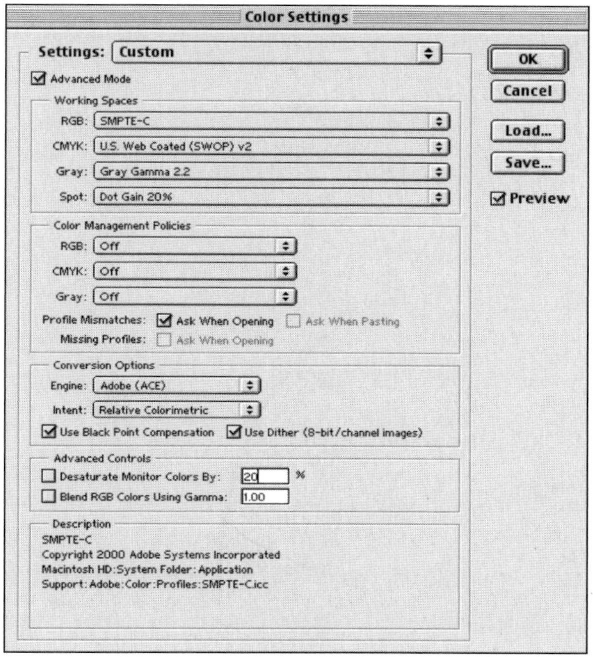

● 3.24

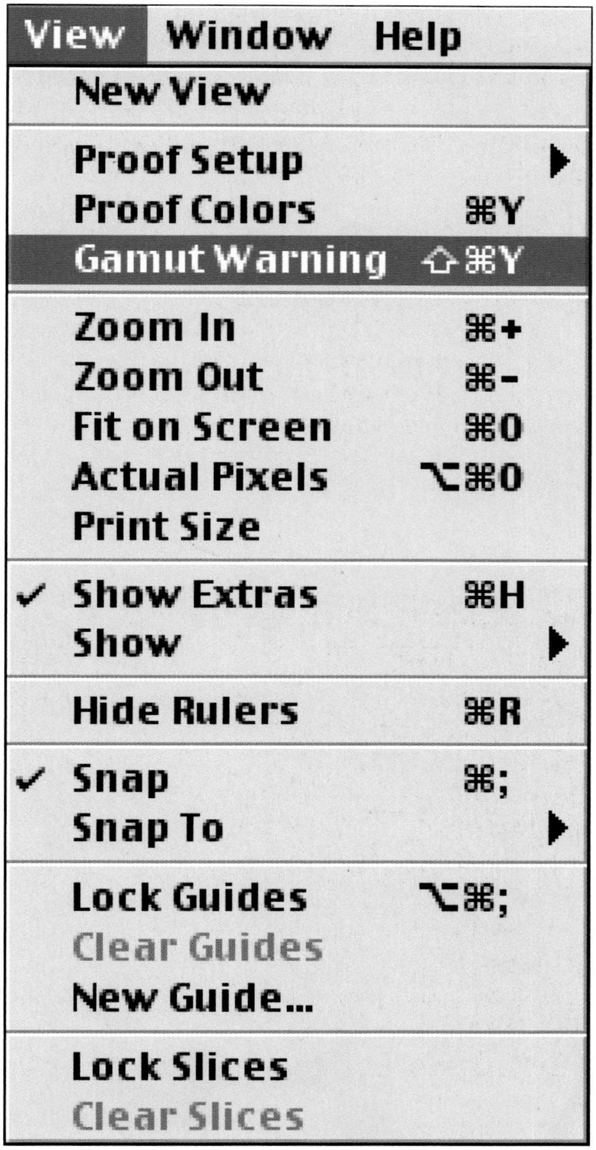

● 3.25

Another method for creating television-safe color is the NTSC Colors Filter. After you have finished creating your image, you can use this effect to restrict the use of colors that fall outside the gamut suitable for television. To do this, select your image and then choose Filter→Video→NTSC Colors (3.26).

Another application that lets you control the use of color for a video project is Adobe's After Effects, the industry standard animation and effects software.

After Effects

The television-safe capabilities of After Effects help you to identify areas that may be a problem (3.27). After Effects also provides you with different options for how you want to treat colors that may be unsafe for broadcast.

After you have created a composition, you may add a special effects filter to constrain the type of colors present in your project. This step is particularly important if you are using any graphics that were created from scratch because they are more likely to have colors that are optimized for a computer display and not a television set.

Choose one of the following options from the Broadcast Colors list under the Video menu in the Effect drop-down menu (3.28, 3.29):

- **Reduce Luminance:** This option adjusts colors that are not safe for video by lowering their brightness (or grayscale) values.
- **Reduce Saturation:** This option adjusts colors that are not safe for video by lowering the amount of saturation applied to them.
- **Key Out Unsafe:** This option literally removes the offending colors from the composition window so that you may see where the problem areas are located. Use this tool to view the changes that you have applied with the other Broadcast Colors options.
- **Key Out Safe:** By keying out the safe colors, only those that are unsuitable for video remain

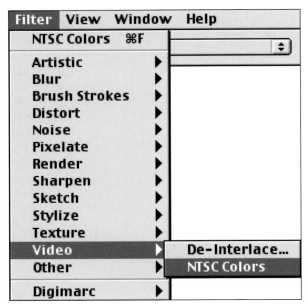

● 3.26

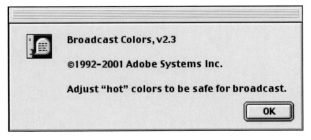

● 3.27

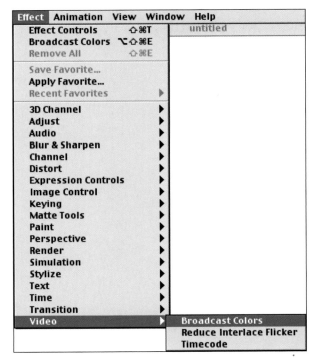

● 3.28

in the Composition window. This may be easier at times than simply keying out the unsafe colors, particularly with a complex graphic or background. To make it even easier, you can apply a temporary background layer with a solid color beneath your graphics. Doing this should help you view areas that are affected by your changes.

CONCLUDING THOUGHTS

We've covered a lot of technical details about the differences between vector and raster images, and between computer displays and television displays, as well as various formats and critical production issues. With this information in hand, you can proceed with confidence when creating your next Flash-for-video project.

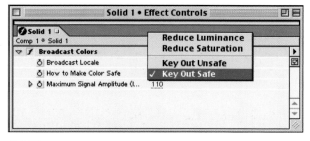

● 3.29

Chapter 4

Flash Video Capabilities and Limitations

Instead of avoiding Flash altogether for broadcast animation, we can be aware of the limits of Flash, push them as we dare, and get a lot done in the meantime.

Flash was originally designed to work with the lightweight media of the Web, and though it's grown up a lot, it hasn't grown beyond its original design at a basic level. It needs some hand-holding to work with large media assets. At the same time, Flash MX has some excellent new video features that allow you to work with video directly within Flash itself.

FLASH LIMITATIONS AND WORKAROUNDS FOR BROADCAST

We talked about what Flash is good and at not so good at in general in Chapter 1. Let's now get into some specifics that apply when you go out to broadcast quality video.

MAXIMUM FRAMES, LAYERS, AND SYMBOLS IN FLASH

There's an upper limit to the number of frames you can have in a Flash movie. Besides number of frames, according to the Macromedia Technote, "How big can a Flash movie be?": "The number 16,000 is a limit to other things in Flash as well. It is the maximum amount of layers that Flash can export and the maximum amount of loaded movies that Flash can support. In addition, the maximum amount of symbol instances allowed in a Flash movie is also 16,000. Combining these limits together would create greater risks, as using them together would most likely create other problems. Keep in mind that Flash and

the Flash Player are optimized for normal circumstances, and testing the extreme limits of Flash can cause memory and other operating system issues."

[NOTE]

You can see the full Macromedia Technote: "How big can a Flash movie be?" at www.macromedia.com/support/flash/ts/documents/bigflash.htm.

So there are limits on the number of frames, layers, symbols, and other things in Flash — by necessity. A software application is not infinite, nor is RAM. But what Macromedia is saying points again to the culprit of many Flash-to-broadcast woes. Flash simply wasn't designed to be doing this stuff in the first place. But it does do it. Instead of avoiding Flash altogether for broadcast animation, we can be aware of the limits of Flash, push them as we dare, and get a lot done in the meantime. Hopefully, Macromedia will someday consider rewriting the kernel of Flash to support more heavyweight uses:

- **Frame limit workaround:** Though it's unlikely you'd be working on a Flash document that is 16,000 frames long (about 17.8 minutes at 15 fps), the general wisdom among those who push Flash to its limits is to work in small chunks — break the animation up into separate FLA files. Some studios break longer animations into scenes, and some studios, if they have a big team, break the animation into very small FLAs consisting of

49

single shots of a few seconds. If you are working with large files to go to video, you'll likely be stitching everything together later in postproduction, so breaking Flash documents into small scenes works well.

- **Layer limit workaround:** When you're doing involved animation, it's not completely unusual to find yourself working with an insane number of layers — as we see in a screen shot from unit9's "Ursa Major" (4.1). If you are using many, many layers, it may be a factor in causing Flash to become unstable.

One particular case when you may find yourself working with a large number of layers is if you must merge scenes together in Flash. The reason is that the technique of putting together layers in Flash involves pasting the layers from one scene into new layers of another scene, so the number of layers of the merged scene is the sum of the layers in each of the individual scenes. Though it's hard to imagine bumping up against the layer limit, it's generally a good idea to avoid merging scenes together with lots of layers in Flash. Besides, the method is very tedious — there's no "merge scenes" feature in the current version of Flash. (See the "Merging Scenes in Flash MX" sidebar.) Wait to stitch the scenes together in postproduction, after they've been converted to video or image sequences.

- **Symbol limit workaround:** We have never spoken to anyone running into the limit of 16,000 symbols, but the clear way to avoid that

is, again, to break up the animation into small FLA files for each scene. You should also periodically delete unused Library items. Libraries that contain more than around 1,000 symbols can

Merging Scenes in Flash MX

Merging scenes in Flash MX is not the most enjoyable way to spend your spare time. But if you absolutely have to, here are the main steps.

1. Work backwards, copying one scene (let's call it Scene 2) and pasting the layers of Scene 2 at the end of and below the last layer of the previous scene (let's call it Scene 1).
2. Prepare Scene 1 (the one you are pasting into) by putting a new blank keyframe into the last frame of every layer. Doing this prevents the symbols in those layers from bleeding into the scene you're pasting at the end of this one. Also, below the very bottom layer in this scene, create a new empty layer (4.2).
3. Then go to the scene you are copying (Scene 2). Select all the frames of all the layers by clicking in the first frame of the top layer and then Shift-clicking in the last frame of the bottom layer. Choose Edit→Copy Frames and hold your breath (4.3).
4. Return to the scene you are pasting into (Scene 1). Select the last frame of the new empty layer you created and choose Edit→Paste Frames. All the frames and layers should now be in Scene 1 (4.4).
5. The layers you pasted retain their original names. Now you can delete the old scene.

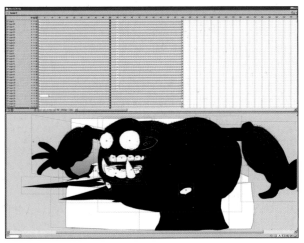

● 4.1   © 2001 unit9 Ltd.

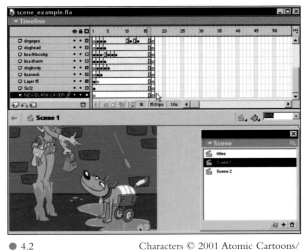

● 4.2   Characters © 2001 Atomic Cartoons/
                                         Honkworm International.

take a very long time to open, even if you have a lot of RAM.

[N O T E]

If you're using Flash 5, you'll notice that for some reason, Flash created a lot of extra frames at the end of layers from the original scene. You can just delete those frames. Also, Flash 5 doesn't preserve layer naming in the layers you pasted and instead numbers them sequentially. (Another reason to switch to Flash MX.)

CRASHY FLASH FILES

Flash files are prone to crashing if they are bigger than 50MB. The reasons this could happen vary. Besides the possibility of bumping up against the frame, symbol, or layer number limits, Flash doesn't like large files, whether the size is caused by complex graphics, lots of sound, or long durations. The problem is universal, PC or Mac.

Workaround: You guessed it — split FLA files into small chunks. This doesn't work well for Web delivery (because then you usually need to stitch the pieces together again to play them back), but it works fine for broadcast, where the pieces are often put together in postproduction. Because a large file size is often due to the sound, you can also work with placeholder sound by using lower resolution sound (for example, 22 kHz mono), or compressed sound while you're animating, then apply broadcast-quality sound when you go out to video.

SKIPPING FRAMES DURING PLAYBACK

If you're working with movies created at 720x540, or some other large video size, the real-time rendering speed is slow, and Flash skips frames during playback. This makes it difficult to see how smooth your animation is while you're working.

Workaround: To preview your animation, zoom out from the Stage and view it at a small window size. Broadcast studios are full of animators hunched over their screens watching postage stamp–sized Flash animation that at least runs smoothly. Scrubbing back and forth on the timeline manually also works well. Alternatively, you can export to a small QT or compressed AVI to preview, or you can export to SWF and watch it in a very small window. The more RAM you have and the faster your processor is, the less this is a problem.

VIDEO IS NOT INTERACTIVE

Video is linear. Formats such as QuickTime video (as opposed to a QT Flash track) and AVI do not support any sort of interactivity. Movie Clips or animation that uses ActionScript to move symbols around on the Stage or changes the colors of Symbols will not be exported when you go out to video.

Workaround: If you know that you will go out to video, just say no to Movie Clips. Don't Load Movies, Tell Targets, or do any other fancy cool stuff that works so great for Web delivery. Avoid Frame Actions, which are ignored on export to video. If you already have Movie Clips in an animation, break them into animated graphic symbols (see the following

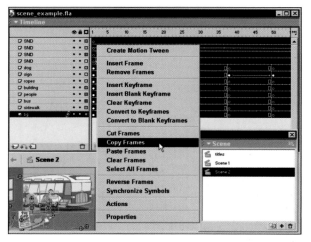

● 4.3   Characters © 2001 Atomic Cartoons/ Honkworm International.

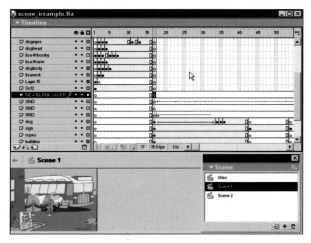

● 4.4   Characters © 2001 Atomic Cartoons/ Honkworm International.

sidebar). If you are adapting an animation for the Web to go out to video, remove any preloading sequences or games.

RAM, HARD DRIVE, AND OS CONSIDERATIONS

As with most applications, the more RAM and hard drive space you have for Flash MX, the better. Studios putting out a lot of animation typically have 1GB RAM, and at least 1 gHz processors.

On a PC or Mac, we recommend using 256MB RAM at the minimum, and you'll get better performance with 512MB RAM. You can get away with less RAM, and then you can get up and have a cup of coffee while you wait for files to open. (That can even happen with lots of RAM.)

The hard drive space requirements for creating animation in Flash aren't a lot more than what many desktop computers ship with — 20GB is fine. But if you're going to do audio or video editing, you'll need more.

The 2GB File Limit

Video files over 2GB are not supported on many operating systems, especially older ones. You may not have run into this if you haven't edited video, but it

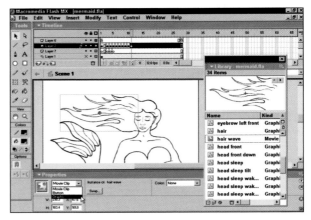

● 4.5   © 2001 Janet Galore

Converting Movie Clips to Animated Symbols

If you use Movie Clips to hold animation for walk cycles, eye movement, blinking, or other cycles in your animation, you'll need to convert these to animated graphic symbols if you want that animation to export to video. Otherwise, only the first frame of the Movie Clip is exported.

First, you need to change the symbol property, and then you have to make necessary adjustments on the Timeline so that all the frames of the animated symbol will play.

1. Select the Movie Clip on the Stage and use the Properties menu to change the property of that instance to Graphic (4.5). If the Movie Clip has multiple frames, doing this will automatically make it an animated graphic symbol.

2. Next, set the instance behavior of the animated graphic to Loop, so it will play back in the Timeline (4.6).

3. Test the playback of the animated symbol by scrubbing on the Timeline or playing the scene back in Editing Mode (you don't need to "Test Movie" since it's a graphic now). If it works, you're all done.

4. If it is not playing back all the frames, then you need make more room for the number of frames it needs to playback on the Timeline. This may involve moving the symbol to a different layer, or it may only require that you delete a keyframe that appears after the animated symbol in the same layer (4.7).

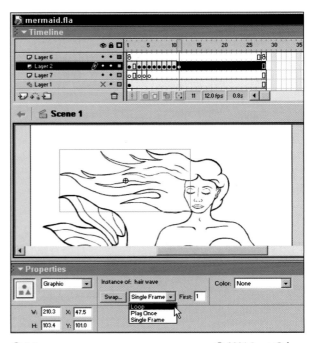

● 4.6   © 2001 Janet Galore

quickly becomes an issue when rendering or saving large files.

To work around this, if you're on Windows, make sure you are using an NTFS file system, and upgrade to Windows NT or 2000. If you're on a Mac, you need the HFS+ file system. These hard drive configurations allow files up to 1,000GB, but regular AVI files are still generally limited to 2GB. You can save AVI files larger than 2GB if your video-editing application supports the OpenDML specification. For example, if you are running Windows 2000 with an NTFS file system, Premiere 6 enables you to save AVI files up to 1,000GB. Unfortunately, Flash is not OpenDML compliant. Alternatively, you can work with smaller pieces in Flash and stitch the rendered pieces together in postproduction. Or better yet, you can export image sequences from Flash and avoid the large file size issue all together. Many Flash-to-broadcast studios use this solution.

[N O T E]

To read more about 2GB file limits and the OpenDML format, check out: "Working with File Size Limitations in Premiere 5.x and 6.x" at www.adobe.com/support/techdocs/100d2.htm.

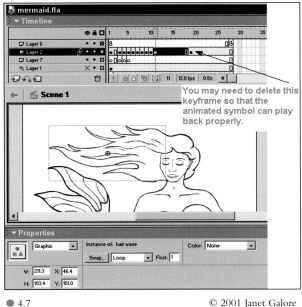

You may need to delete this keyframe so that the animated symbol can play back properly.

● 4.7   © 2001 Janet Galore

FLASH MX VIDEO IMPORT CAPABILITY

Our focus is generating full-screen, broadcast-quality video with Flash and, unfortunately, Flash MX doesn't have any new features that directly relate to exporting video. (Video export functionality is discussed in detail in Chapter 12, "Exporting Video from Flash.") But Flash MX does have some great new features that allow you to incorporate video natively within a Flash project.

It used to be that if you wanted to incorporate video into a Flash project, the only way to do it was to generate an image sequence from video and import the sequence of frames into Flash. That worked okay, but it wasn't efficient in terms of file size or bandwidth consumption — Flash didn't have a way to compress the video when exporting; it only used JPEG compression on the individual frames. The only other option was to import a QuickTime movie into Flash, integrate it within a Flash project, and then export the entire project as QuickTime. In this case, any Flash interactivity became a track within QuickTime. This option worked, but it required the viewer to have QuickTime software installed in order to watch the movie.

Now, with Flash MX and the Sorenson Spark video codec, you have a whole new range of options to choose from.

FLASH MX AND SPARK

In Flash MX, the Sorenson Spark codec has been integrated within the application so that you can work with video natively in Flash. Spark is a true *video compression* codec, allowing you to make adjustments in overall quality, keyframes, and scaling while keeping the overall file size small. It also lets you import audio and synchronize a video clip to a Flash movie's framerate.

Importing Video

In Flash MX, when you want to import video, simply choose File➔Import and locate a video file, such as a QuickTime movie, AVI, or MPEG. Some video formats are available only if you have QuickTime 4 or later installed on your system. See the Flash MX documentation for a complete list of supported formats.

When you select a file, you get the option of embedding it or linking to an external file (4.8). Embedding is the way to go if you later plan to export the movie to a video format.

Import Video Settings

When video is imported, the Sorenson Spark window is triggered (4.9), which gives you a number of options for adjusting the video for import. You may want to leave the default settings alone if you have prepared your video exactly as you like it prior to importing. But it's very helpful to have the ability to scale, adjust quality, and so on. You can also choose to adjust synchronization of the video to the Flash movie, either converting the framerate of your source material or matching it exactly. In Figure 4.9, a 320x240, 15 fps QuickTime movie is scaled 50 percent to 160x120 pixels, and the framerate is converted to 12 fps.

After a video file has been imported, it shows up as a new item in the Library; a new type of Library item known as Embedded Video (4.10). An alternative to

the approach we've been showing is to use the Library drop-down menu to create a New Video and then import a video directly into a blank Library Video item.

When working with your embedded video, the Library gives you the ability to update the video item or re-import, which is handy for situations where you make a change to the video file in the video editing application and don't want to replace the video in the Timeline (4.11). Note that the properties for the movie in Figure 4.11 reflect the properties of the *embedded movie*, not the original one.

[TIP]

You can also use the import feature to "re-compress" an embedded video, in a situation where you want to try different compression settings.

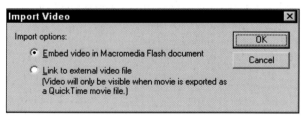

● 4.8

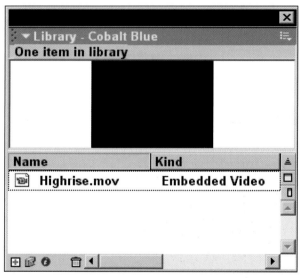

● 4.10

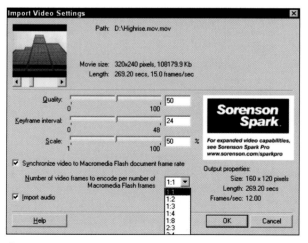

● 4.9

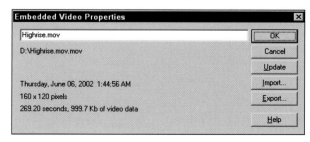

● 4.11

Going Beyond Spark: Sorenson Squeeze/Spark Pro

For Flash MX users who want to squeeze higher quality out of smaller file sizes, Sorenson offers an upgrade to the Spark codec that ships with MX. It's called Squeeze, a standalone application available from Sorenson (`www.sorenson.com`), which represents an upgrade from the standard Spark codec to Spark Pro (4.12).

In comparison to the regular Spark codec, Spark Pro, as delivered through the Squeeze interface in Flash MX, gives you the ability to have higher quality with even smaller file sizes, including such additional features as Two-Pass Variable Bit Rate (VBR) encoding, better processing of motion within video, and advanced batch compression features.

In a typical workflow, you import a video file into the Spark Pro interface and have the ability to export into a variety of formats, including the Flash Video (FLV) format for use as embedded video within Flash.

Squeeze allows you to capture video directly into the program for encoding and gives you the ability to do some powerful video filtering, such as fade ins and outs, as an alternative to using a video-editing application (4.13).

[N O T E]

For a great tutorial on using video in Flash MX, see Macromedia Technote "Using Embedded Video in Flash MX," by Robert Reinhardt, at: `www.macromedia.com/desdev/mx/flash/articles/flashmx_video.html`.

SUMMARY

The main difficulties inherent with using Flash to create broadcast-quality animation arise from the fact that Flash was never designed to work with large assets. However, if you know what to watch out for, and are creative and careful with how you push Flash, it can be a very useful tool for creating animation destined for TV or video.

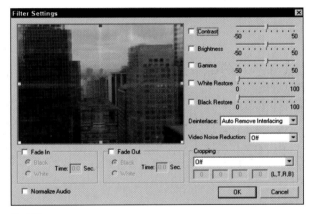

● 4.13

● 4.12

Chapter 5

Visual Storytelling in Film and TV

Thanks to Damian Payne for helping with this chapter.

Even though Flash doesn't provide a real camera, thinking like a cinematographer with a camera puts you in the right frame of mind to take storytelling to a new level.

Those trained in traditional animation often take advantage of the rich history of visual storytelling from film and television. But Flash is so easy to pick up that many of the early Flash animators started animating without first taking a step back to consider what their storytelling options were.

If your goal is broadcast-quality animation, looking beyond the simplest solutions for setting up a scene and taking inspiration from the "visual grammar" of film and television will improve your animation tremendously. Consider where these established techniques can open up new possibilities.

FILM VERSUS WEB

Film has an established style of visual storytelling that audiences understand, accept, and expect. Sequences of camera shots have particular meanings. If a vampire moves towards the camera menacingly with his hands outstretched, viewers interpret that they are seeing the scene from the victim's point of view and empathize with the victim. Even individual scene compositions have shorthand for complex meaning.

When television came about, it borrowed from the visual grammar of film. The technical details of creating television shows (such as the need to produce programming quickly and shorter show durations) caused some divergence of television storytelling style from film. Though you can pick out differences

between television and film style, they borrow from each other and you can find many similarities in the mechanics of how stories get told in each medium.

Animation, as a distinct medium from live action, has largely borrowed from the live-action styles of film and television (often exaggerating them) but also has its own storytelling shorthand.

Storytelling on the Web is still evolving, and there's still a lot of debate as to when (and if) broadband entertainment will really take hold. Clearly, though, the smaller screen size and technical limitations of the Web have a lot of implications about the best way to tell a story on the very small screen. The well-established visual grammar of television and film must be adapted so that it makes sense when played back through a media player or Flash window. The aspect of interactive narrative also adds to the mix.

THINKING LIKE A CINEMATOGRAPHER

Even though Flash doesn't provide a real camera, thinking like a cinematographer with a camera puts you in the right frame of mind to take storytelling to a new level.

Also, more and more animators are mixing Flash with 3D animation software, using virtual cameras in 3D environments (see Chapters 9, "The Movable Camera: Flash and Toon Boom Studio" and 10, "Flash with 3D Applications: Making a Music

Video," respectively.). So there's no excuse not to look carefully at as many great films and animations as you can, to pick up techniques you can exploit.

COMPOSITION

The composition of a scene not only conveys literal meaning, such as where the subjects are located and spatial relationship, but it also conveys narrative meaning.

Aspect Ratio

The aspect ratio of your target screen size is very important in determining how to set up the elements in a shot. Check out the series of three shots of the same subjects, composed for television [1.33:1], HDTV widescreen [1.85:1], and movie widescreen [2.35:1] aspect ratios (5.1). Note that more and more of the environment is visible the wider the aspect ratio. Movie widescreen is closer to the way we actually see.

Nowadays, animated TV series are often composed for HDTV delivery at the same time as NTSC/PAL delivery. The scene is set up so that most of the action takes place within the action-safe zone for NTSC, but the composition continues beyond that area at the sides, so when it is shown on HDTV the shot is filled out (5.2).

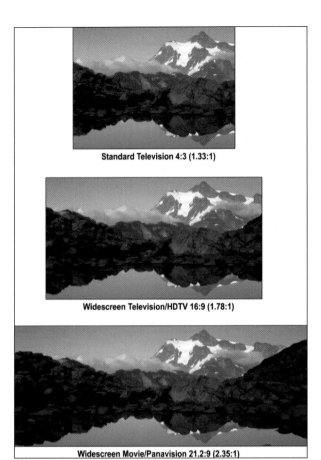

Standard Television 4:3 (1.33:1)

Widescreen Television/HDTV 16:9 (1.78:1)

Widescreen Movie/Panavision 21.2:9 (2.35:1)

● 5.1

Interview: Damian Payne, Honkworm International

Janet Galore talked to Damian Payne about cinematography for animation.

JG: Could you tell us a little bit about your background?

DP: I basically started at the bottom in the UK working as a Production Assistant at a commercials production company. For my money, this is the best way to start out in the business — do two years of this and then go to film school if you're still convinced that all you want to do is direct. I worked my way up the ladder, studied screenwriting at London College

night school, met my wife, moved to the states, and continued working as 1st Assistant Director. I did loads of music videos, some independent features, and tons of commercials. I never really went to film school. Everything I learned I learned on the set and got paid doing it. Film school is really good for building a reel and networking, but I have to say, I know way more people who are making a living in this business who never set foot inside a film school than I do people who did — and of the ones that did, only two of them are actual directors! I finally ended up at Honkworm as a line producer for animation.

JG: What are the differences between the visual grammar for TV versus Film or the Web? Or do we tend to use the same techniques to tell stories regardless of where they are told?

DP: I don't think there are any major differences — they're all the same decisions, "Do I want to show this in a master shot?" "How much coverage do I want to give this scene?" You're probably more limited on the Web with certain master shots because detail can get lost with the screen size. Also, you're probably not going to get away with Batman-esque swooping city establishing shots because the processor will go on strike.

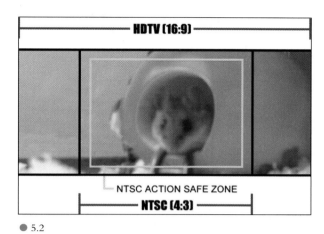

● 5.2

Types of Shots

Here are some examples of common camera shots:

- **Close-up:** If you are looking at a human subject, close-ups show primarily the face or a portion of it (5.3). Close-ups are used more often in television, to bring the action in closer on the smaller screen. This is also true of Web delivery. Extreme close-ups on TV or film can be a little intrusive.
- **Medium shot:** A medium shot shows the subject from the shoulders or waist up (5.4). This type of shot is often used for conversation but is usually interspersed with close-ups and cutaways to keep the scene from getting too static.

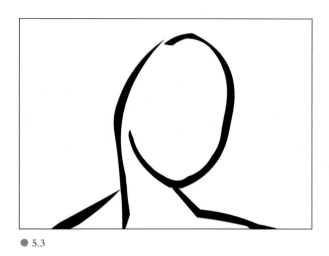

● 5.3

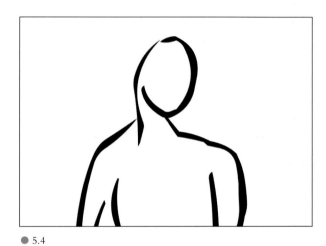

● 5.4

JG: Are some techniques used everywhere, while some are particular to TV or film, for example?

DP: I'd say the good stuff certainly borrows more from TV and film — but once again, those rich establishing tracking shots do tend to swamp the processor. However, there's so much you can do with camera angles and placement and the edit itself that can give a piece a very cinematic feel. Television and film are one and the same now; most network shows are shot on 35mm just as the features are — the only difference is that features usually have more money to make stuff a lot prettier on less of a brutal schedule.

JG: How does not having a real camera affect 2D animation? Do you think animation can fake it? Are there still some lessons to be learned from live action film and video?

DP: I think not having a real camera is actually very liberating. Let's face it; you can basically get exactly the shot you want in animation, but there are a lot of times on the set when you just can't get the lens where you ideally want it. However, on the big features, this problem is solved with money and guess what else? Armies of animators churning out CGI! So are there any lessons still waiting to be learned? I don't think so; it's all

there on the big screen and the TV. Watch, borrow, and expand on it — that's what the business is about at any level.

JG: What's the most important thing a cinematographer (or director) should remember?

DP: Be careful whom you yell at on the way up, because they'll get the last laugh when you're on the way down. Oh yeah, and a comfortable pair of boots; always remember to pack a comfortable pair of boots.

- **Full shot:** This shot shows the entire subject from head to toe (5.5). This shot is often used to establish a new person entering the scene, when you want to show exactly who it is at a glance.
- **Wide shot, panoramic shot:** Use this shot to establish the layout of a new scene, to introduce the viewer to new setting (5.6). The panoramic or extra-wide shot is even farther away from the scene. Extremely wide shots don't work well on small screens to convey information of any detail.
- **Master shot:** This shot is the main shot that the scene is built around. It shows all the significant aspects of the scene and the characters in the scene.
- **One-shot, two-shot, three-shot, group-shot:** Shots focusing on one, two, or three people (5.7), or a group of people, usually a medium shot.
- **Over-the-shoulder shot:** This shot is used primarily in a two-person conversation, where the camera is placed over the shoulder of one person, looking towards and focusing on the second person (5.8). You can typically see the shoulder or some other part of the first person in the corner of the shot.

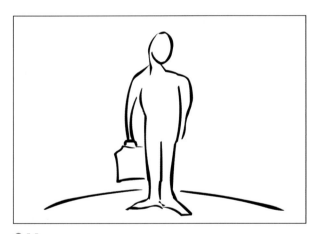

● 5.5

● 5.7

● 5.6

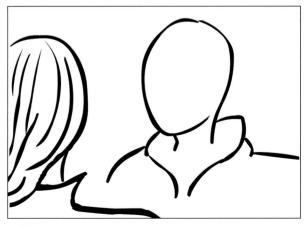

● 5.8

Composition Tips

Here are several composition tips:

- The way that the subjects in a shot relate to each other communicates a lot about what's going on in the story. For example, a wide shot with a single subject in the frame can communicate loneliness or isolation (5.9).
- Subjects in a shot rarely have a perfectly balanced relationship to each other and to the environment, so don't set up shots that are perfectly balanced (5.10). Think about what's important in the scene and call attention to that by adding some dynamic tension (5.11).
- Don't forget the action/title-safe area. Leave about 10 percent of the screen free at the edges where actions and titles do not appear. Keep the main action nearer the center of the screen.
- Think about depth — just because you're working in 2D doesn't mean your characters have to live in a 2D world. Set up over-the-shoulder shots and play with depth of field (what is in and out of focus).

Camera Angles and Perspectives

Using creative camera angles and perspectives is another way to say a lot about what's happening (or what is about to happen) in the story.

- Dutch angles, where the scene is shot at a skewed angle (think of the fight scenes in the old *Batman* live-action TV show), can evoke a feeling that things are wrong, off-kilter, a little crazy (5.12).

● 5.9

● 5.11

● 5.10

● 5.12

- A perspective shot that foreshortens the scene, such as showing a man dangling from a building from above, reaching toward the camera, can give a great dramatic effect (5.13).
- A depth of field shift, where focus is kept on the subject, but elements in the background seem to change in focus and loom ominously, communicates awe, surprise, or realization.
- A camera angle looking up at a character can make them look powerful. For example, in Russ Meyer's *Faster Pussycat Kill Kill*, actress Tura Satana was almost always shot from below to make her look more menacing and intimidating. Likewise, looking down on a character makes them look submissive.

Transitions

Transitions move the action of the story from one scene to another. The way a new scene is brought in can be funny, terrifying, neutral — you name it. Typical transitions are cuts, wipes, dissolves, and fades. There are many types of each — pick some films and practice identifying which transitions are used and why. Here are some examples of transitions to look for:

- **Action wipe:** An object moves in front of the camera to reveal a new shot. For example, a truck drives through a shot of two people in the park, entirely obstructing the view. As the truck passes by the camera, it reveals a new scene of a busy city street.
- **Smash cut:** A very fast cut with motion blur, which often conveys "meanwhile . . ." or "at the same time but in another place."
- **Iris in/iris out:** A "cartoony" way to change from one scene to another. This special type of wipe shows the scene being overtaken by black, where a circular portion of the original scene gets smaller and smaller until there is only black left (5.14–5.16).
- **Match cut:** This is a special type of cut that matches the action, contour, or placement of a subject from one scene to the next. Often the action in one shot flows directly into the next shot. A great example of match action cutting is a TV commercial Nike made called "Move." A kid running down the street in one scene turns into a hockey player skating in the next scene, who turns into a soccer player kicking a ball in the next scene, and so on.

● 5.13

● 5.14

- **Dissolve:** The elements of one scene dissolve into a new scene.

Editing and Continuity

A story is told through editing. The goal of editing is usually to make the action of the story transparent, so what is happening to the characters from scene to scene makes sense. The way you edit, however, determines how that story unfolds.

Visually, action and suspense are all built in the edit. You set something up, for example, a gun in a desk drawer. Will the kid who's snooping around find it? When he does find it, will he shoot himself or someone else? All this is built in the edit — where he looks, what he does, the decisions he makes.

Here are some editing examples and suggestions to consider while studying your favorite films:

- Watch for familiar patterns in editing: establishing shot, master shot, two-shot, over the shoulder, cut to other person, cutaway to new person who's entered room, and so on.
- Look for patterns that set up a question and then answer the question in the next few shots. For example, a car pulls up with tinted windows, and a window rolls down. Is the person inside friendly or trouble? A woman on the street looks in the car, concerned. The next shot shows a hand reaching out with some flowers — the person in the car is a friend.
- Look for sequences that show cause and effect, such as a person throwing a ball and then a shot of a window breaking.
- Watch for sequences that have implied meaning because they are part of the established visual grammar of film. For example, cutting back and forth between two people running from opposite sides of the screen implies they will meet. A subject moving from right to left may imply returning, or going back to something; moving from left to right may imply venturing out. A subject walking away from the camera is interpreted as leaving, and walking toward the camera implies arriving.
- Movement from one shot to another is often anticipated with a turn of a head, or a sound off-screen. Watch for how the director motivates transitions from scene to scene. Motivated scene transitions can really pull the viewer into the story. For example, a person can get up and walk out of the frame and then another person can get up and follow him out, but the camera now

● 5.15

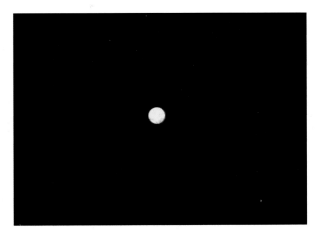

● 5.16

follows the second person. We are now expecting something to happen between the two people, and we want to follow along.

- Look for scenes that build suspense. For example, focusing on one person's point of view after establishing someone hiding in the room that they don't know about. The more close-ups you keep, the more claustrophobic you can make the scene.

Lighting

Consider your options for lighting to establish setting, mood, and the passage of time:

- The most memorable action and suspense scenes take place at night. Things can lurk in the shadows, and the lighting is always going to be more dramatic (think of those great film noirs).
- Shadows contrasted with light, chiaroscuro, add drama any time.
- Harsh lighting on the subject conveys focus, or maybe that the subject is in trouble, singled out.
- Soft lighting can be sexy, cute, or dreamy.

Color

With animation, you have complete control over the use of color, but frequently color is taken for granted. Look at the use of color in TV and film to get some fresh ideas.

- Colors can be realistic, or highly saturated and comic book–like, as in the film *Dick Tracy*.
- Science fiction films, such as *2001: A Space Odyssey* or *Star Wars*, use cool tones to convey a clean, sterile, futuristic environment, while other darker sci-fi films, such as *Blade Runner*, use dark browns and blacks to convey a future that is more bleak and grimy.

- Extremely desaturated color can imply bleakness or depression.
- Black and white has a very different feel in live action as opposed to animation, but it's still interesting to consider its uses. It bucks the tradition of vivid, full color animation.

ADDITIONAL INFORMATION

If you'd like to read more about editing and cinematography, check out *Film Directing Shot by Shot* by Steven D. Katz.

Chapter 6

Working with Sound

Thanks to Christopher MacRae for helping with this chapter.

Trust your ears.

CHRISTOPHER MACRAE

Sound can make or break an animation, Flash or no Flash. If your dialog sounds bad (is unintelligible or sonically inferior), it can damage the visual storytelling. It's better to be silent than have bad sound. On the other hand, sound can make a simple animation captivating, and can fill out a scene with a whole world of ambience, making the animation seem to flow beyond the edges of the screen and into the living room of the audience. Sound is the part of your work that actually reaches out and touches the audience, making physical contact with their ears and the hairs on the backs of their necks — so make it good.

In this chapter, we get a behind-the-scenes look at recording and working with sound in Flash from veteran audio engineer, Christopher MacRae (see Appendix E, "Contributor Profiles"). If you've worked with audio in Flash or other animation programs before, this chapter offers a personal perspective and practical tips and tricks to get the best sound possible. If you are new to working with audio, you'll come away with an understanding of some of the issues involved with achieving broadcast quality audio for Flash animation.

THE RECORDING/MONITORING ENVIRONMENT

Even if you are not planning on setting up an audio recording studio, it's helpful to understand the basic components of one. The equipment and theory behind all of it can be daunting at first. But audio is not hard to figure out if you keep the *signal path* in mind — that is, if you can trace where the sound comes from and where it goes to. The functions of the various components and the hows/whys of their connections will start to make sense.

SCENARIO 1: THE BARE BONES SETUP

A simple audio recording setup into a computer is comprised of a *microphone* (often with a mic stand), mic *cable*, mic *pre-amplifier*, and a cable from the mic pre-amp to the *analog* input of the *sound card* (6.1).

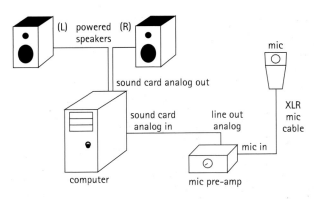

● 6.1

Function Summary

- **Microphone:** sound input
- **Mic cable:** carries signal from mic to pre-amp
- **Mic pre-amplifier (pre-amp):** boosts signal for recording
- **Analog input:** most mics have an analog (non-digital) signal
- **Sound card:** converts analog signal into digital format for recording digitally in computer

To monitor audio from your computer, you can connect a cable from the analog output of the sound card to the inputs of powered speakers (or from the sound card, to a power amp, to the speakers). Expect to pay around $800 for an entry-level pair of high-quality studio speakers (also known as "monitors" in audio-speak). It's worth it. Avoid the cheap plastic speakers that come with a separate subwoofer — those systems are meant for gaming and music, not professional monitoring. Go to a professional audio equipment store with your favorite CDs, or perhaps a CD of something you are working on, and listen to a few different systems before you buy. Most speakers are magnetically shielded to keep them from messing with your computer monitor's colors, but always double-check.

The simple system in Figure 6.1 gets the audio into the computer, but lacks headphone monitoring for the vocal talent, which is not ideal. A good voice-over talent may be able to keep their voice at a consistent volume, but will always want headphones to hear how his or her voice reacts with the mic. If your budget requires that you stick with a simple setup, try using a mic pre-amp with headphone monitoring built in.

The audio levels to the speakers in this setup are controlled via a software panel that comes with the soundcard. The main inputs to the computer are also controlled this way, along with the ability to monitor what is coming in from the microphone input.

[T I P]

On your computer, before monitoring your recording, turn off your system sounds. There's nothing worse than turning the volume way up to listen to a quiet music passage or sound effect and then clicking something and having an error sound from the computer blast your nerves and hearing, not to mention damaging your power amps and speakers!

SCENARIO 2: BETTER MONITORING

To allow for more variety in monitoring, this suggested setup has more flexibility, especially with the added benefit of controlling what comes into the headphones (6.2).

This setup includes more ways to shape the sound coming from the mic. As with the last system, we have a mic preamp that allows us to adjust the microphone level. Beyond the pre-amp, we can now:

Interview with Christopher MacRae

Janet Galore spoke to Christopher MacRae about his philosophies on working with sound.

JG: What's your background, how long have you been working with sound and with Flash?

CM: I've been a musician/songwriter for as long as I care to remember. I started recording and editing dialog for Honkworm in 1998 and got more involved with using Flash a year later or so.

JG: What's your definition of "broadcast quality" sound?

CM: Broadcast quality, to me, is getting the best sound you can for the medium it is released in. But that is no excuse to record tracks of inferior sonic quality. At least record at 44.1 kHz sampling rate, 16-bit depth. Be sure your computer's CPU and drives are as fast as possible, and you have the hardware to back up your data. I like removable hard drives that are dedicated to the project at hand. When the next project comes up, you can start with a new drive. To paraphrase Beatles producer George Martin's philosophy about taping everything, "Drive space is cheap!"

JG: What audio editing tools would you recommend?

CM: Pro Tools or Digital Performer are the industry standards for Mac. On the PC side, Sonic Foundry Sound Forge, Vegas Video, Nuendo, WaveLab, Sequoia are good choices.

JG: What's your philosophy on sound and music in animation?

CM: Less is more (sometimes). Silences are not all bad — I don't try to fill all silent

- Use an *EQ module* to adjust the equalization (remove or add bass, mid, and treble frequencies).
- Use a *de-esser* (to remove annoying sibilants that stand out too much — for example, the hissy parts of *s* and *f*).
- Use a *compressor* to compress the dynamic range (basically lowering the volume when someone speaks too loud and raising the volume in a quiet passage).

(Although you can remove or fix some of these defects after recording, you have a much better source to work with if you record only the cleanest sound, the way you want it.)

The A/D Converter

From the mic preamp/equalizer/compressor combo, the signal enters the advanced *A/D converter* (analog to digital converter). Having the signal go through an external A/D converter is an advantage over the system in the first scenario, where the signal simply came from the mic pre-amp and entered the A/D converters on the sound card within the computer. With cheaper sound cards, the noise from CPU cycles and video card and PCI channel noise all get amplified by the sound card's onboard A/D converters in the computer, which degrades the audio signal. With better-engineered sound cards, this is less of an issue. However, most folks prefer an external A/D converter that converts the signal outside of the computer and sends it digitally to the digital input of

the sound card, thus eliminating a conversion process performed within a noisy computer case. (Note: Some mic pre-amps have an A/D converter built in, which is a nice touch.)

Mixer

When you add a separate mixer to your system, you can monitor your digital inputs and the analog outs from the computer simultaneously, adjust their levels separately, and then send them to either headphones or speakers. If a voice-over talent is overdubbing voice on top of music, for example, the ability to adjust the levels of their voice to music in their headphones is important so that they can get in the mood and fire off a great take.

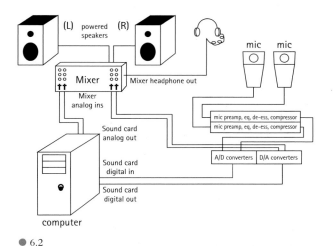

● 6.2

---

areas with a sound effect. Watch the rhythm of the animation if possible to establish a flow that the audio will work with. If no animation is available, close your eyes and try to picture the dialog, music, and so on that you record – if the dialog doesn't sound believable, the animation won't save it. Don't be afraid to start over even if you've worked on something for a while and it isn't working. You never want to feel obligated to explain away some perceived technical flaw to anybody because you were too lazy to fix it at the time. Be tough but fair on yourself, and the quality and focus of your work will reflect your dedication.

JG: What are the biggest pitfalls when recording voices (or processing the audio), and how do you avoid them?

CM: Watch your gain structure from mic to computer! Be sure the mic pre-amp isn't overloading, the level to computer isn't distorting. Watch the *p* pops and excessive sibilance — try moving the mic if this occurs. While trying not to distort, record the hottest signal level to computer as you can. Trying to save a quiet track by raising the gain, normalizing, or excessive limiting will also raise the background noise of the track, and the signal (waveform) will have a harsher, brittle sound due to the sharper, more acute angles introduced into the waveform.

JG: What's the most important thing a sound engineer can do to improve the quality of his or her sound?

CM: Trust your ears. Get good monitors so that you know what you're actually hearing, and a large diaphragm mic for general-purpose recording and then acousticize (foam) the space you're in to more accurately hear what you're working on. Make a CD of your work and listen to it on as many different systems as you can — when it starts sounding good on more and more systems, you know that you're getting somewhere.

A mixer also provides a convenient knob to turn the volume up and down, rather than having to resort to using a simulated knob or slider on the screen all the time.

WORKING WITH VOICE TALENT

If an animation has speaking parts, the dialog has to sound clear and needs to be a convincing performance. Here are some tips for working with and recording voice talent.

USE A SOUNDPROOF ROOM

To get clean sound while recording voices, you need to eliminate the effects of voices bouncing off the walls and ceiling in the recording studio as well as get rid of other room sounds. To this end, voices are usually recorded in a soundproof room. An acoustically dead, accurate signal is easier to mix in with your animation than a voice that has traces of room ambience or echoes. You can always add reverb or room ambience to a signal; however, taking reverb away from a signal already recorded is an exercise in futility.

Recording voices can be done in a small area, like a closet, provided that walls and ceilings are covered in an acoustic open-celled foam, such as Sonex, which soaks up all the ambience and echoes and keeps them from entering the recording. Closets do get stuffy, though. A prefabricated vocal recording booth, such as the Whisper Room from Whisper Room, Inc., is ideal because it isolates the source to be recorded in a small (or large, depending on budget) moveable space, has a quiet fan for ventilation, and has jacks already in the wall for easy setup.

[N O T E]

If you are recording in a noisy environment, foam will not stop low frequencies or loud noise from entering the recording, so check out the environment to make sure it's quiet before investing time and energy to set up a soundproof room.

MICROPHONE TIPS

The most important sounds you'll record with your mic are usually the vocal tracks. Use the following tips to get the most out of your mic when recording voices:

- Some engineers prefer large diaphragm condenser mics for recording vocals. A condenser mic uses power from a mic pre-amp, which allows the mic a greater range of sensitivity.
- Using a pop filter in front of the microphone is important to eliminate "plosives" from the letter *p* and keeps wind from breath noise to a minimum. You can either pay the price for a fancy clip-on pop filter, or you can make one from a coat hanger, which works just as well. (The coat hanger is bent into a circle and a couple layers of pantyhose are stretched over the frame and placed a couple inches in front of the mic.)
- Keep an eye on your mic volume (also known as *gain*) and try not to distort the inputs of the device you are going into. Digital distortion is nasty and can ruin a take.
- Use the equalizer sparingly. If your mic input source sounds less than ideal, try moving the mic into a better position or have the vocalist move around, before adjusting the equalizer settings.

DIRECTING TIPS

There's only so much that equipment can do to rectify a poor voice-over performance. Getting the right cast together and getting the most out of their performances is the best way to improve the quality of your sound!

- **Use professional talent:** Professional actors, union or not, are essential to getting broadcast-quality dialog. Though it may be cheap to use your neighbor or the FedEx delivery person, people who are not trained actors, unless they are naturally gifted, need more takes, tire quickly, tend to give stiff and unconvincing performances, and are not as versatile as professional actors. Of course, you can do the voices yourself, but after you've worked with someone who can blow the lid off a scene in one take, then switch voices and do the same thing again, you won't want to go back. In our experience, professional actors can do in 20 minutes what it takes 2 to 4 hours to do with inexperienced performers, and you get better results.
- **Hold auditions:** Either by phone or in person to make the best choice from a selection of talented people. Most voice talent reps can be

found in the phone book, and they'll send you demo tapes for free.

- **Get to know the talent before you record:** Give them the scripts well ahead of time, and talk about the characters when you meet. Show them storyboards and character art, so they can see what kind of character they are breathing life into. If you can, find out how they like to be directed and how they are used to working.
- **Rehearse:** Don't forget to schedule time to rehearse, ideally before the day of the recording. Rehearsing makes everyone more comfortable with the material and loosens things up when you do record, allowing for more creativity.
- **Don't staple scripts:** When you give the cast scripts for recording, each person should have his or her own script, and staples should be avoided so that paper-rustling sounds are not recorded. Give voice talent pencils and highlighters so they can make direction notes on their scripts.
- **People need food and water:** Some recording sessions can last a few hours, or more if you have breaks. Make sure to feed people so that they don't burn out, and give them plenty of fresh water to prevent dry mouth. Actors should avoid milk before and during the recording session, unless you want lots of lip smacking and tongue noises along with the dialog.
- **Record characters together:** If your setup permits, we recommend setting up mics for every character in a scene (within reason) and recording them at the same time. The different voices can be recorded on different tracks. This leads to more natural interaction among the characters, and is a lot more fun (albeit challenging) than recording one person's character at a time. If you need to record one person at a time, consider setting up a situation so that he or she can still hear and interact with the other characters in the scene while only they are being recorded.

[N O T E]

The more people you record, the more acoustic isolation you will need among people to minimize crosstalk into each other's tracks. It's also important to make sure all the actors are within view of each other, because eye contact is important.

- **Don't be afraid to ask for another take, or another, or another:** Work in chunks. The last resort is fixing it in the mix — which makes a huge dent in your pocketbook from studio editing time and generally does not yield a convincing performance. For example, if you love a certain take, but you can't make out the word "poodle," but you can hear it in another take you don't like, then you can try to cut and paste to make it work. That should only be a last resort. It's better to really listen while you are doing the recording, and make sure that you can hear and understand all the words. One trick is to have four tracks going. You can record them two or three times through and then take the best line from each take and move it to the fourth track. This procedure is called *comping*.
- **Improvise, improvise:** After you've got a few good takes of the scene the way it's written, consider allowing the cast to do a take or two that includes improvisation and goofing around. Some of the funniest exchanges ever recorded happened just that way.
- **The sound engineer is your friend:** If you can afford professional studio time, it usually comes with a nice person who knows how to work all the equipment. Besides those basics, many recording professionals can help you keep track of which takes were good, what scene you're on, and can listen for problems with the audio, allowing you to concentrate on how the lines are being delivered. Treat them as a partner, and you'll have an easier time editing later.

EDITING SOUND

If you are editing your own sound, here are some tips to get good results in audio applications outside Flash.

USING MULTIPLE TRACKS

A great way to record a number of takes with different characters is to use multitrack recording, one character per track. Doing so allows you to easily choose among the takes and see how they flow together.

Figure 6.3 is an example of using multiple tracks to manage takes in Vegas Video, a useful video/audio tool from Sonic Foundry (www.sonicfoundry.com).

We recommend that you choose your takes and do a rough edit while still in the studio from the recording session — don't let things get cold. You may think that you will remember which takes you like best, but doing the rough edit is much easier when everything is still in your short-term memory.

EDITING OUT CROSSTALK

If you've recorded multiple character voices at the same time, one potential problem is *crosstalk*. Sound from one person is picked up in another person's mic, which occurs when several people are standing there in the room at a time.

In most cases, when you record, you want to completely isolate sound sources. However, when you record voices for animation, putting people together usually makes the recording better because the actors can interact and improvise.

If you record more than one person at a time, you may need to deal with two types of situations where crosstalk could occur:

- **Stepping on Lines (Do It Over):** People may "step on lines," for example, talk at the same time or quickly one after another. Sometimes this is desirable, as when one person is interrupting another. But often the exchange will need to be recorded again. Regardless, it's a good idea to record another take where only one voice is recorded at a time. That way, when you choose

among the takes, you can decide if you want to use the one that has the overlapping voices, or replace them with the clean takes and overlap them later in editing.

- **One at a Time (Editable):** If people are talking one at a time, it's not a big problem to edit out crosstalk, as you can see the following example using SoundForge.

Two voice-overs can be recorded at the same time (6.4). Notice the crosstalk from the right channel (bottom) to the left channel (top).

The waveforms representing the crosstalk (the sound that is bleeding through) can be selected and muted (6.5).

This is the crosstalk from the waveform in the second track.

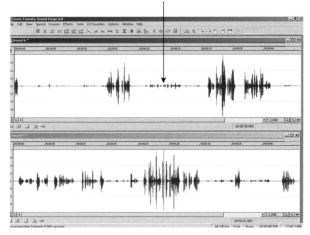

● 6.4

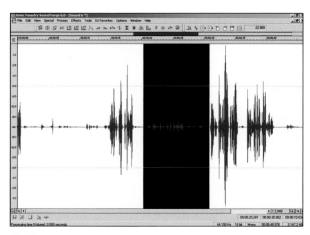

● 6.3

● 6.5

In Figure 6.6, we see a close up of the end of a sound segment after the crosstalk has been muted. The flat line to the right of the waveforms represents silence. In this example, you see how a fade out is applied to the voice after the crosstalk has been removed. Usually, the edges of the mute need to have a fade in or out applied to minimize the audible transition from sound to silence.

CLEANING UP THE WAVEFORMS

After the takes have been chosen from a recording session and a rough edit has been made, listen to each audio track separately and listen for any pops, glitches, or other gremlins that may appear. If you find that your tracks are excessively noisy, use a good noise reduction plug-in to filter out the noise. (If your audio-editing program doesn't include one built in, you can often purchase specialized plug-ins from third party software companies.) Use the noise reduction plug-in to filter each problematic track before mixing the overall production down.

[T I P]

As a matter of good digital housekeeping, when you record audio you should keep all the original audio files intact. After recording, the first thing you should do prior to editing is make a copy of the original files under a new filename so that you can go back to the original versions if you need to.

You may also want to boost the meat of the voices, and minimize the transience, plosives, fricatives, and so on. This is called *limiting*.

Take a look at the vertical dimension of the sound waveforms in Figure (6.7) and notice how the majority of the audio information falls within a certain range. Waveforms that jump out of the general range and cause distortion are known as *transients* and typically occur in a recording environment due to the way people talk, if they accidentally hit a mic, and so on. In this example, the goal is to chop the transients off -8.5 dB and then raise the level of the waveform to -1 dB. Doing this will raise the volume of the dialog without distorting it.

In Figure 6.8, you can see how the Waves Ultramaximizer plug-in is used to chop off the transients, with Threshold set to chop the waveform at -8.5 dB and raise it up to -1 dB.

● 6.7

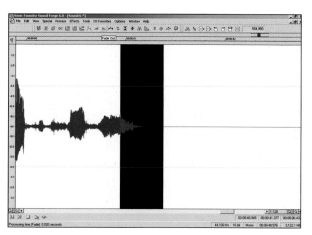

● 6.6

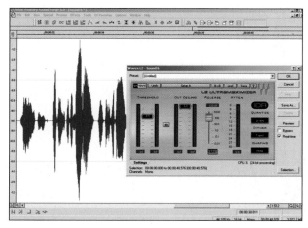

● 6.8

After processing, you end up with the final, "limited" waveform (6.9). Notice how at -8.5 dB on the vertical scale, the sound waveform has come up against the threshold we established and has a flat edge — this is what limiting accomplishes.

This tweak should be used as a final touch rather than a cure for a poorly recorded (quiet) track. The limiter raises the background noise of the track along with everything else. Another reason to record the best track you can before editing!

THE SOUND OF SILENCE

Unless a continuous ambient audio track or music is underneath the voices, you should consider recording the sound of the empty studio where the voices were recorded, also known as *room ambience*. Putting a background layer with looped room ambience in the Flash file prevents audible differences in the quality of the audio between when characters are talking and when they're not talking. (Or you can do this in postproduction.) If you have edited the waveforms of the voices and muted the areas between the voices, having a loop of room ambience can even things out nicely. Using an ambience loop is particularly important when you export the audio for broadcast or video — any defect in the audio that might not have been noticeable on a home computer comes through loud and clear on TV or video.

THE FINAL VOICE BED

After you complete the rough edit of the voice track (or voice bed), typically you'll want to apply the

● 6.9

voice bed to the animatic (a movie with storyboards and the basic dialog). In the animatic, you can make various edits to refine the timing of all the scenes, cuts, and dialog. Only after the timing is perfected in the animatic should a final voice bed be mixed down. At that point, the voice bed (as well as the timing of the scenes) should be locked. This allows the animation to be refined based on a stable dialog track.

[N O T E]

If the voice bed does not have to be locked down timing-wise, some studios break up the voices into chunks that can be placed in the Flash file as the animators see fit. Generally, this is not done in traditional animation studios or on projects with big teams, where keeping the timing consistent is imperative.

DEALING WITH BROADCAST QUALITY SOUND IN FLASH

Throughout this chapter, we're assuming that you've been recording and editing audio at 44 kHz, 16-bit. But good sound makes for huge file sizes, and Flash is not designed to handle long, heavy audio files.

As described in Chapter 4 "Flash Video Capabilities and Limitations," Flash files over 50MB tend to crash even the most robust machines with lots of RAM and disk space. To avoid this, it's best to work in small chunks and plan on adding the final sound in postproduction. It's possible to work with Flash projects as long as five minutes with full-quality sound, but we don't recommend this.

If you are going out to broadcast from Flash, it's common practice to break up the animation into 30-second to one-minute pieces, each in it's own FLA file. The final voice bed is simply cut into pieces, and the pieces are imported into the FLA files for animating. The audio can be imported at a lower quality to keep the file size down. When the animation is complete, all the pieces are stitched together later in postproduction, and the final, full-quality sound is mixed in at that point.

SCRUBBING

One nice feature of Flash MX (and 5) is sound *scrubbing*. Scrubbing allows you to grab the Playhead in the Timeline and drag it over consecutive frames and hear the sound as you go back and forth (6.10). To use this feature, set the sync for the sound to Streaming. Scrubbing is very helpful for lip synching and getting timing right with sound effects.

EDITING SOUND IN FLASH

Flash has some rudimentary sound editing tools built in, such as fades, volume, and setting in and out points (6.11). However, for broadcast quality, we don't recommend using these to edit your sound unless you're in a pinch. These settings will be exported when going out to video or exporting the audio separately, but you'll get much more control over the sound if you edit the sound file in an external application, such as Sound Forge.

SOUND DESIGN

Dialog may be the heart of most narrative animation, but sound effects, ambience, and music give the story an immersive quality and often a believability that wouldn't be achievable with voices alone.

SOUND EFFECTS

Invest in a basic sound effects library that you can build on. For example, the Hollywood Edge SFX library has inexpensive starter libraries to get you going. We've included other sound effects library sources in Appendix D.

But don't settle for what's there — make your own effects. Use libraries for sounds that are difficult, but experiment with the easier ones. Besides getting clever with kitchen implements, your biggest tool is *pitch shifting*. Pitch shifting refers to changing the pitch of a sound up or down. For example, Alvin and the Chipmunks' voices were created by pitch shifting normal voices way up. Don't be afraid to take any sound you hear and pitch shift it up or down. A chirping bird outside your studio window may just be the alien you want when pitched down an octave.

Experimentation is mandatory when creating your own sound effects. Can't find a sound effect for the USS Missouri firing on Iwojima? Be creative. Hit a pan lid, pitch shift it down 24 semitones, add some reverb, and roll the high end down to 500 Hz — someone will think it's real. That just saved you $600 on the latest "Authentic Sounds from WWII Collection."

AMBIENCE

Ambience is the sound of the world around you when you're not listening to it. It gives character and tone to a scene. Again, you can use ambient loops in stock libraries, but you can easily record your own ambient sounds.

In the field, you'll likely want to equip yourself with a mini-disc recorder or digital audio tape (DAT) recorder. There are many arguments about these technologies, which generally boil down to the fact that mini-disc compresses the audio, and DAT does not.

Mini-disc recorders are inexpensive (about $150 in the United States) and easy to conceal. So, for sneaky situations, a small stereo mic/mini-disc setup can work well. Check out such places as bars, grocery stores, shopping malls, and state fairs. Walk around with a mini-disc recorder in a handbag and a stereo mic (you can Velcro it to the handbag pointing forward so it's not noticeable). This way you can get unbiased, sleight-of-hand ambient sound.

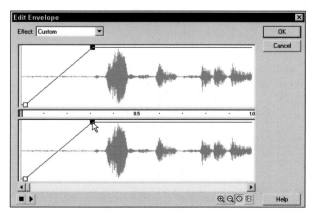

● 6.10

● 6.11

[NOTE]

Avoid the automatic record setting on the mini-disc, to avoid a pumping and breathing compression effect created from the mic automatically adjusting the recording level. Instead, manually adjust the recording level before starting. Watch the level in a loud setting for about 1.5 minutes for peaks, and if it's not maxing out, leave it alone and have fun.

For quieter ambiences where you need to turn the microphone gain up (fields, forests, recording a small child in St. Paul's Cathedral from the rear pew), a portable DAT is better because it has a lower noise floor (records quieter). It's also the solution if you need perfectly uncompressed quality. You can expect to pay as much as $4,000 in the United States for a portable DAT with a quiet, phantom-powered condenser mic/preamp or $800 in the United States for a serviceable, battery-powered stereo mic/DAT combo.

[TIP]

Ambient stereo WAV files take up twice as much space as mono, but a stereo field allows the voice-overs to be in the center, and the ambiences to spread around them. Spreading sounds out makes for an easier mix.

MUSIC

Many good freelance composers are out there. Unfortunately, you also find a lot of bad ones. Ask for demo tapes. If you want to have a real orchestra or brass band, plan on spending more for real instruments than you would for synthesized versions. You should also expect to pay for the studio time and recording costs of the performers as well as the performance fee and composition fee.

Alternatively, there are plenty of royalty-free (buy-out) libraries of music that allow you to pay once to use the music for a very, very long time, or "needle drop" music which charges a per-use royalty. These are often worth investigating if you don't need something custom, and you can find them online. For example, you can check out CSS Music at www.cssmusic.com. Be sure to read the licensing agreement carefully before making a purchase because there are many types of licenses, usually with restrictions on how you use the music.

CONCLUDING THOUGHTS

When your tracks are done, listen to the soundtrack without the visuals. It should be convincing and make sense. Don't think of sound effects as distinct elements separate from each other — you are creating an aural world, just like the visuals.

If a sound effect conflicts with the visuals, don't be afraid to take it out. If you've spent ten hours trying to make the perfect battleship effect, and it's just not working, take it out. If you leave it in, that bad sound effect will be there for you to hear over and over again.

Even if you are not doing the recording, editing, and sound design yourself, the information we've covered should help you understand the issues involved with broadcasting sound in Flash, and will hopefully help you maximize the use of your time in the recording studio.

ADDITIONAL INFORMATION

To understand the basics of digital audio, follow up with a read of *Streaming Media Bible,* by Steve Mack (Wiley Publishing, Inc.).

To get the basics of working with sound in Flash, check out *Flash Studio Secrets,* by Glenn Thomas (Wiley Publishing, Inc.). There's a chapter with an excellent introduction to applying sound in Flash animation. You may also want to visit Flashkit.com, (www.flashkit.com/tutorials/) and check out the audio tutorials and downloads.

For further reading on audio equipment and working with digital audio, check out the following Web sites:

- Pure Digital Audio: www.puredigitalaudio.org/home/index.shtml
- ProRec.com: http://prorec.com/
- Electronic Musician: http://electronicmusician.com/
- Home Recording.com: http://homerecording.com/

For help in putting together an audio editing system, talk to the folks at Sweetwater Sound (www.sweetwater.com). They carry just about everything under the sun as far as music equipment and software goes and can put you in touch with in-house experts for more demanding situations.

Applied Animation Techniques

Chapter 7

Working with Digital Puppets

Thanks to Sandy Debreuil for helping with this chapter.

A digital camera is your best friend.

SANDY DEBREUIL

In this chapter, we present two case studies of projects that use bitmaps and "digital puppetry" techniques in Flash. We're assuming that you're already familiar with basic Flash animation methods. *Digital puppetry* is a term used to describe how characters can be animated like puppets, instead of animated frame by frame. Characters are broken up into pieces (head, hands, arms, legs, mouths, eyes, noses, and so on), and each piece is stored as a symbol in Flash. Characters are then put together on the stage, and the pieces are moved from frame to frame (or tweened), rather than redrawing the whole character. There are many variations of this technique, and it can be used with hand-drawn art as well as bitmap-based art. Here we focus on projects created using manipulated photographs.

In this first case study, Janet Galore talks about her experiences creating art and animating the *FishBar* series, and some of the issues encountered in adapting a Web series to television.

CASE STUDY: FISHBAR

FishBar is an animated Web series featuring characters based on photographs of real animals, tending toward the oceanic variety. The series began simply enough, as a collaboration between Noah Tannen, Johan Liedgren, Janet Galore, and Christopher MacRae at Honkworm International in Seattle. Today, there are over 30 episodes, each from two to four minutes in length. In 1998, MTV's *Cartoon Sushi* (the successor to *Liquid Television*) showcased a couple of the *FishBar* episodes. To our knowledge, this was the first time Flash animation appeared on television.

FishBar's photosurrealistic art direction is based on photographs that have been manipulated in Photoshop. Photocollage works great when you are going for a look that is a little surreal and clunky, and most of the action takes place in a single plane, or series of planes, so you have a rather flat look, sort of "2½ D" instead of 3D (7.1–7.4). The master of this technique is Terry Gilliam, who did all the animation for *Monty Python* (among other things).

CAPTURING SOURCE MATERIAL AND WORKING IN PHOTOSHOP

The fish and crustaceans that populate the *FishBar* world were recruited at the local fish market in Seattle. Noah would bring back various candidates to audition, and the fish with the most personality made the cut. After their photo session was over, they were retired to the freezer, only to be taken out on special occasions.

To capture the source images, we used a digital camera. Any decent digital camera will do — a resolution of 2 megapixels is plenty. You want to be able to work close to your subject if you are photographing props and characters, so be sure to get a camera that allows a depth of field so that the whole object is in focus, otherwise you have to do a lot of retouching in Photoshop. It's also important to have even lighting and to avoid shadows. If your subject is time-sensitive (like dead fish, which don't look or smell so good the next day), be sure to grab all the angles and rotations you need in one session (7.5–7.8).

Next, I imported each of the images into Photoshop and adjusted for color and contrast, and painted the image as I pleased, making heavy use of the Cloning tool. I erased the backgrounds (I prefer to do it by hand with the Eraser tool), and cut up the main body parts into pieces, so they can be moved around in Flash. Each piece goes in its own Photoshop layer. You can test the animation by turning layers on and off and by moving pieces around. For *FishBar*, I tried to preserve the original personality of the fish, while

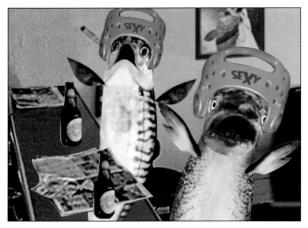

● 7.1

● 7.2

● 7.3

● 7.4   Photocollage works well for "2½ D" art direction.
© 1997–2002 Honkworm International.

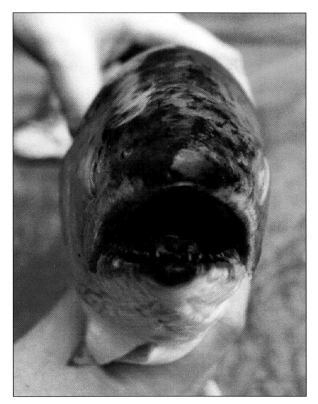

● 7.5

enhancing the character with new eyes, textures, or tweaks to the face and body. Figure 7.8 shows a fish that got a lot of enhancement. When I got one complete look for a character, I made the other rotations (usually just front, back, and side, because *FishBar* uses simple animation), including rotations of any hats or

● 7.7

● 7.6

● 7.8

costumes (7.9). If a character was particularly complex, I did each of the rotations as separate layered Photoshop files (7.10 and 7.11).

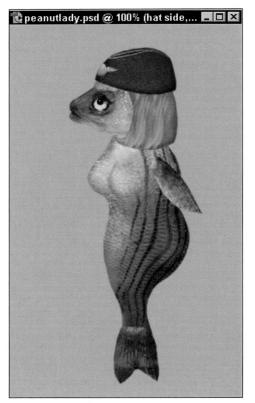

● 7.9   *FishBar* character © 1997–2002
                         Honkworm International

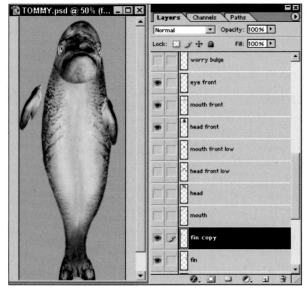

● 7.10

As far as image resolution goes, at the beginning of the series, I created the characters at a very small size because we were delivering on the Web and needed to keep things small. Later, we found that it works best to create the characters at least 900 pixels high, so you have high-quality base art. Then you can scale down on export if needed. As a rough guide, I figured the characters should be big enough so that they were a little bigger than NTSC resolution (720x540 pixels).

EXPORTING LAYERS FROM PHOTOSHOP

Early in the series, before Flash supported the PNG format, we exported each layer from Photoshop as a JPG and cut out the backgrounds in Flash using the Eraser tool. This was a lot of work, but as a result we had vectors defining the edges of all our symbols that used bitmaps, giving a very clean edge even if the bitmap was low resolution. Now using much PNG is much simpler, and it supports 24-bit color with transparency and imports nicely into Flash.

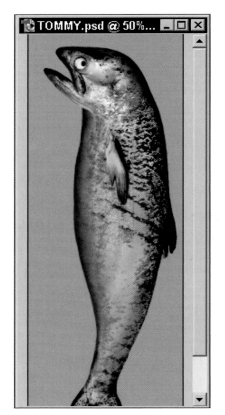

● 7.11

[N O T E]

Photoshop 5.5 gives poor results when exporting PNG, due to color management issues. It's better to upgrade to Photoshop 6 or 7 or use Corel Photo-Paint.

Exporting from Photoshop 6 and 7 is as simple as turning off all layers except the one you want to export (turn off the background layer as well). Then choose File➔Save for Web . . . and select PNG-24 with Transparency selected (7.12).

Save the file and repeat with all the layers you need to export, putting everything into one folder. After the PNG files are exported, you can use the Image➔ Trim command to make each of the PNGs as small as possible (7.13, 7.14). The Trim command allows

you to crop to the nearest nontransparent pixel in your image. Trimming is very important for Web delivery, but is also nice to keep the working file size down in general.

By using the automation tools in Photoshop 6 and 7, exporting lots of little layers can be simplified. You can easily record a set of actions that can take care of trimming and exporting the layers. See your Photoshop documentation for more information.

[C A U T I O N]

If you want to alter the original bitmap after you've used it in an animation, you can easily swap in a revised image (see next case study). However, if you do this, make sure that the new bitmap you are swapping in has the same dimensions and has the object in the same position as the original. Otherwise, the replaced images will be off in the animation, and you'll need to do a lot of tweaking.

IMPORTING ART AND CREATING CHARACTERS

To import the art into Flash, use the File➔Import command to import each PNG element into the Library. Bring all the bitmaps into the library, so you can begin constructing the characters. I suggest starting with a fresh Flash project to build your characters, so things don't get confusing. When the characters are finished, the Flash project containing the characters can later be opened as a Library and copied into the animation project file. Be sure to use the same document/stage size and framerate you'll be animating at. For

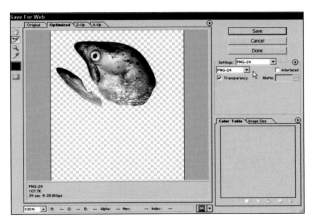

● 7.12

● 7.13

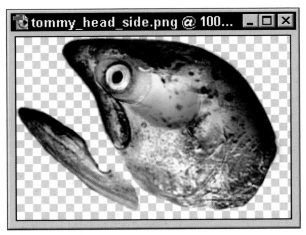

● 7.14

FishBar, we worked at 320x240. Framerates for the series varied from 8 fps to 12 fps, eventually settling at 15 fps for Web or video delivery.

After importing the bitmaps into Flash, I saved each bitmap as a separate symbol. Doing this makes swapping out elements easier later if you need to change something, especially if you need to swap in higher resolution artwork (see the Swapping In High-Resolution Bitmaps sidebar). Then I would assemble a "base" figure for each angle of the character (7.15). This basic figure can be dragged onto the stage and broken up so that the parts can be moved frame by frame.

Building a base character in Flash with properly nested symbols can speed up the animation considerably. Think about how the various parts of the character are naturally connected (knuckles are children of the fingers, which are children of the hand, which is a child of the wrist, which is a child of the lower arm, which is a child of the upper arm, which is a child of the torso, and so on). This technique is similar to how characters are built in 3D animation. Even with the simple characters found in *FishBar*, it's much easier to drag a whole character into a scene and break it up to manipulate symbols that are connected in a logical structure than it is to drag in the same pieces and reposition them.

[C A U T I O N]

If you do use nested symbols to build your characters, when you drag the character from the Library to the Stage, be sure to break up the main character symbol first (Ctrl+B) to gain access to the parts. If you don't, when you double-click the nested elements, you'll be changing the character symbol everywhere and not just the instance of the character. If you want to, you can save the modified character instance as a new symbol.

We also created basic behaviors, such as walk cycles or certain gestures, as animated symbols in the library. Figure (7.16) shows a walking cow cycle as an animated symbol that can be placed in the main Timeline (yes, that's a periscope coming out of her head). Remember not to use any Movie Clips if you plan to go out to video — only use graphic symbols. After you have a walk or sequence of moves as an animated symbol in the Library, copying those frames into a new symbol and modifying the movement to create a new behavior is easy.

[N O T E]

For step-by-step details on creating walk cycles and other character animation techniques, check out *Flash Studio Secrets*, by Matt Rodriguez and Glenn Thomas, as well as *The Art of Cartooning with Flash*, by John Kuramoto, Gary Lieb, and Daniel Gray.

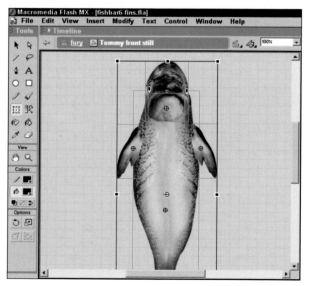

● 7.15   Bitmap elements are saved as symbols and combined into one symbol for the base of the character.

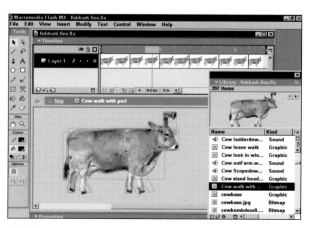

● 7.16

ADAPTING FOR BROADCAST

When we first exported *FishBar* to video, it was an experiment. We had created the series at 320x240 pixels, which is TV aspect ratio (4:3). So outputting to video was just a matter of scaling up. But unfortunately, bitmaps don't scale. We had focused so much on getting the file size small for Web delivery, the size of our bitmaps was accordingly pretty tiny, certainly not 720x540. First, we made sure to change the JPG compression for all the bitmaps so that they were not compressed at all. Then we exported to video and hoped for the best. What we found is that the smoothing option when exporting to video from Flash made up for a lot of the lost quality.

Also, because we had cut out each of the bitmaps by hand by erasing the backgrounds in Flash with the Eraser tool, the edges of the bitmapped symbols were defined by vectors, and so they had a very clean edge, even after scaling. The other thing working in our favor was that the art direction was intentionally rough, so the low-tech look translated well. If we had been going for higher production values, we would have had to swap in higher resolution bitmaps and increased the framerate of the animation to achieve a decent result (see the "Swapping in High-Resolution Bitmaps" sidebar). Increasing the framerate would have meant re-animating a lot. We had used 22 kHz 16-bit mono sound, which ended up working okay, but it was not broadcast quality.

As we progressed with the *FishBar* series, we learned a lot of lessons and got much better at going out to video. We used 44 kHz 16-bit stereo from the start and no sound compression when going to video. We increased the framerate to 15 fps and redid the character art at a higher resolution so we could get better results. We still worked at 320x240 in Flash, but used bitmaps that were about 900 pixels high for the characters, scaling them down to fit in the small 320x240 stage. For Web delivery, we just compressed the bitmap images like crazy (usually setting JPG compression at a quality of around 15), and because the images were scaled down to fit in the 320x240 stage, the high JPG compression didn't look bad at all. For television delivery, we simply exported the video at 720x540 with no JPG compression, so the bitmaps were then scaled up relative to the Flash document size, but were not bigger than their original import size.

Swapping In High-Resolution Bitmaps

If you've already created animation that uses bitmaps for delivery on the Web or other low bitrate environment, you can swap in higher-resolution art without having to re-animate the whole thing. Unfortunately, you can't simply use the Update command in the Bitmap Properties dialog box (double-click on the bitmap in the Library to bring this dialog box up), because the new bitmap will be a lot bigger than the original and will distort any symbols that use it. Instead, import the higher resolution art (Ctrl+B). If you first made symbols from the bitmaps and built off of those symbols instead of the actual bitmap, replacing the bitmap is easy. Here's how:

1. First, make a backup copy of your project — replacing bitmaps is risky.
2. Open up the symbol that contains the original low-resolution bitmap.
3. Add a new layer and move the new layer below the original bitmap layer.
4. Drag the high-resolution bitmap from the library into the new layer. Use the Info panel in Flash MX to scale and position the new high-resolution bitmap so that it is the same size and position as the original low-resolution bitmap. To do this, simply note the width, height, and (x, y) position of the original low-resolution bitmap and then select the high-resolution bitmap and enter those values into the Info panel for that object (7.17). The new bitmap snaps into the same position as the original.
5. Delete the upper layer containing the low-resolution bitmap, and you're set. The high-resolution bitmap now replaces the low-resolution bitmap wherever this symbol is used and is scaled so that it fits properly.

If you didn't make symbols from your original bitmaps first, you can still replace them, but doing so is a little more work. For each bitmap that you want to replace, create a new symbol (Ctrl+F8) and drag the low-resolution bitmap from the library into the scene, centering it. Now follow the steps outlined above to replace the low-resolution bitmap with the high-resolution bitmap (so that the high-resolution bitmap is scaled to be the same size as the original). Use the new high-resolution bitmap symbol to replace the old low-resolution bitmap wherever it is used in another symbol.

FishBar is a great example of how Flash can be pushed to work with art based entirely on bitmaps. As long as you keep in mind that bitmaps don't scale like vectors, there are some tricks you can use to get good results in video, even when you are repurposing Web-based animation.

CASE STUDY: FOX SPORTS NETWORK MAJOR LEAGUE BASEBALL SPOTS

Produce 130 animated commercials for a national TV broadcast in less than three months? No problem.

● 7.17

This project was created in 1999 for Fox Sports Network. Wongdoody was the advertising agency for Major League Baseball on Fox Sports Network, and they liked the art direction of Honkworm's *FishBar* series (as seen in the previous case study). So the folks at Wongdoody approached Honkworm, and together they created the concept for the spots. Two main characters, Phil and Woody, were guys at the local neighborhood bar, commenting about baseball. The 30-second spots were done in a goofy photocollage cutout style at an intentionally low framerate, so the motion was a bit jerky — not lifelike but "animated."

The catch is that Fox Sports wanted ten different commercials localized for 13 different markets (that's ad-speak for geographic regions), one for each major team in the league, totaling 130 ads! And they wanted the spots fast — over a period of a few months, on a tight budget. Debreuil Digital Works, an animation studio in Manitoba that has done a lot of animation for Honkworm over the years, came to the rescue. Sandy and Robin Debreuil developed new production methods that enabled them to produce the ads in record time. Sandy Debreuil told Janet Galore all the secrets of how they managed the feat and made Fox Sports Network happy.

CREATING THE ART

JG: How did you create the art for the characters, props, and backgrounds? What programs and equipment did you use?

Localizing on a Budget with Flash

Interview with Dan Pepper, Chief Operating Officer of Honkworm International

JG: How did you come to work with Wongdoody and Fox Sports Network?

DP: Wongdoody was considering using animation for a Fox Sports Major League Baseball campaign, so I approached them with samples of *FishBar*. After we had their attention, we created a demo to

show how the technology would translate to broadcast format. We also needed to demonstrate that we could handle the scale of the project affordably. Flash was the only way to accomplish what we did on time and on budget.

JG: Who came up with the ideas for the spots, and how was the writing done?

DP: The agency writers developed the script outlines, but depended on Honkworm to provide input and direction based on the

production design and nuances of animation. It was a collaborative effort that — as in almost all creative production processes — was bettered by working as a team with the agency.

JG: Why did you decide to use Flash?

DP: The bottom line was, well, the bottom line. Where else could you produce over a hundred 30-second spots for what equals the average cost of one, live-action spot?

Also, Flash provided a unique look. That was as much a selling point as the budget.

SD: For the characters, we worked with Honkworm to choose a couple of male models everyone felt would be suitable. After the models where chosen, they were photographed from every conceivable angle that we could think of, following a shot list we gave to Honkworm (7.18, 7.19). We also took shots of various facial expressions we could cut up.

Using those photos as the raw materials, we came up with a series of looks, which the clients would comment on, and then we'd do a series of revised looks, and so on. To create the looks, we used Corel Photo-Paint, which is basically Photoshop with bells and whistles. The breakthrough to get the looks was to drag the saturation bar to 100 percent, giving the characters that intense, splotchy look.

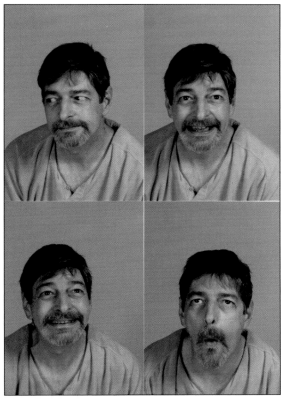

● 7.19   Facial expressions ready to be cut up.

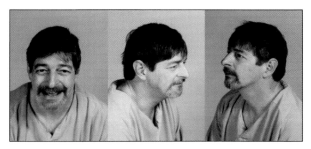

● 7.18   The character model is photographed from many angles.

JG: How much work was done in Flash versus postproduction?

DP: The work we did in Flash was 90 percent of the work — the postproduction was really like adding a frame to a finished painting. We worked hard to templatize the process in order to crank out the work and make a margin. The broadcast portion of the job consisted of:

• Transferring Flash to QuickTime to NTSC broadcast format

• Creating end title sequences

• Editing to time

• Sound sweetening/mixing

JG: Are there any other comments you'd like to add about the project and how Flash was involved?

DP: I believe the technology and process introduced by the technology affected the end product in a positive way. The finished media of any creative process is the summation, or derivative of that process. For that reason, I believe that the campaign is truly unique and unlike anything created before or since. Flash provides not just the tools, but an alternative process from which to create "new" (and I mean that in every sense of the word) media.

JG: What advice would you have for other studios that want to do advertising work?

DP: Understand your client's needs and expectations. Communicate clearly. Make the creative/production process easy and fun for them. You should under-promise and over-deliver.

After we had the looks, it was basically a matter of cutting out pieces from different images to do the collage-style animation (7.20–7.22).

We created a base head with no eyes, nose, or mouth and then created a series of mouths, eyes, and so on, which were layered on top. On a lot of pieces we also alpha-faded the edges so that they would blend in better with the base head (7.23). We then exported the image as a PNG (because PNG had the 24-bit alpha channels) and brought that into Flash, where we turned it into a symbol, ready to animate.

The other big trick with the characters and a lot of the props was to use a mask in Corel Photo-Paint and then create the to-be-localized artwork inside it. For example, in each localized animation, the characters are wearing the local team's baseball cap. So we'd make one cap, create a mask around it, save the mask, and then when we'd go to create the next 13 caps, we'd open the mask and make sure that the new teams cap would fit within the mask. This saved a huge, huge amount of time when it came to localizing each episode, because we didn't have to go in and tweak every animation; we could just replace the symbols and we knew they would match up perfectly (7.24–7.27).

For a lot of the localization art, we didn't have any actual props to photograph, so we just built what we needed in Photo-Paint, using the assets we had as a base. For example, we didn't have most of the team caps, but we had an official book of team logos. So we'd scan in the logos, photograph a hat and airbrush out the logo, and then paste on a scanned logo from

● 7.20

● 7.21

● 7.22

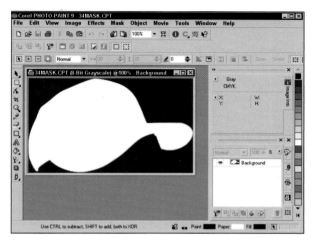

● 7.24

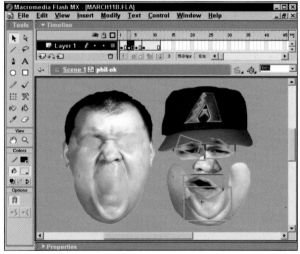

● 7.23

● 7.25

● 7.26

the team we needed. That, combined with using masks, made sure everything was the right size. With a little cleanup, the localized hats looked fine.

The backgrounds, however, were a little trickier. We had a bunch of photos of a bar in Seattle which we used as a reference and a source of textures, but a lot of the backgrounds were created completely from scratch in Photo-Paint (7.28). The reason for working from scratch to create the backgrounds is that we never seemed to have just the angle we needed.

All the baseball paraphernalia on the wall behind the two characters were from stock photos that were simply pasted into Photo-Paint. We then blended them together, added some texture to the bulletin board, added some noise to fade it back a bit, and just kept tweaking it until it looked right.

After we had the first one done, the localizations were easy, though time consuming (7.29–7.31). We kept notes of what filters, colors, and so on that we used, which sped up creating the new artwork.

● 7.29   Phil and Woody localized to Chicago, Pittsburgh, and Seattle. © 1999 Fox Sports Network

● 7.27

● 7.30   © 1999 Fox Sports Network

● 7.28   Bar background collaged together from various sources.

● 7.31   © 1999 Fox Sports Network

LOCALIZING THE ARTWORK

JG: How did you keep track of all the art assets? Did you use shared libraries, or just clever folder organization?

SD: We used Flash 3, and we kept track of all the assets using folders. I don't know if you could call it organized or clever, but it seemed to work. We had a bit of a naming convention set up, and we gave each team a folder to dump any localized artwork into, to avoid confusion. We had a lot of duplicated artwork in the different folders, but that wasn't really a worry. As an example, the directory structure would be. . . /teams/chicago/pngs/wFhat_chi.png. So every team would have it's own directory, and the localized, finished artwork would be in the PNGs directory. When it came time to localize the Chicago animation, you'd open up the Library in Flash, click Update on the graphic you needed to change (for example the hat, front view), go to the Chicago PNG directory, find the file named 'wFhat_chi.png' (Woody's hat, front view, Chicago), and boom, once the PNG was updated (7.32), the entire animation had the new, localized hat in it, and it always fit perfectly because we'd used the masks I mentioned earlier.

So localizing an animation took about 10 to 15 minutes, after the artwork was done. But it would have been a nightmare had all the artwork been different shapes and sizes; we'd have basically had to re-animate the whole thing. One other note on that: We'd rename all localized artwork in the library, putting a 'zz' in front of it, just to make sure that we didn't miss any PNGs, which was our biggest worry.

JG: What framerate and Flash document size did you work in?

SD: We used 15 fps, with a window size of 720x540. At the time, with Flash 3, this seemed really big and fast. Because it was so large, it was hard to see how they would play back on the computer using Test Movie or exporting in Flash. To test animations, we'd export them as AVI, and look at that for timing, and so on.

Sharing Libraries and Swapping Symbols

In Flash 5 and in Flash MX, you can swap a symbol with another symbol from a library, which is a big improvement over just being able to update bitmapped graphics. (You can still update bitmapped graphics, too, even from the stage.) If you click on an instance and swap in a new symbol, the new symbol will only replace that instance (7.33). To globally replace a symbol throughout a movie, simply drag a new symbol with the same name into the Library and click Replace when the program asks you to resolve the conflict between the new and the old symbol.

You can use the technique of swapping symbols to share a library on a network so that all artists are working with the same version of artwork. However, at this time, a shared library can only be opened by one person at a time.

Flash MX also has a feature that allows you to share library assets at runtime via the Web, but for video output, only sharing libraries at author time is applicable.

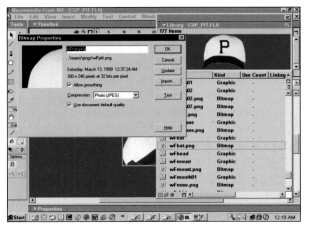

● 7.32

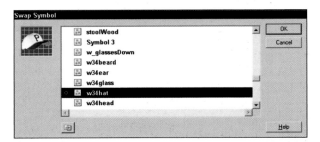

● 7.33   Swapping out a symbol in Flash MX.

JG: How did you swap out the art for all the different locations? Did you have 13 separate versions of each ad? How did that work out?

SD: It worked out great. That was the biggest worry going in, and it turned out to be the easiest part in the end. We did one version, revised that until everyone was happy, and then just replaced any PNGs that were localized (which was most of them, all the backgrounds, clothing, hats, players, and so on). We would end up with 13 versions for the client, but 95 percent of our work was done in a single version.

JG: Could you give me a walkthrough of what you had to do to localize one of the ads?

SD: So the client signs off, they're happy with all the artwork, the animation, timing, and so forth. We localize the artwork in Corel Photo-Paint. For example, we take the original piece of art for the background wall and replace all images that pertain to Seattle with images that pertain to New York. We change the color of the trim, using the NY team colors. Add any NY touches we can think of, but make sure the image stays the exact same size. Then using the mask from the original image, export the localized version. After all the localized art was finished, it was just a matter of updating the PNG file in Flash.

JG: Would you have done anything differently now if you had the same project again?

SD: I'd move somewhere with better bandwidth. As far as the actual computer/animation work went, it ran pretty smoothly, better than we'd hoped. I remember promising everyone that it would be no problem to do 150 animations in a few months and then wondering how we were going to do it. But as far as the technical side went, I was pretty happy with how it turned out.

PREVIEWING ON A TV MONITOR AND SETUP TIME

SD: One thing I would have done differently is that I would like to have set it up so that we could have seen the output on a TV screen. We started to do that, but had no time at the beginning, and then it was too late, because we were locked in with the look. We had a lot of problems with communication because there were so many parties in the chain, and the lack of communication screwed us up more than a few times. It would have been really nice to have had more time up front, as we had to come up with

the looks, the first animation, the organization, and figure out a way to localize all this in the first few weeks, which was insane; then after the first few spots were out the door, we had more time than we needed for the last few. I might also have whined a bit more about getting assets earlier; we pulled a lot of all-nighters.

MORE TIPS AND TRICKS

JG: Are there any special techniques or tips you want to mention?

SD: A digital camera is your best friend. We took hundreds of photos of hats, newspapers, shirts, and so on, and if we needed a new one, it just took a few seconds (7.34–7.36). It was really hard to anticipate the shots we'd need, so having the digital camera gave us a lot of flexibility.

● 7.34

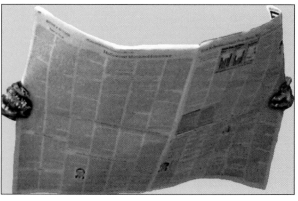

● 7.35

Another tip is to keep track of settings and parameters when you're creating artwork that will have to be localized. At the beginning of the project, there were a few times when we were creating different looks of the characters for the clients to choose from, and we'd be cranking out five or ten different variations a night. The next day someone would say "I liked number seven, make it more like that," and we'd be wondering how we made number seven. Especially considering that number seven was done at 4:30 a.m. and was probably the result of having your face fall on the keyboard, creating this really cool effect. So then we started keeping notes of anything that we did that was weird or different. Like turning the saturation up to 100 percent.

[T I P]

The History panel in Photoshop 6 and 7 is indispensable for remembering what you did (7.37). But as soon as you close the file, the history is gone. Remember that you can record a sequence of modifications as a Photoshop action for future reference.

SD: We found that sometimes fewer pieces of artwork worked better than more; for example, we'd build ten different arms built for an arm swing, it didn't look as good. Then we'd use only three, and it would look perfect. Part of that was the style of animation, but also your eye fills in a lot if you let it. We'd do a lot of the animation pose to pose; he starts here, and 13 frames later, he has to be here, now fill it in. You'd often change the last frame anyway, but setting up the pose was a good guideline to aim for.

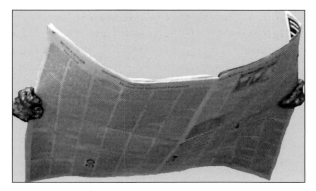

● 7.36

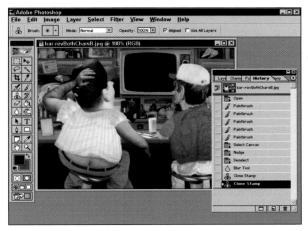

● 7.37   © 1999 Fox Sports Network

Chapter 8

Working with Traditional Animation in Flash

Thanks to Trevor Bentley for helping with this chapter.

All the artists on our Flash production teams are animators and designers first. They use Flash like they would use Photoshop or use a paintbrush.

TREVOR BENTLEY, ATOMIC CARTOONS

In this chapter, we take a look at how a traditional animation studio has embraced Flash as a part of its production process for broadcast animation.

Atomic Cartoons is a lively and talented traditional and Flash animation studio in Vancouver, Canada, founded in 1999 by Directors Trevor Bentley, Mauro Casalese, Olaf Miller, and Emmy winner Rob Davies. It is a full-service animation preproduction house, offering finished animation in Flash as well. (For more information on the studio, please see Appendix E, "Contributor Profiles.")

Atomic Cartoons is one of a growing number of traditional animation studios that are now using Flash in their broadcast production process. The approach, as with other traditional animators, is very different from a Web animation approach. Instead of starting with bandwidth-stingy digital puppets, Atomic Cartoons has figured out a good way to make Flash work with traditional cel animation techniques. They also use Web Flash techniques, such as tweening, but judiciously. The philosophy is to design and animate using traditional techniques that yield very high production values, and then use Flash to economize and streamline certain aspects of that process. This gives them the ability to fine-tune the level of detail (and thus cost) of the final product, while maximizing the quality.

THE ATOMIC BETTY PILOT

Atomic Betty is an animated television series created by Atomic Cartoons. They are pitching the pilot episode to various networks. The series is about Betty, a sweet and brainy little girl who, unbeknownst to her family and schoolmates, also happens to be Intergalactic Rocket Jockey and Defender of the Universe (8.1–8.4).

Atomic Betty was developed with cross-purposing in mind, so the animation can be delivered on the Web, TV, even as a game. However, Atomic Cartoons took a classical approach to designing the characters, layouts, and most of the animation.

On the Atomic Cartoons Web site (`www.atomiccartoons.com`), you can find information about the series as well as an animated promotional video and an *Atomic Betty* game (8.5–8.7).

Janet Galore spoke with Trevor Bentley, Mauro Caselese, and Rob Davies at the Atomic Cartoons headquarters in Vancouver, B.C.

USING FLASH IN A BROADCAST STUDIO

JG: Where do you use Flash in your production process, and what types of projects?

TB: We use Flash on occasion to produce the boardamatic [animatic]. We also use it to combine 3D elements with traditional 2D, and sometimes to ink and paint traditional 2D.

JG: Do you ever use other programs like Toon Boom Studio?

TB: No, we generally avoid that.

JG: When would you *not* use Flash in a broadcast situation?

TB: If we were doing a realistic action-adventure show, we wouldn't use Flash, but if the style were more wonky squash and stretch, we'd be more likely to use Flash.

JG: How long does it take to animate a half-hour TV program — is it quicker with Flash?

TB: Flash will allow you to cut some corners, but it comes down to how well you have planned the show before you start animation. Flash can be quicker, but it can also be more work. As far as a time frame to produce 22 minutes of Flash to broadcast, if you have all the pre-production done and are in the middle of

● 8.1   Atomic Betty © 2001, Atomic Cartoons.

● 8.3   Atomic Betty © 2001, Atomic Cartoons.

● 8.2   Atomic Betty © 2001, Atomic Cartoons.

● 8.4   Atomic Betty © 2001, Atomic Cartoons.

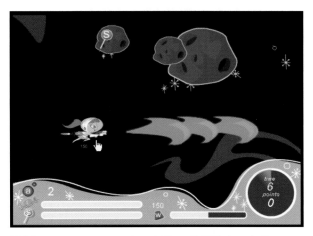

● 8.5   Atomic Betty © 2001, Atomic Cartoons.

● 8.6   Atomic Betty © 2001, Atomic Cartoons.

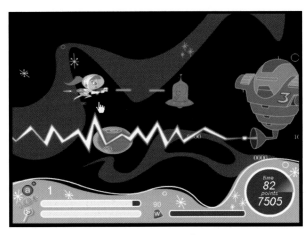

● 8.7   Atomic Betty © 2001, Atomic Cartoons.

the production (everything is running as well as it can), I'd say somewhere in the 20 week realm. But again, it depends on how complex the animation is.

JG: Can you give an example of when it would be more work in Flash?

TB: It's always more work up front to create the correct library elements and cycles, but over the duration of a production it evens out a bit.

THE TEAM

JG: What types of people do you have on your broadcast Flash team, or is it mixed in with the regular animation production team?

TB: All the artists on our Flash production teams are animators and designers first. They use Flash like they would use Photoshop or use a paintbrush. We tend to stay away from Flash-only animators.

MC: We've found a lot of good animators from Capallano College in North Vancouver, which is an excellent Flash and traditional animation school.

RD: People need to know how to draw and animate first. Once you have that, it's easy to learn Flash, and we have our own specific techniques we teach them.

JG: How many animators do you usually have on a project?

TB: It totally depends on the schedule, budget, and style. I'd say both *Dirty Lil Baster* (another Flash-based TV series) and *Atomic Betty* have crews of under ten people. (In Figure 8.8, an animator at the Atomic Cartoons studio analyzes some storyboards while

● 8.8

drawing at his table. The animation tables are equipped with the standard traditional animation equipment — pegs to hold the paper in place, and a rotating drawing surface for drawing a variety of angles easily. Figure 8.9 shows an animator working in Flash on a computer, and Figure 8.10 is another animator working traditionally.)

THE PRODUCTION PROCESS

JG: Describe your process from Flash to broadcast.

TB: When we are planning to produce animation for broadcast utilizing Flash, we start planning prior to the storyboard. In fact, we think about the process during the scripting, if we have that opportunity. The style of show you are doing relates to all the planning leading up to the actual animation. With *Atomic Betty*, we are trying to keep things simple (pose to pose), we try and keep the action going left to right. You know, like all the good old cartoons produced in the '40s and '50s.

(Figure 8.11 shows storyboards for another Flash to broadcast series, *Dog in a Box with Two Wheels*, and how those storyboards translated to the final scenes in Figures 8.12–8.20.)

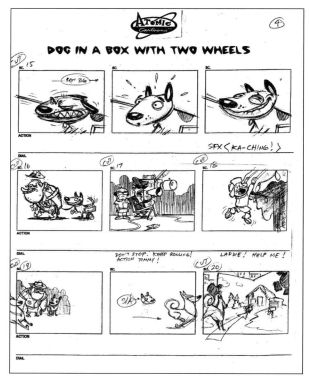

● 8.11

● 8.9

● 8.10

● 8.12

● 8.13

● 8.14

● 8.15

● 8.16

● 8.17

● 8.18

Once the board is done, with this in mind, we go through it and pick out the scenes that will be animated traditionally using pencil and paper, and the ones that can be animated in Flash. We go ahead and start animating. Once that's done, we import animation frame by frame and drag it into its respective scene. We time it and sync it up to any dialog or music. Once all the scenes are complete, we will export it and dump it on tape.

JG: Do you use shared library features of Flash, and if so, how? How do you manage version control?

TB: For both streaming and broadcast it's pretty simple — don't alter symbols in the library. But it isn't as important if you are going to broadcast and you never end up merging the separate sequences in Flash, and you merge the scenes in postproduction.

ANIMATION TECHNIQUES

JG: How do you decide which parts will be Flash and which will be pencil?

TB: We just look at how difficult the scene is. If it is a close-up and there isn't too much action, we will do it in Flash. If it's a really subtle acting scene, we will probably do it traditionally.

JG: Do you animate differently in Flash than using traditional methods? What are the differences?

TB: Every show is different. We usually mix the different animation styles on any given show. It just depends on what the board calls for. There's no big difference other than the time involved cleaning up traditional animation.

JG: When you scan the hand-drawn work, do you use any special software or special scanning setup?

TB: No, we use Photoshop. You can also scan in through software (like Toon Boom or Adobe Streamline). We scan the pencil sketches (8.21, 8.24) and then do the inking and coloring in Flash (8.22, 8.23, 8.25) — but again, it depends on the scene and how we've chosen to animate it.

[T I P]

If you're drawing cels that will be scanned, registration marks can help you align the drawings in Flash after they are scanned in.

JG: When you scan in the sketches, do you only scan extreme poses and then do the in-betweens in Flash, or do you scan in everything?

TB: Well, we may do a cheat, but usually if we've decided to do a scene in 2D, we scan in everything, cel by cel.

JG: It looks like you use a combination of the pencil and brush tools in Flash to do the inking for Betty.

TB: Yes — we use whatever the character calls for. But you have to be careful about how lines scale in Flash. We usually export to QuickTime to do a test to make sure the line weights are coming out the way they should.

● 8.19

● 8.20

JG: You also did animation on *Thugs on Film* for Mondo Media (8.26). Is the animation method for *Atomic Betty* different than what you did for *Thugs on Film*?

TB: I guess they are the same in that there are moving parts and we use a library, but not much else. *Thugs on Film* was probably the simplest show to do once we were up to speed because Mondo had its systems down. We always followed a system to produce every show. We never added any actual hand-drawn animation or messed with the stock library. With *Betty*, we have a stock library, but it is pretty small. Every scene has many more individual symbols because we rely on more traditional animation. Mondo was also very strict on file size because we were working on the Web version of *Thugs*. We don't have the same constraints since we're going out to broadcast.

● 8.21

● 8.24

● 8.22

● 8.25

● 8.23

● 8.26   Thugs on Film © 2001 Mondo Media. All rights reserved.

TECHNICAL DETAILS

JG: What platform do you prefer to work on, Mac or PC, and how much RAM do you typically have?

TB: We work primarily on Macs, but we do have a PC around in case a Mac has a problem opening up a really huge file. Sometimes PCs handle that a little better, we hate to say. We have at least 500MB RAM on the Mac G4s, and at least 256MB on the PCs.

JG: How about pixel dimensions?

TB: We use 720x486 — for NTSC standards.

JG: How do you get around the file size limitations for the FLA project files?

TB: You can't really escape file size. If you are doing streaming Flash, that's another thing, but for broadcast obviously you don't have to worry about dropping frames and chugging. As long as your computer can manage your file you should be fine. Just keep the sequences down to a manageable size.

JG: What framerate do you use for broadcast in Flash? What framerate do you export out to in post?

TB: Currently we use 30 fps. That way we can animate on twos, but go to ones if needed.

[N O T E]

Animating on "twos" or "ones" refers to the technique of using a new drawing on every other frame (twos) or every single frame (ones). Animating on ones is usually done for very detailed or fast movement.

POSTPRODUCTION

JG: What type of postproduction system do you use to print to video, or do you send it out?

TB: We usually get things to a point then send out for transfer. We will export a sequence of files from Flash and import them into After Effects or a similar program to get it just right. Then we dump it onto whatever the broadcaster requires.

JG: What elements of the animation are done in post versus in Flash, for example, titles?

TB: We find that titles are best done in post. In Flash they tend to look unclear. All the animation is rendered inside Flash.

JG: What are the main pitfalls you run into using Flash to go to broadcast?

TB: The biggest pain is file size problems and transfer costs. Once you start producing animation at 30 fps for any duration over a few minutes you start to run into file size troubles. If a 2-minute FLA comes in at 60MB, you can imagine what is going to happen for longer pieces. It just becomes tough to manage. I hate to say it, but it's easier to open some of the bigger files on a PC. The trick is to break down your work into manageable segments. Then comes the transfer — get out your bag-o-money.

JG: I have found the same thing, that's for sure. I have had Flash crash regularly on sizes over 50MB, and Flash also seemed to double the file size on bigger files when you save unless you do a "Save As." Have you found the same thing?

TB: Yes, we have found the larger the FLA file, the more weird little problems you discover. It's a pain, but the best way is to keep the work in smaller segments. We operate in chunks of 30 seconds to one minute. That keeps the file size reasonable.

BROADCAST TV NOTES

JG: Do you think Flash has a stigma against it in the broadcast television world?

RD: Well, it's frustrating that TV broadcasters seem to think that if you are working in Flash, it should be super cheap. But the reality is, if it looks like real animation, it will cost the same as real animation, regardless of whether you're doing it with pencil and ink or in Flash. Detailed, realistic animation requires time and skill, and using a different tool doesn't change that.

MC: Besides, Flash isn't the first time people have figured out a way to do animation economically — look at shows from the '70s like *The Hulk* and *Spiderman*. It was all sliding and zooming on static characters. So it's just a matter of figuring out what you're going for and doing what's required.

JG: Can you give us any tips on creating original programming for TV or doing a pilot?

TB: Keep positive! It is a war of attrition. Keep your pitches short and to the point. They need to be clear — and if you use animation to sell the show, make it lively.

Chapter 9

The Movable Camera:
Flash and Toon Boom Studio

Thanks to Mark Simpson and Sixty40 for helping with this chapter.

Shadows, special effects, focus blurs, and motion blurs are vital to giving a job a special look to bring it out of the flat-Flashness.

MARK SIMPSON, SIXTY40

Flash is pretty versatile, but as many agree, it's lacking in certain animation features. One feature present in more expensive, professional 2D software is a movable camera. A movable camera allows the animator to arrange 2D elements in a 3D environment, so that objects in the distance appear physically farther away than objects nearby. A camera can be moved through the 3D environment along a path, so you can do push-ins, trucks, and even follow behind a character walking through the environment.

USAnimation is a suite of professional (very expensive) 2D animation tools that provides a movable camera, among many other features. Recently, the makers of USAnimation, Toon Boom Technologies, Inc., developed a scaled-down, stand-alone animation tool, called Toon Boom Studio (TBS), that creates Flash output for the Web and provides a 3D scene planning environment with a movable camera. Being the smart people that they are, Toon Boom Technologies realized that many animators want to be able to go back and forth between TBS and Flash.

So, with the release of Flash MX, Toon Boom Technologies created a plug-in for Flash called the Toon Boom Studio Importer (TBSi) that allows Flash MX to import native TBS files. This means that you can create characters, backgrounds, and animation cycles in Flash, bring it into TBS to do the camera movement, then import those layers and scenes directly back into Flash for further animation work and export to video. This is just one possible production pipeline; some animators may work entirely in TBS and use Flash for the last few steps.

3D multiplane effects in Flash, previously only possible by painstakingly tweening each plane of an environment by hand, is now something that can be done simply and naturally. TBS and Flash MX together form a suite of tools that can streamline work and raise production values of animation created in Flash.

TOON BOOM AND FLASH MX

Let's take a look at how Toon Boom Studio works with Flash MX. Animation can be developed in TBS and then imported into a Flash project via the Toon Boom import module.

[N O T E]

Flash MX ships with a version of the Toon Boom Studio importer pre-installed, but you may need to download the latest version of the plug-in from the Toon Boom site in order to be able to import projects created with more recent versions of Toon Boom Studio (`www.toonboomstudio.com/product/ tbsi_plugin.ch2`).

To import a Toon Boom Project file in Flash MX, you choose File→Import and locate the appropriate .tbp file (9.1), and then you work in the Import dialog box (9.2), which gives you several options for controlling input. Then the TBS animation appears in the Flash environment, with layers automatically named and appropriate files in the library (9.3). Names of layers and symbols are preserved.

THE TBS INTERFACE

The Toon Boom Studio interface is designed from the bottom up with animators in mind, with a suite of tools that offer capability that goes above and beyond Flash.

The scene-planning mode (9.4) is the heart of TBS, with standard elements such as a Timeline and Properties palettes. The scene-planning mode contains advanced controls for camera angles and other adjustments, including a Camera View window (9.5), providing the ability to see the field of view of the camera and the elements in a scene from the top or side. Motion paths for objects and the camera can be created as well.

● 9.3

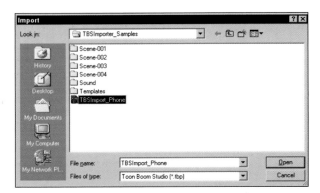

● 9.1

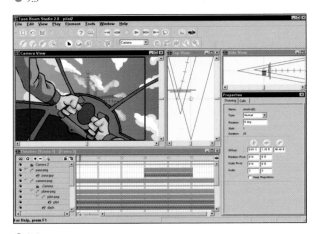

● 9.4

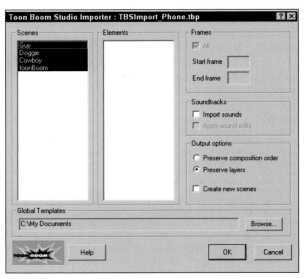

● 9.2

● 9.5

• TABLE 9.1: SIXTY40: THE NUTS AND BOLTS

PEOPLE	HARDWARE	SOFTWARE
Mark Simpson: Interactive, broadcast design	4 x Macintosh G4 256MB RAM	Flash 5 / MX Toon Boom Studio
Scott Collin: Sound design	Matrox RT Mac card for quick and dirty video previewing	After Effects 5 / 5.5
Matt Taylor: Character Design + head animator + illustrator	DVD burner	Adobe ImageReady / Photoshop
Ben Pietor: TV director	Wacom Intuos II tablet	Final Cut Pro 2.2

There is also the Drawing Mode (9.6), oriented toward the creation of individual elements, which includes such tools as the Exposure Sheet palette (9.7). In professional animation, an exposure sheet ("dope" sheet) is a method of keeping track of the cels that make up each frame of an animation, including tracking dialog per frame and camera instructions. In TBS, the Exposure Sheet palette is similar, showing layers and frames for each element used in the animation.

There are many other interesting features of TBS, including a lip sync tool introduced in version 2, which will help you to analyze the sounds in a voice track and generate a "lip chart," which can help with the process of syncing the mouth motion of a character with underlying dialog.

GETTING STARTED WITH TBS

With a street price of around $350 in the United States, TBS can pay for itself in the time it can save and the new possibilities it can open up. There is a learning curve for folks not familiar with traditional animation, and it helps to have a little knowledge about working in 3D environments, but there are a number of helpful tutorials that come with the program, and the investment of time in learning the program is worth being able to give real depth to your Flash animations.

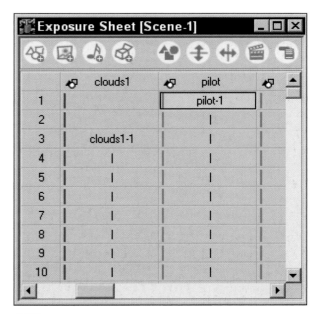

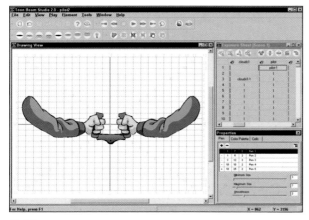

● 9.6

● 9.7

For more information, visit www.toonboomstudio.com. You can register and download a free trial version, or go through several online tutorials (including an overview of how the Flash MX importer works) and ask questions of experienced Toon Boom users in the User Forum. You can also submit an animation for consideration to be played in the online Theater, where you find such categories as Promotional, Music Video, and Student Projects. Try visiting the product information page, where the workflow section can help you get a sense of how Toon Boom works.

Case Study

Qantas Airlines TV Spots, by Sixty40 Pty. Ltd.

Sixty40 Pty. Ltd. is an animation studio in Sydney, Australia (see Appendix E, "Contributor Profiles"). Their work is renowned for its offbeat slant and high production standards. This case study features a TV commercial they created for Qantas Airlines using a combination of Flash and Toon Boom Studio.

Janet Galore spoke with Mark Simpson and Matthew Taylor from Sixty40, about how their studio is set up, how they created the spot, and why they used the tools they did.

About Sixty40

JG: Tell me about Sixty40 and what you do.

S4: Sixty40 was founded to take advantage of the strong cross-media foundations of its team. By blending experience and knowledge in both traditional and new media, Sixty40 attempts to provide a unique suite of services for clients and media of all shapes and sizes.

The core of Sixty40 is formed by four young specialists who cover sound, animation, interactive, and film/TV production (see Table 9.1). Still enthused by the prospects of the advertising and media world, we plunge in to conceive, develop, and produce what we believe is both innovative and effective.

In terms of services, we cover animation, DVD, online, TV, and sound production. We collaborate on most jobs and find the cross-disciplinary attack to be effective in coming up with some excellent creative and production techniques for different jobs.

Cross-media delivery is an excellent motivation for incorporating Flash into the production process — elements from the TV job can be used online in e-cards, site design, screensavers, mobile devices, and so on. In an ever-changing media landscape, it's vital to have a broad base of media components upon which one can develop a multitude of media executions. Using the tools smartly means that a small company can provide the client with cost effective and sexy media.

JG: What are your backgrounds?

Mark Simpson: Eight years in the interactive world, returned to the real world for a break. Now does motion graphics too.

Matt Taylor: Experienced illustrator and animator. Draws a lot. Made his own sweatshop and employed himself. Started in comics, still in comics.

Scott Collin: Sound design and music composition. Sits in a room with lots of music equipment . . . knows what it does.

Ben Pietor: TV Promo producer, independent filmmaker and freelance commercial ya-ya.

JG: Do you consider yourselves traditional animators, or Web animators, or . . . ?

S4: Computers and the proliferation of desktop tools gave us the opportunity to develop our traditional animation skills. As a company we simply use the tools available. We have no particular affiliation to the Web or any aversion to it. Whatever works the best to deliver a good product on time. We use paper and pens. We're not Web animators in the sense that the Web has traditionally spawned crap, but we're not traditional animators, as we've never been invited to a Disney sweatshop.

JG: How do you define "broadcast quality?"

S4: It goes on TV without shame.

Flash in the Production Flow

JG: How is Flash usually involved with your work? Why do you use it?

S4: It's important to remember that producing animation in Flash isn't an end unto itself. It's a tool that helps to produce work efficiently and effectively. We often use Flash as a part of a production arsenal, and by identifying its strengths and flaws in a production flow, it has become an excellent tool.

Flash is an extremely versatile animation tool, and works well for teams of all sizes, from an individual animator to jobs that require the cooperation of a team.

Vectors rule in so many ways, with the same material being able to be output for the Web, film, or print, it allows small numbers of people to produce work on a previously unpractical scale. Additionally, scalable vectors mean that single drawings can leap tall buildings as well as appear on mobile devices without much re-working or re-inking.

JG: So what's a typical production flow like?

S4: Depending on the job, we animate sequences and character loops and scene elements in Flash and then use Director, Toon Boom Studio, or After Effects to composite, move characters, do panning shots and zooms.

As required we'll go out of house to get high-end equipment. For example, we'll take final QuickTime movies rendered out of After Effects to a Flame box for final effects if required.

We find that Flash is a great tool for illustration and animation production, but left to its own devices tends to have a very flat look that we find requires a final finishing off in something like After Effects or Flame (depending on the job). Things like shadows, color correction, special effects, focus blurs, motion blurs, are vital to giving a job a special look to bring it out of the flat-Flashness.

JG: "Flat-Flashness" — you've coined a new term.

S4: I believe there is a paradox with Flash. The pay-off of the privilege of ease of use and accessibility is that much of the artistry of traditional animation is lost on Flash production work. Backgrounds, use of non-line-based media, and real-world media (like paint and pastels) need to be incorporated and considered in order to put Flash back in its place: as a part of the production process in achieving a desired look. Already we see Flash being identified as a cheap and dirty way to make cheap and dirty animations. Case in point: South Park, which made the world sit up and say, "Cheap, fast animation rocks!" But in fact, tremendous effort was put into recreating the paper textures and drop shadows, which are the coup de grace of the show's visual stylings, and it was all re-created in 3D.

JG: What are some tools you've used in conjunction with Flash?

S4: Toon Boom Studio (TBS) is a tool designed to solve a very specific production problem, the laying up of 3D scenes using Flash components. As in Flash, all of this was possible previously but the tool automates and regulates tasks that would otherwise have been done by hand or more particularly, by eye.

We also like TBS because it ties in traditional animation vocabulary and concepts (dope sheets), which saves Flash animators from reinventing the wheel for every job. Production tools like color palettes, lip

synch, libraries, shared server support all mean it can help in the production process.

After Effects 5.5 — After Effects is also a vital tool, now allowing the importing of SWFs and the laying out in 3D of scenes. Again, useful replacements for stuff we had to do by eye.

Director 8.5 — Good tool for the real-time laying out of scenes and mocking up for client and internal review. Imports Flash, text, and big bitmaps.

Pencil + paper version 1.0 — The original, and the best. Pencil and paper provide quick storyboarding functionality with multiple version-saving on different sheets including an eraser function for on-the-fly updates. Easy cross-office transportability and "flick through" display mode.

The Qantas Airlines Spot

JG: You guys did this TV spot for Qantas Airlines, which aired in Australia for a summer (Boxing Day!) sale. Who came up with the concept and how did it develop?

S4: It was an agency concept, but Sixty40 came up with the production strategy and executed the concept. We worked with their script.

[N O T E]

To see other work by Sixty40, visit the Flash Design for TV site, at www.wiley.com/go/ftv.

JG: How did Flash impact your work on this project — was it absolutely necessary to use?

S4: Flash sped up the production process enormously.

By tracing straight into Flash, a lot of the cleanup process is at least halved and since the line work is in vectors, the animator has greater versatility in reusing work at different sizes. Certain elements can be penned directly into Flash using a Wacom tablet.

Features such as reusable libraries mean that elements can be shared across scenes, and color palettes mean a more streamlined colouring process as uniformity is guaranteed. Flash also provides intuitive illustration tools with easy line and fill manipulation, both of which save hours of redrawing and/or mucking around in other software.

JG: Was Flash faster, or cheaper, or somehow better than other options?

S4: Our competition for the job pitched a 3D concept that relied upon an expensive 3D toon-shader

9.8

9.9

9.11

9.12

9.14

9.15

● 9.10

● 9.13

plug-in to give it a hand-drawn look. Flash proved the right tool to deliver the job as specified.

JG: You used Toon Boom Studio as well. Why?

S4: TBS was used mainly for its 3D scene layout features.

JG: How were the scenes set up?

S4: Each scene is broken down into key elements. All the animated elements are made into graphic symbols as opposed to movie symbols, so the animation is exported properly if going from Flash to QuickTime. The simple style of the Qantas character design meant most of the animation was in the camera moves and scene changes.

JG: Can you give us a description of your typical step-by-step production process?

S4*:* I'll describe the steps we take as follows: Storyboarding, Animatic, Layout/Keyframing, Animation, Compositing, and Finishing.

Storyboarding

Pencil and paper. Still sketches to illustrate style and movement, including "camera move" notes and any special effects required.

Animatic

Storyboard panels are imported as JPGs into Flash. The rough sound cut is laid out in the timeline and still panels are arranged according to script (9.8–9.22).

Layout and Keyframing

Scenes are broken down in terms of keyframes, keyframes are sketched on paper and brought into Flash for tracing and coloring of key elements such as character movement and the wave effects and so on.

● 9.16

● 9.17

● 9.18

Animation

Flash sequences are imported into Toon Boom Studio for camera moves (9.23–9.27), zooms (9.28–9.30), and cut-aways (9.31–9.33), exported as SWFs, and then timing is refined.

Compositing

SWFs are imported into After Effects 5 and combined with other sequences, text, and graphics.

Finishing

In After Effects, we do the final shading, sound synch, and visual effects.

● 9.19

● 9.21

● 9.20

● 9.22

[TIP]

Mark and Matthew recommend putting a 0.3 Gaussian blur over finished video to remove jaggies and provide a smooth finish.

JG: Are there differences between how you'd animate to go to the Web versus broadcast only?

S4: Animation for the Web requires several rounds of optimization to ensure smooth playback. Broadcast animation has a priority of smooth 25 fps motion [for PAL], so obviously requires more detail and attention to tweening.

JG: Did you have to do anything special to the art to optimize for broadcast?

S4: We added secret Sixty40 love.

● 9.25

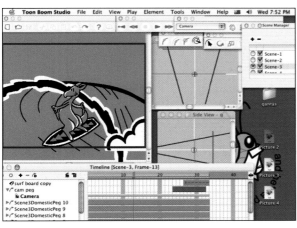

● 9.23

● 9.26

● 9.24

● 9.27

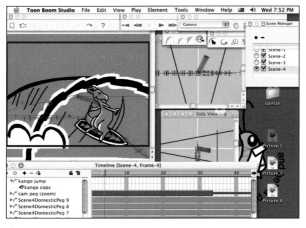

● 9.28

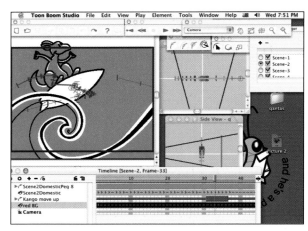

● 9.31

● 9.29

● 9.32

● 9.30

● 9.33

QANTAS ANIMATION: CAMERA MOVES

Figures 9.23–9.27 are shots of the camera moves mentioned earlier in the interview with Sixty40. These shots illustrate how TBS can move the camera in a scene, without having to move the elements themselves.

QANTAS ANIMATION: ZOOMS

Figures 9.28–9.30 are shots of the zooms mentioned earlier in the interview with Sixty40. A zoom is a particular type of camera move, where the camera is moved closer to the elements of a scene, moving the viewer closer to the action.

QANTAS ANIMATION: CUTAWAYS

Figures 9.31–9.33 are shots of the cutaways mentioned earlier in the interview with Sixty40. Note the lines of the camera motion are broken in these shots, indicating the camera is cutting from place to place in the scene.

Chapter 10

Flash with 3D Applications: Making a Music Video

Special thanks to Tom Sacchi and unit9 for primary development of this chapter.

Key to the success of a coherent campaign across different media is a strong sense of continuity in style and theme.

TOM SACCHI, UNIT9

unit9, located in London, is a digital production company that specializes in updateable sites, digital marketing, media, and animation (10.1). Co-founder and Director Tom Sacchi was kind enough to give a personal tour of how a music video for the band Mint Royale was created, using Flash, Softimage, and USAnimation — in just four weeks. This chapter is a rare, behind-the-scenes look at cutting edge techniques using some of the best animation tools available, in Tom's own words. The production credits appear at the end of the chapter (see Table 10.2).

THE CONCEPT: PROJECT INTRODUCTION

The animated promo for Mint Royale's single, "Show Me," is just one part of a large-scale branding exercise, spanning a CD and 12" record cover, and a microsite complete with game, card game, viral e-mail, and even purchasable action figurines.

Key to the success of a coherent campaign across different media is a strong sense of continuity in style and theme. The concept of Minty was born out of a common passion for manga among unit9's designers as well as an appreciation of the many different incarnations of a manga character. (*Manga* refers to a traditionally Japanese type of animation and comics that uses cute cartoon characters.)

The relationship between the actual single "Show Me" and the 12–inch album cover, video, game, card game, Web site, and action figures is very strong.

"If you're born as a character from a manga comic, you'll soon begin moving through different media — you'll become animated, and you'll be turned into 3D, then be on key chains and card games, toothbrushes, T-shirts and toilet seats, and on and on . . ." says technical director Yates Buckley, "until eventually you become a kind of new pagan deity that has a meaning much wider than the original drawing does."

● 10.1

● 10.2

Ben Hibon, unit9's lead designer, came up with the central character of the campaign: Minty, a Pokémon/manga-style creature. Figure 10.2 shows Ben working in After Effects with the character and storyboards. The video portrays a dream-type sequence that follows Minty around through its short, happy life (10.3–10.7). The online game sees Minty flying around Star Island, collecting other creatures from the video. A look at the Star Island game as a companion piece to the "Show Me" video can be found in Chapter 16, "Cross-Purposing Flash for Web, TV, and DVD."

A diagram of all the different incarnations of Minty and his world is shown in Figure 10.8.

● 10.3

● 10.5

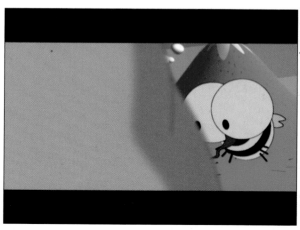

● 10.4

● 10.6

● TABLE 10-1: SOFTWARE USED IN MAKING THE SHOW ME VIDEO

SOFTWARE	PRIMARY USE	SECONDARY USE
Flash	Character development	Drawing
Flash	Frame by frame animation	Drawing
Flash	Textures for 3D	For coherence and color control
Softimage 3D	Modelling—Minty's world	
	Clouds scene	
	Nasty Flower action animation	
USAnimation	Inking and painting Final compositing	Xsheet provides complete control over toon elements
After Effects	Broadcast color correction	
	Flicker reduction	
Media 100	Off-line edit	

CREATING THE "SHOW ME" VIDEO

The video took one full month of very solid work to complete. The workflow went through storyboarding, character design, art direction, more detailed planning of the scenes with the animatic, 3D modelling and animating plus 2D animation, effects work in After Effects, and then finally editing.

THE CHALLENGE

With less than a month to complete from start to finish, technical issues and rendering times proved critical for the project. The biggest challenges for the team in producing the "Show Me" video related to combining 3D background sequences with the 2D Flash animations of the characters.

Because the 2D depended on the 3D for reference, and the time available meant it all had to happen at the same time, it was a challenge to make sure the scenes were moving along the production line at all times and that the 2D team was always supplied with reference background sequences.

TOOLS

The production flow was largely determined by what tools we used, and how they all fit together (Table 10.1).

● 10.7   Stills from the Mint Royale music video "Show Me" used courtesy of Faith & Hope Records Ltd.

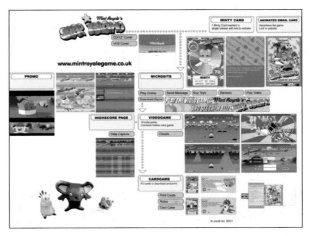

● 10.8

Flash + Wacom Tablet

- Use to create the 2D animated character drawings.
- Use to replace the pencil and paper part of the process.
- Use to allow for fast drawing of frame-by-frame animation. Has the added benefit of allowing the option to animate using the Tweening tool. Onion skinning is used to preview adjacent frames of animation. In this respect, Flash is an animator's dream.

Softimage 3D

- Use to generate the background stills and sequences.
- Use for subtle camera movements to help create a more cinematographic feel.

USAnimation

- Use to vectorize the animations made in Flash. (Flash sequences had to be rasterized for technical reasons.)
- Used for linking and painting the individual cells.
- Use to provide ultimate control over the animation.
- Use to scale the animation moves over the background with its virtual camera.
- Use for compositing the 2D and 3D sequences into the final rendered frames.

After Effects

- Use to import final rendered frames.
- Use for color correction and flicker reduction.
- Use to output QuickTime movies.

Media 100

- Use to edit QuickTime movie sequences, and cut to music.
- Use to output final product to tape.

THE TEAM

The team consisted of a Project Manager, a Technical Director, and two separate teams of animators — a 2D team working in Flash and USAnimation, and a 3D team working in Softimage | 3D.

PROCESS OVERVIEW

Each scene was numbered, arranged by importance, difficulty, duration, and render overhead, and arranged in the production timeline accordingly. "Render overhead" refers to how much time it will take to render out all the frames, which can be hours or days.

- The 3D animator directed the camera around the virtual environment, and then output sequences of low-res stills at 24 fps.
- The low-resolution renders were then brought into Flash as a sequence, just as a reference for the 2D animator.
- The 2D animator animated at 12 fps and exported the action as a series of black and white drawings.
- These were then imported into Toon Boom's USAnimation and batch-vectorized.
- Arranged by scene, all the stills were brought to 24 fps using the Xsheet feature in USAnimation.
- The characters were inked and painted in USAnimation, and shadows and effects were added.
- Characters were composited with the backgrounds.
- Color correction was done in Adobe After Effects and, finally, the video was edited in Media 100.

THE PROCESS: STEP BY STEP

Let's take a detailed look at some of the main steps in creating the "Show Me" video. As with most animations, once the narrative is determined, the first step is creating storyboards.

Storyboard

With the campaign's theme and the stylistic approach decided, a detailed storyboard was produced (10.9, 10.10).

The storyboard was then developed into an animatic to define the speed and pace of the shots. The animatic was extremely useful in establishing the emotional content of each shot — it's sometimes difficult with storyboards alone to get the "feeling" and timing of the shot. This is particularly relevant in music videos, because they are often cut to the music.

We originally got the job based on the strength of the storyboard and animatic we made. Time scales were very tight, and there was no time for client intervention once production had started. The guys at Faith & Hope Records were great. They made small adjustments to the story, sat back, and took a leap of faith (well, they thought so).

The final video edit is very close to the original storyboard, emphasizing the importance of story-boarding this type of project (10.11, 10.12). With no time to waste and rendering and hard drive over-heads spiraling, we couldn't afford to spend any time on material that wouldn't make it into the final edit. The clock was ticking.

The storyboard was fundamental to the structure of the project, as we coordinated the workflow of each team.

Creating a Test Scene

The tricky bit of the project was combining these separate techniques originating from separate software packages to look as integrated as possible in the final product. Also, there are many ways to skin a cat — do we do this or that in package A or package B? How does it look, how long will it take and who is going to do it on what machine?

Creating a test scene was essential to establish and test the procedure we would be working on 24/7 for the next month. So we tested the entire production

● 10.11

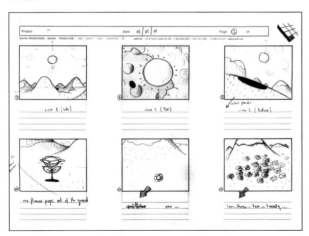

● 10.9

● 10.10

● 10.12   Stills from the Mint Royale music video "Show Me" used courtesy of Faith & Hope Records Ltd.

● 10.13

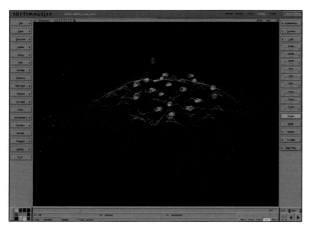

● 10.14

line and viewed the final results on a monitor out of Media 100. We tested various options, tweaking the process until we were satisfied that it would give the desired results and would work within the time frame that we had. Figure 10.13 is a shot of the test scene we decided to do.

In creating the test scene, we needed to determine:

- The overall look and feel of the 2D/3D Animation composite.
- How the colors would come out in the PAL color spectrum.
- The rendering time versus quality ratio for the background sequence.
- The rendering overhead for FX in After Effects.

To address the main output issues of flicker and PAL color spectrum, we adjusted the color and design of the textures in Flash, after importing to Softimage, and in the render settings.

We then controlled the final effect with After Effects filters: Effect➔Video/Broadcast Color➔PAL and Effect➔Video➔Interlace Flicker.

We tested various lighting solutions and different texture resolutions as well as different rendering parameters to get the highest quality render possible for our limited time budget. We found it was quicker to add more detail in the textures, render at a slightly lower aliasing setting in Softimage, and not use Mental Ray for rendering.

Modeling in Softimage

Ben Hibon initially sketched out what he wanted and passed it along to Roberto Simoni to recreate as a 3D environment (10.14).

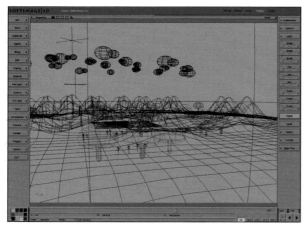

● 10.15

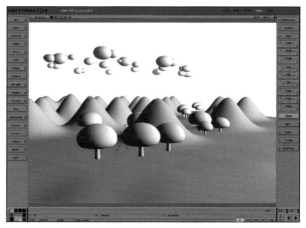

● 10.16

Once the overall model was in place, we constructed several separate "sets" to better suit specific shots from the storyboard (10.15, 10.16). The great thing with 3D is that you can move and scale items around in space to suit the camera.

Flash-to-Softimage Textures

The look of the 3D was going to greatly affect how the Flash and 3D components would come together. To make sure that the backgrounds would then fit correctly in the final composited scene, very simple cartoon-like textures were generated in Flash for:

- Sky (10.17)
- Snow peaks (10.19)
- Trees (10.18)
- Grass (10.20)

These were exported as high-resolution stills from Flash, which were then scaled and manipulated in Photoshop before being introduced to Softimage.

● 10.17

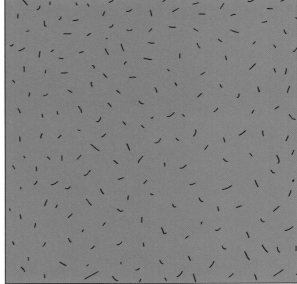

● 10.19

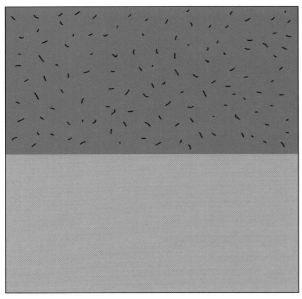

● 10.18

● 10.20

Working with 3D Sequences in Flash

To create the 2D animation in Flash, the 2D animators needed stills from the 3D backgrounds as a visual reference. But it wasn't going to be possible to give the 2D animators full-quality 3D backgrounds to work from. This is because rendering PAL-sized finished sequences in 3D takes time, which means that the 2D artists would be kept waiting. Also, Flash can't handle long sequences of large images.

To solve these problems, we decided to export low-res images from Softimage at 1/2 PAL resolution, rendered with low-quality settings. Doing this reduced the rendering times to minutes, and we could leave the high-quality PAL 768 x 576 renders to happen overnight. (The high-quality backgrounds would be brought in later, into USAnimation.)

The half-size, low-quality background stills were then batch processed with Graphic Converter and Photoshop to convert from Softimage PIC format,

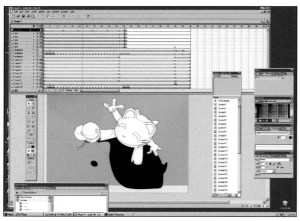

● 10.21

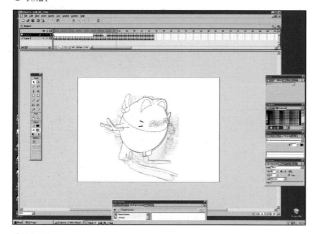

● 10.22

and to double the size so they would be at the proper PAL size before bringing into Flash (which didn't add appreciably to the file size). The 2D animators could then begin working.

Animating in Flash

Each scene was numbered as per storyboards and started with a new PAL-sized FLA at 768x576 pixels, 12 fps. Then title safe and image safe guidelines were imported, and the PAL-sized low-quality JPGs of the background stills were brought into a separate layer. The character animation was then drawn over the top (10.21).

The characters were drawn directly into Flash using a Wacom tablet. A modified, frame-by-frame style of animating was used. After a pose is perfected on a keyframe (using the Zoom tool to tweak the lines), the pose is copied and pasted in place on the next frame, where the lines are pulled to develop the motion (10.22). Old school animators are bound to frown, but it really works very well and has several benefits. The interface really facilitates frame-by-frame drawing, while at the same time allowing for animation techniques.

[N O T E]

We used the Pencil tool, which has better control at various zoom levels, but, unfortunately, won't work with the USAnimation swf2Paint converter.

Exporting Flash to USAnimation

USAnimation provides an SWF to USAnimation converter called Flash2paint. "Wonderful!" we thought, "lets keep it all vector, speed the production along, save disk space and have a nice time."

Unfortunately that was not to be the case. There are, of course, as always, some limitations. The guys at USAnimation tech support were great and helped us identify the problem. It turned out that Flash2paint only works if you have drawn your character using the Brush tool in Flash as opposed to the Pencil or Line tool.

But the Brush tool did not work well for us, because the Brush tool paints at a different size, depending on the level of zoom you are using. The Pencil tool maintains the line size constant as you zoom in and out, and so worked much better for the animation technique we were using. Flash does have a Convert Lines to Fills feature, but, unfortunately, it produces quirky results.

So we had to find a workaround. We bit the bullet and rasterized the stills coming out from Flash by exporting the animation from Flash as a series of PAL-sized PNGs. We had to use PNGs, because it's the only still image format shared by Flash and USAnimation.

USAnimation Workflow

First, the series of 2D character stills from Flash (PNGs) were imported into USAnimation as if they were a bunch of scans from a traditional pen and paper animator. These stills were then batch vectorized (10.23), and ink and paint were applied to each of the frames. After the toon is in USAnimation, it becomes very easy to control all aspects of it, such as color, framerate, and line thickness (10.24, 10.25).

USAnimation's Xsheet environment was used to match the 12 fps Flash animation to the 24 fps of the Softimage generated background (10.26). Then the high-resolution PAL-sized background images were imported. Effects such as shadows were added, and the final scenes were composited (10.27). The final image sequence was output to a TIFF sequence to use in creating the video.

● 10.25

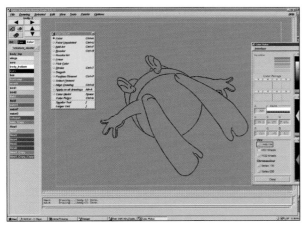

● 10.23

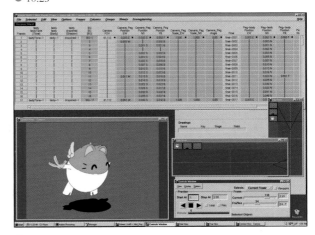

● 10.26

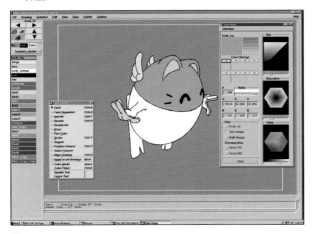

● 10.24

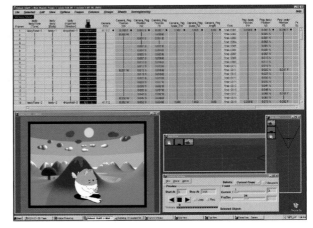

● 10.27

• TABLE 10-2: CREDITS FOR THE UNIT9 SHOW ME PROJECT

ARTIST	Mint Royale
TRACK	"Show Me"
COMMISSIONER	Amul Batra, Faith & Hope Records
CREDITS VIDEO	Concept, Design, and Production by unit9 ltd. for Faith & Hope.
	Directed by Ben Hibon
	Producer: Piero Frescobaldi
	Art Director: Ben Hibon
	Technical Director: Yates Buckley
	Project Manager: Tom Sacchi
	2D Animation: Ben Hibon
	3D Animation: Roberto Simoni
CREDITS VIDEO GAME	Gameplay design: Chris Peck, Yates Buckley, Ben Hibon
	Copy: Yates Buckley
	Illustrator: Ben Hibon
	Programming: Chris Peck
CREDITS WEB SITE	Art Director: Ben Hibon
	Programming: Yates Buckley
	Web Development: Heikki Rantakkari
CREDITS CARD GAME	Gameplay design: Yates Buckley, Ben Hibon
	Copy: Yates Buckley, Ben Hibon
	Illustrator: Ben Hibon
	Programming: Yates Buckley
CREDITS FIGURINES	Design and modeling: Ben Hibon
TECH. CREDITS VIDEO	2D Animation in Flash and USAnimation
	Hand drawn textures on 3D environment modeled and animated in Softimage 3D
TECH. CREDITS VIDEO GAME	unit9 developed the game using Macromedia Director and a proprietary software developed in-house.
TECH. CREDITS CARD GAME	Flash
HARDWARE	Apple Power Mac G4s, various dual-Pentium NT workstations
DETAILS	Faith & Hope Records: www.faithandhope.co.uk. unit9: www.unit9.com

Chapter 11

Creating a Television Series in Flash

Thanks to Ron Crown for helping with this chapter.

Repeat after me: Flash is just a tool.

We've shown you the wide variety of ways that Flash has been used by Web animators and traditional animators to create broadcast-quality animation. Now we turn to one of the largest Flash production operations in North America, the in-house broadcast Flash team at Bardel Entertainment, located in Vancouver, British Columbia. We will get a special, behind-the-scenes look at what their process is and the types of issues that arise in an environment where many animators work on the same project simultaneously.

The team is led by Ron Crown, Creative Director at Bardel Entertainment (see Appendix E, "Contributor Profiles"). He develops and implements new animation techniques for broadcast productions, and he is currently working on three different series for television, all using Flash. Janet Galore spent an afternoon at the studios of Bardel Entertainment talking with Ron Crown about the ins and outs of the process he's developed over three years and his thoughts on the current state of Flash in the broadcast production studio.

JG: How many people do you have animating here?

RC: We have about 35 traditionally trained people animating in Flash (11.1–11.3). One really cool thing about Flash to broadcast is that it's allowed us to bring animation back into the studio instead of sending it overseas.

JG: Tell me about the projects you've been working on in Flash.

RC: Well, we are working on a series for a major TV network that keeps us very busy, but, unfortunately, we can't talk about it. It will be the first Flash series to air on a U.S. network.

JG: They are shy about the fact it's being animated in Flash?

RC: Yes, they'd prefer to keep that under wraps.

● 11.1

● 11.3

● 11.2

● 11.4

JG: I'm sorry to hear that . . .

RC: But we are working on a Bardel property called *The Christmas Orange*, which will air this holiday season on the ABC Family Channel and Teletoon in Canada, and we've also animated two short pieces for the *Drew Carey* season premier for last season. I can also talk about the series called *Stories from the Seventh Fire*, which aired on CBC, and *The Mr. Dink Show* (11.4–11.7).

THE MR. DINK SHOW

JG: *The Mr. Dink Show* is something you created, right?

RC: Yes, and I've licensed the rights to Bardel for television distribution. It was originally created as a broadcast property that simultaneously opened on the Web as well. All four five-minute episodes have appeared on the Comedy Network here in Canada. The whole show is animated completely in Flash.

● 11.5

● 11.7   Mr. Dink © 2001 Bardel Entertainment, Inc.

● 11.6

THE CHRISTMAS ORANGE

JG: *The Christmas Orange* **is a very nice looking show. It's hard to believe it's done in Flash with the art direction looking so much like watercolor** (11.8–11.10).

R.C: The show has hand painted backgrounds. The bodies are animated traditionally, frame-by-frame, then vectorized in Streamline, and then colored in Flash. The heads and faces were built and animated in Flash. The whole thing is then composited and effects applied in After Effects.

JG: How do you scan in the traditionally animated artwork? Do you use any special techniques?

R.C: We use Photoshop or other scanning software to scan, but we use Adobe Streamline to vectorize

the artwork, mostly because of the batch processing. We set up the scanner with animation pegs to preserve the alignment of the cels. Streamline hasn't been updated for a long time, but it works well — you have a lot of control over how the drawings are vectorized, with the vector Conversion Setup dialog box (11.11). For *The Christmas Orange*, we did most of the bodies in 2D and used streamline to vectorize the lines, and we did the heads in Flash.

We decided to do the heads in Flash because they have no line for the hair — there are many layers of watercolor-like color that would be very difficult to animate traditionally (11.12). The heads are built with multiple layers of hair, about seven pieces, so we have the ability to do some animation on the hair, like settles.

[N O T E]

A *settle* is an animation term that refers to a specific kind of secondary overlapping action. Organic things tend to move just past their stopping point and then settle back to the stopping point. So when hair settles, it does just that – if you flick your hair with your head, your hair follows the movement of your head, moves past the point your head moved, and then it settles back into place.

Important characters, such as Anton, have about nine rotations of his head in Flash, so we can turn his head as much or as little as we want, all with full

● 11.8

● 11.9

● 11.10   The Christmas Orange © 2002 Bardel Entertainment, Inc.

mouth comps, full eyes, all the expressions. It's a lot of setup work, but after we get going, it's fast.

CLIENT EXPECTATIONS WITH FLASH

JG: You've worked with a lot of different broadcast clients. How do they respond to the idea of using Flash for broadcast?

RC: Some clients balk at the cost and time it takes to set up a broadcast Flash project. But if we have the time and money to set up properly, they get a big benefit. Compare the setup time to doing 10,000 drawings of even one head you'd have to do by hand — it's not the same. People aren't used to spending their money up front. But you'd see this for anything digital — 3D or Flash; you need to be very prepared. If you're prepared when you begin, the

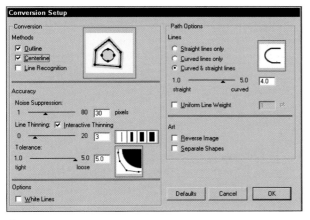

● 11.11

● 11.12

production can go very fast. The smoothness and speed of production is where you're going to save your money.

JG: It seems like people look at Flash as coming from the Web and its reputation for being inexpensive (they assume everything's cheap on the Web), so they think Flash animation should be really cheap.

RC: We find this all the time — clients want to pay us less for working with Flash than they would pay for traditional animation, but all our animators have all the experience that traditional animators have, plus they have all the computer skills, plus they know Flash inside and out, plus they know a handful of other applications that they use to mix and match. If anything, they're far more versatile with their skills than a traditional animator. They shouldn't get paid less — they should get paid more.

We can save money in production because of how fast we can produce. Our animators produce about 50 to 60 seconds of animation per week per person, in color, and traditional animators can't even come close to that.

With the show we're currently working on, the team is putting out close to five to seven minutes of animation a week. If we were a traditional studio, we'd have to have three times as many people. We also have time and money savings due to the fact that when an animator finishes a scene, it's done — it's colored, it's already digital. It's ready for post. Some time needs to be spent coloring the characters the first time, but then you only do that once, and that colored character might be used 5,000 times in the show.

So we get a lot of savings, but it's not so much that you can chop budgets in half or in quarters and still get good results.

REPEAT AFTER ME: FLASH IS A TOOL

JG: I think people in the broadcast world have some misconceptions about Flash, about the quality you can achieve with Flash animation.

RC: Flash is just a tool we're using, and if it's not the right tool for the job, we won't use it. All the pre-production for Flash animation stays the same as traditional animation — you still need good scripts, good storyboards, and good character design.

We're not going to attempt to do a full Disney-style animation in Flash. That's a criticism I hear often about Flash, "Well, you can't do this and that." Well, we don't want to do that. I'm not going to use a hammer when I should use a screwdriver — it doesn't make sense. It's a tool, and you use it for production on the right shows. It's like 3D — you wouldn't use it for something that 3D doesn't do well.

The Internet got Flash off on the wrong foot. Anyone in their basement could make a cartoon, which was cool, but because everybody in their basement did make a cartoon, there's this backlash. Everyone thinks that the quality of the animation is determined by the program used, as opposed to what the artist does. We're using Flash to make real, broadcast-quality animation. I don't go to a museum and look at the sculpture and wonder what kind of chisel the guy used. If it looks great and moves the way it is supposed to, who cares how it's made?

The difference between "Internet animation" and "broadcast animation" lies in the quality of the animator, not his or her tools. If the basic principles of animation such as follow-through, overlapping, secondary actions, acting, and solid timing are missing in any style of animation, then it will appear amateurish. The delivery medium (the Web or television) or the tools used (Flash or pencil and paper) is not where the fault lies. When these tools are used by experienced, trained animators in a professional environment, the quality of work falls easily within the expectations of "broadcast animation."

Flash has this stigma that if you use it, the result is going to look like Internet animation. We have to show clients all the stuff we've done, what it can look like, and coax them into it.

That's what happened with *Stories from the Seventh Fire* — we did a big sales pitch to get them to go with Flash. There are four shows in the series, and the first one was made two years ago here at Bardel. It was all traditional hand drawing. To make the next three in Flash, we had to convince them that this was the way to go. We also had to convince them that it wasn't going to look the same as the first one, but it was going to be more true to the paintings (11.13).

STANDARDS FOR FLASH-TO-BROADCAST ANIMATION

JG: In *The Christmas Orange*, are you using digital puppets? It's hard to tell how it was made.

RC: We are switching techniques every scene, every frame — whatever it takes. Obviously, you have to develop some sort of standardized working system. That's one of the main goals for me when working in Flash for broadcast. Anyone animating on the floor that is working on a scene can walk away, and anyone else should be able to sit down and finish or fix it. Most people working in Flash are all over the place with techniques; everyone approaches it differently.

The first thing I had to do was come up with how we would work in Flash. It's not a matter of there being a right or wrong way, but we had to lock it down. So we had to teach the animators our working methods. Some of it's confusing because Flash isn't overly friendly towards traditional animators. Our saving grace is that everyone we had was a trained animator, but very few of them had worked in Flash before. So it was easier for them to learn our methods. And then we went into production, and we adjusted and were flexible, which is very important for working digital. Programs are changing all the time, and you want to be able to take advantage of new discoveries.

● 11.13   © Storytellers Productions, Inc.

For example, we discovered we could use Adobe Illustrator to cut building to about one-third the time, just because we adapted. So you have to be flexible, but at the same time, have working standards.

Each scene we do goes through three people. We have our setup people who put all the stuff together — they break up all the layers, pose the characters out, put in the dialog, and basically take the storyboard and build it into a color animatic using Flash assets. Then that scene will go to the animator who will do all the motion, and then it'll go out for approval. Then it will come back, and we have one person who does revisions. So all three people need to totally understand the same concept, or it gets messy.

FLASH ISSUES

JG: Are you using Flash MX?

RC: As soon as MX came out, we tested it for a couple of weeks and then started using it (except for the big project we can't talk about). I don't even have Flash 5 on my computer anymore. But on the other hand, there's a new bag of bugs now. With Flash 5, we knew all the problems and had our workarounds. With Flash 6, some of the old ones are gone, but there's a new set of problems.

TWEENING PROBLEMS IN FLASH MX

RC: For example, we're building an animatic for *The Christmas Orange*. If you put a symbol on the Timeline, do a motion tween, and then put in a new keyframe with a new symbol directly after the tween, Flash replaces the new symbol in the new keyframe with the old symbol that you were just tweening.

So every time that you put a motion tween on the Timeline, the next symbol reverts to the previous symbol that has the motion tween on it. The only thing you can do is to make a new layer, so for every new symbol you have to make a new layer. And because it literally swaps the symbol, you can't undo it — you have to go back and manually swap the symbol to the one you wanted in the first place. We have looked at this some, and putting in a blank keyframe between the tweens may make a difference, but that's not desirable in many situations.

LINE-POPPING ISSUE

RC: There's another bug with the Pencil tool that happens in both Flash 5 and MX. If you are drawing on the Stage, and you draw thin lines on top of thicker lines, the thin lines will pop behind the thicker ones. That's okay. But if you export that drawing as an SWF, the lines are toast — the thin lines are now on *top* of the thick ones (see the "Pencil Line Popping" sidebar). So if you wanted to work with an SWF, the lines would be totally screwed up. If you export as PNG sequences, it comes out fine and the lines stay the way you drew them. My advice is to avoid lines when you can.

Pencil Line Popping

If you use the Pencil tool to draw a series of lines (11.14) and then change the thickness of the tool and draw additional thinner lines, the thinner lines will be forced "behind" the thicker lines within the Flash preview (11.15).

If you were to export to a bitmap format, such as JPG, you would get the same thing as you have in preview (11.16), but when you export to SWF, the thinner lines appear on top again (11.17).

So, if you work with lines of varying thickness, one solution is to develop the various parts of your drawing on separate layers. But if you want to work within a single layer, another way to do it is to find ways of grouping the lines, which can help to solve the problem.

If you draw a series of lines at a particular thickness, you can then drag-select them all and choose Modify→Group (11.18).

Then, when you draw the thinner lines, drag-select everything or choose Edit→Select All (11.19).

At this point, because you've grouped the thicker lines, you can Shift-click to deselect the thicker lines, leaving the others all selected underneath. Then choose Modify→Group to group the thinner lines, which will now behave. You can use the Arrange command to place them behind or in front as desired (11.20), and both bitmap and SWF export will be consistent with the internal preview functionality of Flash.

CAMERA MOVES

JG: So how do you deal with camera moves in Flash?

RC: We try not to do camera moves in Flash itself because the ease in and ease out function doesn't work like we need it to. That's why I like programs like Toon Boom Studio, because you can use Bezier curves to see the slow in and slow out.

In Flash, you can only do ease in or ease out. The easing slider goes from 0 to 100, but if you put it on 100, there's still some arbitrary distance between the keyframes. And, it's rare to ever have a camera move that doesn't have both a slow in and a slow out. So you have to do one tween to slow in, then one keyframe, and one tween to slow out, but then they don't quite line up, because when it hits that keyframe it changes speed. . . . Controlling easing in Flash is so frustrating that we try to avoid using it whenever possible.

We'll build scenes oversize to be able to do the camera moves in After Effects — we'll over render so

● 11.14

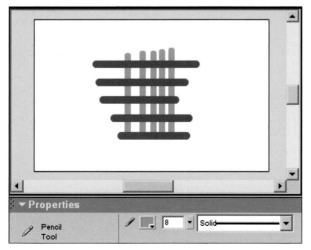

● 11.15

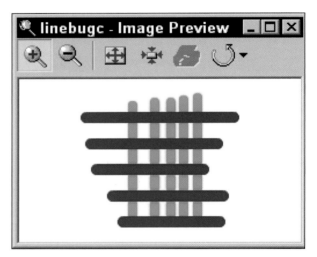

● 11.16

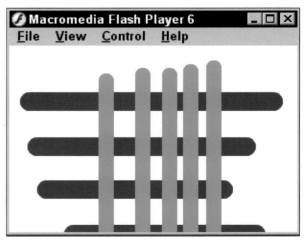

● 11.17

we can scale down and do a truck in. But even then, the vector lines are so crisp on the edge, there's always a staggering that happens when you truck in, especially if you have a rotation; then you really notice it. It's not so bad if you do a straight truck in. The main problem is doing a pan — the edges of the shapes stagger.

Thin horizontal lines are another problem. When they get displayed on an interlaced screen, the display gets confused about which field to use, so the horizontal lines jump around. Even if the line is fatter than two pixels, if you have a certain angle, it still staggers. So we put motion blur on our camera moves, and it made all the difference in making the camera moves smooth. But it caused other problems with the characters, especially with *Stories from the Seventh Fire*. You want to put motion blur on the camera, not on the characters themselves. We spent many, many days trying to figure this out. It's really a

problem with the way the TV is displaying the lines, not with the actual camera move.

ANIMATION TECHNIQUES

JG: Tell me about some of your animation philosophies when working with Flash.

RC: One thing is that we try to avoid scaling and skewing symbols as much as possible with our characters. That's part of what can make Internet animation look amateurish. Inexperienced animators are sometimes squashing a whole character, or using skewing. If you do even very slight skewing, the character goes off-model.

As a fundamental concept of animation, squash and stretch makes sense, but the way that many people approach it in Flash doesn't work; you don't take the whole character and stretch it. If you drew it as a stretch, you wouldn't take your whole drawing and try to make it look stretched. We avoid using scaling tools in Flash, and prefer to draw stretches and squashes when we can. If we have a stretched drawing, we might use the scaling tool to do the in-betweens to smooth out the pop between the hand-drawn keyframes.

If we do use stretching and squashing in Flash, we apply it to individual parts, so the squash you put on the arms would be different than the rest; like the arms might be stretched, while the torso is squashed. It just all comes back to traditional animation skills, like using the rules of animation. Just because Flash, as a tool, does all these things cheap and fast, doesn't mean it makes good animation. You still have to be an animator to understand why you're applying something.

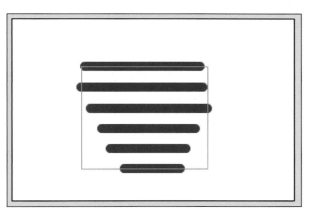

● 11.18

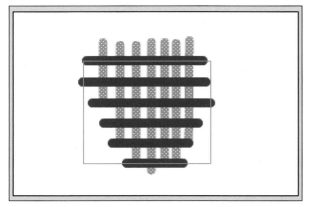

● 11.19

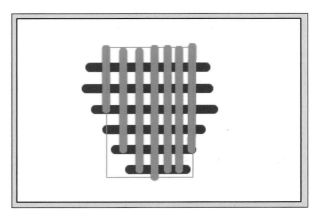

● 11.20

USING ILLUSTRATOR BRUSHES TO MODIFY SYMBOLS

RC: A very cool animation technique uses Adobe Illustrator 10. Illustrator 10 has a brush option that enables you to paste in a vector graphic and use it as a brush. So you can take a character's arm and copy it right out of Flash, paste it into Illustrator 10 and it'll come in as vectored artwork. You can convert the artwork into a brush, and any kind of squiggle you paint with it, the artwork will fit around the curve. So you can create a curved arm in Illustrator, then copy and paste it back into Flash, and you now have a curved arm which can be converted to a symbol. If you could do that from within Flash, we'd love it.

QUICKTIME AND LIBRARY MANAGEMENT

JG: What are some other production techniques you've found work well?

RC: We use QuickTime a lot. I view all my SWFs in QuickTime, mostly because doing so gives me a timecode and the ability to scrub back and forth, which the Flash player doesn't have. For editing, I'll take a whole series of scenes and put them together in QuickTime Pro. It's not perfect; there's a slight slowdown when it pops from one scene to the other, but if you're just working with rough sequences it's really good. You can see how the cuts are working, how the scenes are flowing together.

All our scenes, every scene from our storyboard, exists as a separate FLA file. We never combine anything in Flash because of the problem of symbol duplications, and symbol numbers getting off, and the fact that an FLA can only be opened on one computer at a time. So a "shared" library can't be opened and used by more than one person at a time. Every scene is totally individual. We have hundreds of scenes, sometimes only a few seconds long, according to the storyboard. Having many separate scenes is the only way we can do it. I had hoped we could composite and assemble the cartoon as we animated, but the process can't work that way. A typical half-hour show for us has on the order of 400 scenes, all about 1MB, 2MB so that Flash can handle the file size.

JG: So you don't bring it all together until you go to After Effects?

RC: Pretty much. That's where QuickTime comes in as a nice way to preview how five or six scenes are coming together. It's faster than going into After Effects.

All the scenes live on the main server, and the individual animators copy a scene to their local drive to work on it and then copy it back to the server when it's done.

JG: Tell me more about sharing libraries.

RC: It would be wonderful if we could really do that. Flash 5 and MX have a notion of a shared library, but the sharing happens at run time, so you can have three different movies that all share the assets of one library. But the library cannot be opened by three people at the same time. We have huge libraries of assets that need to be accessed by many animators. We'll have a master character library for a show, and I'll try to open it, and if I'm lucky, no one else on the floor will have the library open and I'll be able to open it. If I'm not lucky, I get a "failed to open document error" and I have to go out there and say, "Who has this library open?" and they have to shut it. We wish Macromedia would put in real shared libraries that can be opened by more than one person at a time.

The other problem with master libraries is that once they grow to a very large number of symbols, it's too big for Flash. If you try to copy and paste something, it takes literally five minutes. You might as well call it crashing — it just freezes. You can't move something from scene to scene. The best you can do is to come in and copy something from the master library and paste it into a new FLA. If you try to do any editing in the master library, there's too much information and it freaks out. We think the number of symbols is what causes this behavior. We have over 5,000 symbols in some of our libraries. That's the reason we have over 10 libraries for a TV series, and even then it's hard. The more libraries you have, the more file management issues you have. We'd like one place where everything lives, and you can go get your assets from that one place, but we don't get that.

STORIES FROM THE SEVENTH FIRE

JG: *Stories from the Seventh Fire* is a very interesting TV series. Where did the art originate?

RC: The artist who made the paintings the series is based on is a First Nations artist named Norval Morrisseau. He founded the *Woodland* school of art, which uses traditional iconography. He's well-known in Canada, and is starting to get more recognition in the States. The series was produced in two languages, English and Cree.

JG: What kind of techniques did you use on *Stories from the Seventh Fire*?

RC: *Stories from the Seventh Fire* was built and animated mostly in Flash with the more difficult animation done traditionally and integrated into Flash. The traditional animation usually doesn't make up a whole scene, but rather a piece of the scene or even a piece of the character. For example, when the character jumps up and kicks a leaf, that little clip is a piece of 2D animation. Generally for this show we used 2D animated arms and legs with Flash bodies and heads (11.21–11.24).

All the waving tree branches were done in Illustrator, using Illustrator brushes. So I'd take one branch symbol, copy it into Illustrator 10, make it a brush, then drew the wave cycle in Illustrator using the branch brush, exported the layers to frames in SWF, and manipulated and duplicated the branches to go on all the trees.

Taking advantage of tools like Flash or Illustrator is a matter of being smart about how you're going to split the work. We plan all the production before we start animating — we have a board breakdown. We communicate with the board artist as to what level of detail we need on the boards, but after that we have a big board breakdown meeting where we go through and decide which parts should be 2D, which parts are too complicated or should be thrown out. Before it ever goes into production, we know exactly how we're going to approach it. But we're also flexible once it gets to production.

● 11.21   © Storytellers Productions, Inc.

● 11.23   © Storytellers Productions, Inc.

● 11.22   © Storytellers Productions, Inc.

●11.24   © Storytellers Productions, Inc.

With this project, we really tried to capture the feel of the paintings (11.25–11.27). We used After Effects for the special effects, such as water reflections. It still all comes down to the animators, though. We have some really great people, which makes all the difference.

WORKING WITH 3D

JG: What other programs do you have in your bag of tricks? You've mentioned Streamline and Illustrator.

RC: We use After Effects a lot. For a new project coming up, we're going to animate the characters in Flash, backgrounds in 3D, and composite in After Effects and do all the special effects on top of it. In my opinion, Flash isn't a strong enough program to work as a compositing tool for broadcast. If you use big files

for backgrounds and so on, the file size gets too large for Flash to handle, and it gets slow and unstable.

To create the 3D elements of the animation, we use Maya, but we're flexible. We work in broadcast size, at 720x486, and when we deliver for Web, we simply scale back down. I like rendering 3D elements out to vectors, but we haven't had to use that yet. I haven't seen many programs that do a very good job of it, but 3D Studio Max has some cool plug-ins.

If we are really going to use 3D elements in a Flash animation, we try not to do any of the animation in 3D. Instead, we render out the 3D elements in all the different angles, convert them to symbols, color them, and then just manually pick the image we want. For say, a car, you could render out five or six rotations and have a library with all these symbols for the rotations. You can store the symbols as an animated graphic, so you can place the car master symbol in the timeline, and tell it to start playing on frame 5 and go to frame 12, and so on. So all we use the 3D for is to build symbols. Then we export the vector lines from the 3D package, and color them in Flash, because coloring in Flash works better to match the rest of the show (which is built and colored in Flash). We have big plans for that technique, especially for backgrounds and vehicles and props . . . not so much for characters.

SOME TECHNICAL DETAILS

JG: How much RAM and hard drive space do you try to have?

RC: As much as we can get. The very minimum is 256MB, and we try to get 512MB at least. Hard drive

● 11.25   © Storytellers Productions, Inc.

● 11.26   © Storytellers Productions, Inc.

● 11.27   © Storytellers Productions, Inc.

space on individual computers is not as much of an issue, because most animators are only working on three or four scenes at a time. 60GB hard drives are fine. In terms of processors, we get them as fast as we can. Most are at more than 1 gHz or higher right now.

JG: Do you use Macs or PCs?

RC: We try to avoid Macs as much as possible. We can't, but internally we all use PCs. Macs are good, but PCs are far more flexible, and you can get bits and pieces everywhere; they're cheap. A new 80GB hard drive for a PC will cost you $100. Macs are more precision-based.

JG: Do you output for a TV-size aspect ratio, 4:3?

RC: For the series we're doing now, we're working at HDTV aspect ratio, at 960x520 pixels. We still use an NTSC guide for the action, so they can crop to 4:3, but it also looks great at HDTV aspect ratio.

JG: What framerate do you create your animations in?

RC: 24 fps. We animate on twos most of the time, sometime ones, whatever is needed, same as traditional.

POSTPRODUCTION

JG: Do you do all your postproduction here?

RC: We're incorporating more and more of our own postproduction as we go along because it saves a ton of money, and post houses are hugely expensive. Now that we're working in digital, we can do a lot more on our end before turning it over to postproduction for final output. We even take it to broadcast safe colors internally. So they do a final check for broadcast safe, and they put it out onto digital beta or whatever the client requires.

Before we worked digitally, it was all inks and paints and paper, and we'd hand it over to postproduction and it would be all mysterious. But now we do the color, the correct aspect ratio, all the scenes are there. The only thing left is to put them together and do cross dissolves, fades ins, and that's really it.

For *The Christmas Orange*, we'll take it as far as we can before going to post, do all our own special effects and transitions, titles, everything. We use mostly After Effects because it's not hugely expensive, it's powerful, and there are so many third-party plug-ins,

it does pretty much anything you want it to do. It doesn't work in real-time, but it's close enough for us. We set up renders all night and come back in the morning. We like After Effects a lot.

For delivery to the post house, we export QuickTime with Animation compressor set to 100, which has great quality, and everyone can read it. In fact, that's what our post house requires. We started out with TGA sequences, but those end up being huge.

JG: What about sound, do you do that in post, or in-house?

RC: With our series, we supply exposure sheets with sound breakdown and lip sync animation, as well as timing notes. We use Magpie to do the lip synching. The dialog is timed to the picture at the animatic stage, which is then given to the animators. Scenes don't change from the animatic that has all the dialog, so from Flash, we just export a WAV file. When we put in all the scenes in After Effects and put the scenes end to end, we drop the WAV file in and everything syncs up. So the sound person gives us one big mixed down WAV file. We drop that file into After Effects, and it works great. Sound effects and music are still done out of house, since we don't have enough work to have a composer on staff.

[N O T E]

Magpie is an inexpensive and popular lip sync application. You can check it out at www.thirdwishsoftware.com/magpie.html. The professional version supports Flash, as well as facial feature synching.

Part III

Postproduction: Working with Flash Video

Chapter 12

Exporting Video from Flash

Special thanks to Chad Fahs for primary development of this chapter.

When you do the export, let the machine do the video rendering and leave it alone — don't try to do other work on the machine. Don't tempt it to crash. Don't even look at it funny.

In this chapter, we take a look at a few approaches to exporting video, discuss some issues that you want to consider when you're developing your project, and we provide a pre-export checklist that you should go through before starting the video rendering.

CHOOSING YOUR EXPORT FORMAT

There are three main approaches to exporting video from Flash, each having its own pros and cons — exporting to AVI, exporting to QuickTime video, and exporting as an image sequence (exporting the sound exported separately). In the typical production flow, after you have the project in one of these formats, it is further processed in postproduction to do color correction, titling, fades, or credits (covered in Chapters 13, "Titles, Fades, and Credits," and 14, "Polishing and Delivering Flash Video," respectively).

The decision to use QuickTime video or AVI format largely depends on your platform. In Flash MX, if you are exporting on a Mac, QuickTime is the only option for video. On a Windows machine, AVI is the only video export option. Some studios find that exporting to image sequences offers the most flexibility and control over the final product.

We cover each of the export options in detail, but first let's address a question that most folks ask when going out to video from Flash.

WHAT DOCUMENT SIZE IS BEST?

You may have read different opinions on what Flash document size (Stage size) to use when going out to video. Even in the case studies in this book, we've seen that different studios use different document sizes. The fact that computers work with square pixels and television uses rectangular pixels, and the existence of so many video formats, doesn't make the task of deciding how big to make your Flash movie any easier. The good news is, there are many, many ways to go out to video, and if something goes wrong, there is usually a way to fix it in post, almost always. The bad news is, there are many, many ways to get the job done, and it's hard to figure out why you'd pick one over the other — everyone has the definitive answer, but no two are the same.

To us, it all comes down to a very simple principle: make your Flash movie at the same *aspect ratio* as your target video format, and all will come out in the wash. Therefore, because most video formats use an aspect ratio of 4:3, you should create your Flash movie at an aspect ratio of 4:3, for example, 320x240, 640x480, 720x540, 768x576 — they all work.

[N O T E]

To determine the "aspect ratio" of your Flash project, divide the width in pixels by the height in pixels. If it comes out to 1.33333. . . , then the aspect ratio is 4:3.

"But," you may say, "if I create my Flash movie at one of those resolutions, won't it get squished when it gets displayed on a TV with rectangular pixels?" The answer is that it would if your video-editing software were dumb. But it isn't. All the major non-linear editing (NLE) applications, like Premiere, Final Cut, Vegas Video, and After Effects, have compensation algorithms so that when you import a video clip or a sequence of images at an aspect ratio of 4:3, the software understands that the imported art uses square pixels. If you have your project set up correctly, the software will convert the square pixels to rectangular pixels and preserve the aspect ratio when you do a final render to video.

Table 12.1 lists standard video formats and our recommendations for Stage size/export size from Flash.

Note that you can create Flash project files for DV or D1 video at 640x480, but your work will be scaled up a bit when you print to video. For best results use 720x540 for NTSC and 768x576 for PAL.

ADJUSTING THE DOCUMENT/STAGE SIZE IN FLASH

Now, what if you are not starting from scratch but converting a Web-based animation to video? If you have created the original Flash project at a 4:3 aspect ratio, you can simply scale up the size when you export from Flash (as we discuss shortly). One great aspect of vector-based animation is that you can easily scale up without affecting the image quality.

If you have not created the original project at 4:3, then you'll need to first change the Document Size (Stage size) of your Flash project so that it is 4:3 (when you divide the horizontal pixel size by the vertical pixel size, it should come out to 1.333333). Otherwise, you may end up having areas of blackness on-screen. If you are going with a letterbox look, that's okay, but we are assuming that you would like the video content to completely fill the screen without cropping.

There are various ways to change the Document Size of your Flash project, none of them for the faint of heart. Assuming your Document Size is smaller than video dimensions, the basic idea is that you want to scale up the objects in your scene, keeping the horizontal and vertical dimensions constrained so your content is not distorted. Then you adjust the positions of objects and fill in the background in the new Stage area as needed. The most straightforward procedure is as follows:

TABLE 12.1: RECOMMENDED STAGE/EXPORT SIZES FROM FLASH

DESIRED FORMAT	STAGE OR EXPORT SIZE FROM FLASH	ASPECT RATIO IN SQUARE PIXELS	FINAL VIDEO RENDER IN RECTANGULAR PIXELS
DV-NTSC (720x480)	640x480	4:3	720x480 (4:3)
DV-NTSC (720x480)	720x540	4:3	720x480 (4:3)
D1-NTSC (720x486)	720x540	4:3	720x486 (4:3)
DV-PAL (720x576)	768x576	4:3	720x576 (4:3)

1. Make sure that you have plenty of RAM — you'll be moving and/or scaling many objects at the same time.

2. Make a backup copy of your project file — this process is prone to hanging and crashing, and your file could get corrupted.

3. Change the document size of your Flash project by choosing Modify→Document→Document Properties and type in new pixel values for the width and height, so that they are in a 4:3 aspect ratio (640x480 or 720x540, for example).

4. You will see that your Stage size is now the correct aspect ratio, but all the artwork is in the upper-left corner. You need to go through the movie, scene by scene, and scale and move all the objects to their correct positions by editing multiple frames simultaneously.

5. Make sure that all the layers you want to adjust are not locked and are visible.

6. If possible, make room in your layout, so you can see all the frames and all the layers. You can use the tiny and short options for the Timeline view and minimize the Property Inspector to help see as much of the Timeline as possible (12.1).

7. Click the Modify Onion Markers button and select Onion All (12.2).

8. Click the Edit Multiple Frames button. You can see beginning and ending markers in the Timeline to indicate that you are now in multiple-frame editing mode (12.3). You'll also see a mess on the Stage — every object in every frame is visible. At this point, you may also want to click the Onion Skin Outlines button so your processor is not taxed as much when you move the objects on the Stage.

9. Choose View→Work Area to see all the objects and use Control-2 to fit the artwork into the available screen area in your layout.

10. Now carefully move your mouse into the Stage area and select all (either by dragging the mouse or by pressing Ctrl+A). All the objects should be selected (12.4).

11. Do some quick math to calculate the scaling factor you'll need. There are a few ways to do this, depending on whether your content is too wide for TV or too narrow. A good rule of thumb is to use the desired horizontal change in scale as a base scaling factor for all objects.

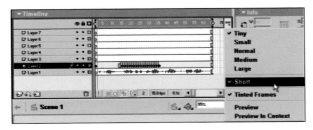

● 12.1

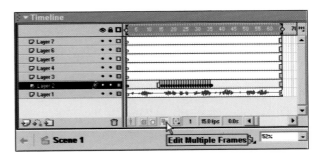

● 12.3

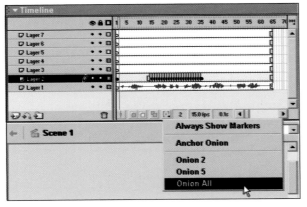

● 12.2

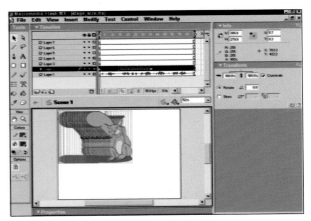

● 12.4

For example, if you are going from, say, 300x 200 pixels to 640x480 pixels, find the factor required to scale 300 to 640. Divide 640 by 300: 640/300 = 2.133, or about 213 percent. That is the horizontal scaling factor needed to get from 300 to 640 pixels, and it will also be your overall scaling factor.

12. Before doing anything, look at the Info panel and write down the x and y position of the selected group of objects.

13. Now use the Transform panel to scale up your objects (while they are still all selected on the Stage) by the percentage you calculated — keep the Constrain check box selected (12.5).

14. Because of the scaling, the x and y positions of the objects will have changed. Now type in the x and y positions that you wrote down earlier. The whole collection of objects should be very close to the relative position on the original Stage, but are now at the proper size and aspect ratio.

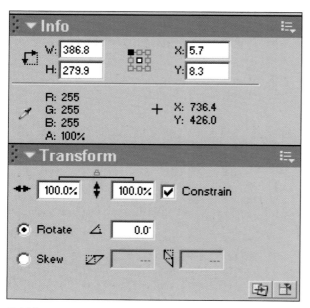

● 12.5

You now have to tweak various objects and backgrounds, depending on how different your original Stage proportions are from the new ones. We suggest doing this layer by layer (or by groups of layers, depending on how your characters are built). Lock the layers you do not want to modify and use Onion All and Edit Multiple Frames buttons to move objects in one layer across the whole timeline by dragging the objects, making sure that all the objects are selected before you start dragging. You may have to adjust motion tweens so that objects that are supposed to move off the Stage actually do move off the Stage.

If you have many scenes that need to be scaled up and adjusted, it gets more difficult. You may need to add "cut away" shots to disguise small differences in layout and positioning across scenes. As you can imagine, this process is difficult, but the results can be worth the effort, and it beats re-animating from scratch.

[T I P]

If your animation is at a smaller Document Size and uses a lot of bitmap images, be careful about scaling up the movie to your target video size. Bitmaps don't scale like vectors do, and if your bitmaps are small, the quality will be degraded if you scale up. As discussed in Chapter 7, "Working with Digital Puppets," you can swap in higher resolution art before exporting to video so that the bitmaps are not scaled more than 100 percent in your final output.

EXPORTING FROM FLASH

In this section, we review the three options for exporting from Flash to go out to video: QuickTime, AVI, and image sequences.

QUICKTIME

If you are working on a Mac, you will be exporting video in QuickTime format. On a PC, you can export to a QuickTime file, but it will not be a video file. (See the "QuickTime Flash Tracks" sidebar).

When exporting into QuickTime on the Mac, you have a variety of options to get to QuickTime:

- QuickTime option in Publish Settings
- Export Movie→QuickTime option
- Export Movie→QuickTime Video option

The first two options are appropriate if you want to include Flash interactivity as a QuickTime "track." For example, you can create a project in Flash that

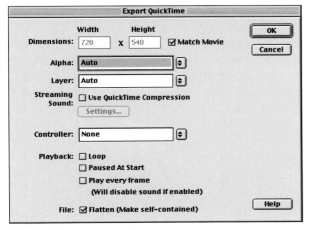

● 12.6

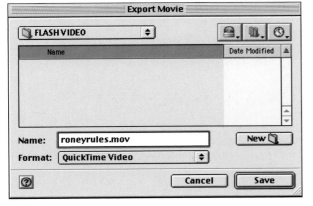

● 12.7

includes buttons, links, and so on and make it into a QuickTime Movie (MOV) file that can be opened by the QuickTime player. This kind of QuickTime export functionality includes a variety of options that relate to the delivery of QuickTime on the Web or on disc (12.6), but with video, you want to use the Export Movie→QuickTime Video option (12.7).

Exporting from Flash to QuickTime on Mac

To export your video on a Mac to QuickTime, follow these steps:

1. Choose File→Export Movie→QuickTime Video.
2. In the Export QuickTime Video dialog box (12.8), choose appropriate options and click OK to export:

- **Dimensions:** Set dimensions to your target delivery size (for example, 720x540 for NTSC, 768x576 for PAL). If you've followed our advice about authoring at video aspect ratio, keep Maintain Aspect Ratio selected.
- **Format:** Always use 24-bit color to maximize image quality.
- **Smooth:** Select the check box next to Smooth if you want to apply smoothing. If you're not sure, try exporting it with and without to see if it will benefit your project. Smoothing can improve the

● 12.8

perceived quality of bitmap images but may affect text adversely.

- **Compressor:** QuickTime video includes a variety of compression schemes. It is possible to select None, but it is standard practice with high-quality video to use QuickTime Animation compression, (12.9) making sure to set the quality slider beneath this choice in the window to the maximum on the far right.
- **Quality:** Always set to maximum quality (far-right) setting.
- **Sound Format:** If you are working with Sound directly in the Flash movie, you want to export

at the highest possible quality setting, which in this case is 44 kHz 16 Bit Stereo.

AVI

AVI is the standard video format for Windows. It's the format of choice when exporting to video on a

QuickTime Flash Tracks

QuickTime 4 and later supports a "Flash track," which means that Flash plays natively in QuickTime with interactivity. This fact is good to know for Web distribution, but when you are exporting Flash to video, it can be confusing. In the old days, if you exported to QuickTime, you could only do so as a video format. Not so any more. On a PC in Flash MX (and Flash 5), the QuickTime option exports to QuickTime 4, but the MOV file is **not** a video format — it is a QuickTime movie with a Flash track, as seen in the QuickTime Player. Figure (12.10) shows Atomic Cartoons' *Dog in a Box with Two Wheels* exported to QuickTime as a Flash track.

You can convert the QuickTime movie with Flash track to a QuickTime movie with a video track by opening the MOV file in QT Pro and exporting it as uncompressed QuickTime (12.11) — then it will be in QuickTime video format, but with no sound. You can check this type of file in the QuickTime Player, and it will show up as a bona fide video file (12.12). But you will have to export sound separately and then import into your NLE. This is why we recommend just sticking to AVI if you are on a PC.

✓ **Animation**
BMP
Cinepak
Component Video
DV – NTSC
DV – PAL
Graphics
H.261
H.263
Motion JPEG A
Motion JPEG B
None
Photo – JPEG
Planar RGB
PNG
TGA
TIFF
Video
Sorenson Video

● 12.9

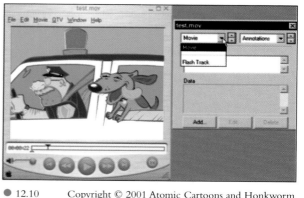

● 12.10   Copyright © 2001 Atomic Cartoons and Honkworm International

PC. In the following section, we examine the Flash MX export dialog box and the steps required to export to AVI.

Exporting from Flash to AVI on a PC (Windows)

To export your video on a PC to AVI format, follow these steps:

1. Choose File→Export Movie→AVI.
2. In the Export Windows AVI dialog box (12.13), choose the appropriate options and click OK to export:

- **Dimensions:** Set dimensions to your target delivery size (for example,720x540 for NTSC, 768x576 for PAL).

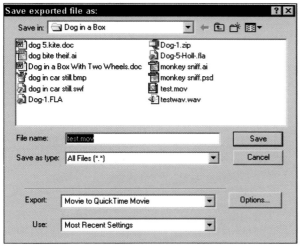

● 12.11

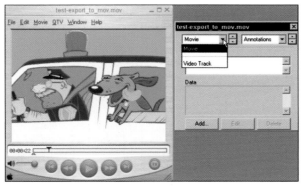

● 12.12   Copyright © 2001 Atomic Cartoons and Honkworm International

- **Maintain Aspect Ratio:** Depends on original document size. If you've followed our advice about authoring at video aspect ratio, keep Maintain Aspect Ratio selected.
- **Video Format:** 24-bit color.
- **Compress Video:** Deselect! For testing purposes compression may be okay, but when rendering the final version for broadcast, you want to deselect this check box. The file size will be large, but deselecting Compress Video will yield the highest possible quality, which is what you want.
- **Smooth:** Select Smoothing. If you have bitmaps in your animation, it often improves the look and gives a nice effect. On text, smoothing tends to make it a bit smudgy if the font size is small. If you are scaling the Dimensions up for export, smoothing should not adversely affect the text.
- **Sound Format:** If you are working with Sound directly in the Flash movie, you want to export at the highest possible quality setting, which in this case is 44 kHz 16 Bit Stereo.

EXPORTING IMAGE SEQUENCES

Many Flash studios that create Flash content for television or film use QuickTime or AVI as an export format, however, some studios prefer image sequences. You may be able to achieve a higher level of quality by exporting as a series of still frame images and then importing that sequence of stills into a video-editing application. The primary reason people use image sequences is that you can avoid

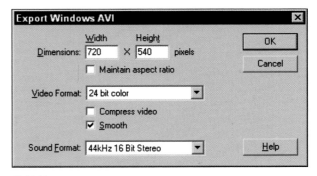

● 12.13

giant, uncompressed QuickTime or AVI files — image sequences are often easier to handle. Also, with some image formats, you have the option of using an alpha channel, so you have more freedom to composite the Flash animation on top of other content in After Effects or a similar application.

You may end up working with a postproduction company that asks you to provide an image sequence rather than a QuickTime or AVI file. Most facilities can handle raw digital video files, and you may end up sending them raw digital video on CD (650 megabytes), DVD-R (4.7 gigabytes), or even a FireWire hard drive. Another option that an image sequence provides is that you can break up a video project into numbered sections that can easily be broken up on separate volumes and then rejoined.

Exporting an Image Sequence

To export an image sequence, choose File→Export Movie. In the drop-down menu in the Export Movie dialog box, choose the file format that you want to export in. There are a few different options for image sequence formats, but in most cases, depending on your platform, you will either want to export in a sequence of BMP (Windows Bitmap) or PICT/PCT (Macintosh Picture) files (12.14, 12.15). PNG is another choice and offers an alpha channel.

[N O T E]

The Windows version of Flash MX does not support exporting in PICT format, but the Mac version will export in PICT and BMP. If you need a PICT sequence on a Windows platform, you can use Equilibrium's DeBabelizer to convert a BMP sequence to a PICT sequence.

PICT, BMP, or PNG format is suitable for exporting where the eventual result will be video.

Note that in the Export PICT or Export Bitmap dialog boxes, you do not have the option to change the aspect ratio. Flash requires the size you specify for image export to always have the same aspect ratio as your original document size.

Interestingly enough, if you compare uncompressed video to uncompressed image sequences, it can work out to take roughly the same amount of space. For example, one minute of uncompressed AVI takes up nearly two gigabytes of hard drive space, and the same project exported into a BMP image sequence can take up the same amount of space.

DeBabelizer

In production environments, when image sequences are exported, often a tool such as DeBabelizer is used to batch process the images, though it may be simpler to process the images after they've been imported to Final Cut Pro or Adobe Premiere. DeBabelizer is an extremely powerful tool that can be used to automate such tasks as applying a television-safe color palette to an image sequence. For example, a red with a value of 255 in the R portion of the RGB scale is going to be too bright for television — and video is especially sensitive to reds, so one approach is to adjust the palette directly in Flash to mute the

● 12.14

● 12.15

reds, bringing the red channel below a value of 235, or just adjust the color in postproduction. But if you're going out to image sequences, DeBabelizer can handle the job.

To get a bit more technical, DeBabelizer's NTSC/PAL Hot Pixel Fixer (12.16) gives some advanced controls over processing the reduction of either color saturation or luminance in relation to sending out image sequences that are ultimately destined for NTSC or PAL format.

[N O T E]

Photoshop 6 and 7 can also batch process sequences of images using its NTSC Colors filter.

Sound Export

If you are exporting an image sequence and have the sound synched in Flash, then you need to export the sound separately, for later resyncing in post-production. Generally, you want to use WAV if you are on a PC and AIFF if you are on a Mac — just make sure that the format you are using is accepted by the software you are going to resync the audio with.

● 12.16

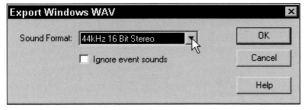
● 12.17

To export your sound on a PC to WAV format, follow these steps:

1. Choose File➔Export Movie➔WAV Audio.
2. In the Export WAV dialog box (12.17), choose 44 kHz 16 Bit Stereo and click OK to export.

To export your sound on a Mac to AIFF format, follow these steps:

1. Choose File➔Export Movie➔QuickTime Video.
2. In the Export Movie dialog box (12.18), choose a name for your file and click Save to export.
3. In the Export QuickTime Video dialog box (12.19), make sure that the Sound Format is set

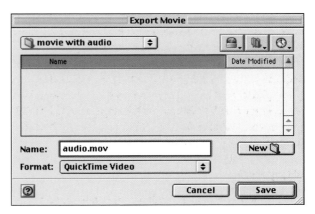
● 12.18

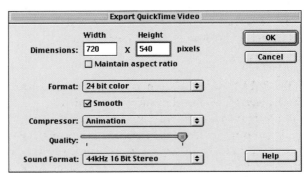
● 12.19

to 44 kHz 16 Bit Stereo. (The video settings don't really matter unless you are going to want to use the video as well — you will be extracting the audio from the resulting video file.)

4. Open the resulting file in QuickTime Pro (available from `www.apple.com`) by choosing File→Open Movie and then choose File→ Export. In the Export dialog box (12.20), choose the Sound to AIFF option. The default settings are probably fine, but the Options button allows you to adjust settings (12.21).

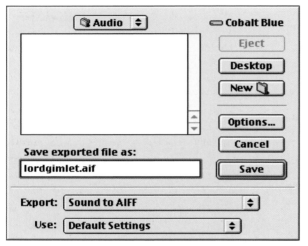

● 12.20

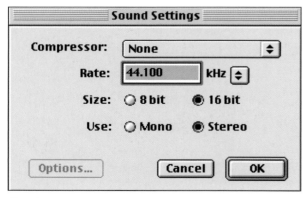

● 12.21

PROCESSING AND STORAGE REQUIREMENTS

Exporting to video is probably the hardest thing for Flash to do. Slower machines, machines that have little hard drive space left, or machines with less RAM, can get bogged down or crash.

Make sure that the export machine has plenty of RAM and hard drive space. In general, you want to have a minimum of 512MB of RAM on a Mac and 256MB on a PC. You want to have about 2GB of hard drive space available for every minute of uncompressed video or image sequences you want to export, assuming 30 fps.

If you usually work with Flash with the intention of delivering on the Web, one of the major differences in working with broadcast-quality digital video is that the file size is considerably larger. In a vector-based animation file, individual frames often consist of information that describes a shape and where it is moving, rather than describing individual pixels. With uncompressed video, every single pixel of every frame is specified, 30 frames per second.

As we've mentioned, practically speaking, one minute of video based on a Flash movie created at 30 frames per second, exported as uncompressed AVI, takes up nearly two gigabytes, depending on the Stage size and whether or not you are including sound. (16-bit 44.1 kHz stereo sound takes up 10MB/min.) The file size varies with the Stage size, because when you are exporting as video, a video file is more or less comprised of a series of digital images and if the size of the individual frames is larger, then the file size will be larger.

USING POSTPRODUCTION/ SERVICE BUREAUS

In some situations, you may want to work with a postproduction studio or service bureau that can take your digital video file (or Flash file in some cases) and generate the desired broadcast-quality master, whether you are talking about developing something as simple as a Mini-DV tape, a DVD, or one of the broadcast-quality tape masters, such as Betacam SP (various output formats are mentioned in Chapter 14, "Polishing and Delivering Flash Video").

You can choose to bypass all that we've discussed here and just hand over the Flash project file (FLA) to the postproduction house. If you do, be sure that it has a lot of experience with exporting and working with Flash and ask to see some examples. In general, we recommend that you export to video yourself and then work with a postproduction house to print to video if needed.

Whether or not you work with a post production studio may revolve around the question of your final delivery format and what equipment you have immediately available. If you need to broadcast on television, find out what format the broadcast facilities accept, and if you don't have that kind of deck in-house, a postproduction facility can generate the master tape for you. Or, if you want to distribute your project on a variety of formats, such as VHS and DVD, a postproduction facility can help you to generate the appropriate master tapes and get the project duplicated or manufactured.

When you consider DVD, getting a DVD "copied" may be different than getting one manufactured. DVD-R discs are compatible with about 90 percent of the DVD players out there, but if you need 100 percent compatibility, you'll need to get it manufactured with a DVD manufacturer such as EMV USA (`www.emvusa.com`). Your postproduction facility probably has the capability of burning DVD-Rs in-house, perhaps even copying short runs of DVD-Rs, and they will likely have a DVD manufacturer they like to work with for longer runs.

Regardless of what your output format is, if you need to get a file to a postproduction studio/service bureau, check to see what kind of formats they will accept. CD-R media will work for very short clips or for image sequences that are split across several CDs;

DVD-R media will work with larger data files (over 4 gigabytes — DVD-Rs are technically rated to hold 4.7 gigabytes, but, because of the way data is stored, may only hold approximately 4.3 gigabytes). The postproduction facility will likely accept a variety of removable media such as Jaz cartridges.

With the advent of inexpensive FireWire drives, if you have a large project, you can probably just send the postproduction house a portable FireWire drive. Prices are always dropping, and because you may consider such a drive simply as data storage, you can probably get away with getting a relatively slow one. The less expensive FireWire drives are probably 5400 rpm drives and are not suitable for video capture, but they are fine for data transfer/storage.

Another alternative is to use one of the small, portable bus-powered FireWire drives. A variety of these devices are available to choose from, with different levels of performance. The nice thing about bus-powered FireWire drives is that they are very small and very convenient, with no need to hook up to a power supply — ideal for working with laptops.

In fact, they often use the same mechanism as hard drives found in laptops, and some come equipped with special chipsets that improve the performance, such as the ones from All4DVD (`www.all4dvd.com`), which are certified for DVD video capture (12.22).

● 12.22

PRE-EXPORT CHECKLIST

After you decide what format to export to, what platform to do it on, and you have files and hardware ready to go, go through a final check of items that can make the export to video go smoothly.

RAM AND DISK SPACE

Make sure that you have at least 256MB RAM on a PC and 512MB on a Mac. You can get away with less, but you run the risk of the hanging or crashing the system. Plan for at least 2GB of storage per minute of video and leave an extra gigabyte free for overhead, just in case.

DOCUMENT SIZE/EXPORT SIZE

Set your Document Size at your target dimensions or plan to scale up your movie upon export (12.23):

- Digital Video or DVD (NTSC): 720x540
- Digital Video or DVD (PAL): 768x576

COLOR-SAFE

Check to see that you used an NTSC- or PAL-safe color palette in your Flash movie (such as the one available on this disc/available for download on this book's official site: www.flashtotv.com), or you are planning on using a filter in your video-editing application (After Effects — NTSC filter, Premiere — NTSC filter, and so on).

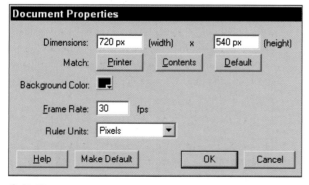

● 12.23

BITMAPS

Make sure that the bitmaps in the movie are not scaled over 100 percent or else they will become blurry or pixelated on export. This is okay for some background images or if there is a quick zoom on a bitmap. However, as a general rule, bitmaps should not be scaled bigger than 100 percent for best results.

FRAMERATE

Verify your target framerate for video: 30 fps for NTSC, 25 fps for PAL.

If your animation was created for the Web, it's likely to run at a lower framerate. If the Flash animation is going to NTSC, and the framerate is a divisor of 30 (10 or 15), then conversion to 30 fps is easy in postproduction by just doubling or tripling the frames. If the movie was done at 8, 12, or some other framerate, you can still convert to 30 fps in postproduction, but a "pull down" issue similar to what happens when transferring film to video is likely to occur.

[N O T E]

For a great explanation of *pull down* and telecine transfer, see the Web site "How Film is Transferred to Video" by Henrik 'Leopold' Herranen, at www.cs.tut.fi/~leopold/Ld/FilmToVideo/.

Remember that if you start at a low framerate like 10 fps, increasing the framerate in postproduction won't make the animation smoother — it just adds extra frames where needed. Changing the framerate in Flash before exporting doesn't help, either — the animation just plays faster. If you want smooth results in video, you need to create the animation at a framerate of at least 15 fps, and better yet, 24 (film), or 25 (PAL), or 30 (NTSC).

ACTION AND TITLE-SAFE ZONES

As discussed in Chapter 3, "Working with Television Display," televisions tend to cut off the edges of video (overscan), and you should review your project with this in mind. Keep characters and other important visual elements within the action-safe zone and keep titles or other text elements within the title-safe zone (12.24).

Generally, the action-safe zone extends out to about 90 percent of the screen in either horizontal or vertical dimensions, and the title-safe zone extends out to about 80 percent. Please see Chapter 3, "Working with Television Display," for details on using an action-safe/title-safe guide layer in Flash.

SOUND

Sound should be 44 kHz 16-bit stereo, uncompressed. You can export a separate WAV or AIFF file if you are exporting an image sequence.

CONVERT MOVIE CLIPS TO ANIMATED SYMBOLS

If you have any movie clips in your Flash file, they need to be taken out or converted to animated symbols as described in Chapter 4, "Flash Video Capabilities and Limitations." Only the first frame of a movie clip will be exported to your video file.

NO ACTIONS

It's actually okay to leave these in, but, of course, none of them will work. Any animated effects done with ActionScript will not show up and will need to be converted to frame-based animation before export.

TEXT SIZE AND FONTS

Make sure that your font sizes are not too small (at least 18 pt). Also, make sure that you have all the fonts used in the Flash project file installed on the machine that will be doing the video render. This step is easy to forget if you're sending out the project file to a postproduction house to render — be sure to include fonts for the platform they are using.

● 12.24

[T I P]

To work around not having the correct fonts installed on the machine rendering Flash to video (especially if it's a different platform than the animation was created on), you can convert all the text to shapes in Flash, before sending it to render on a different machine. To do this in Flash MX, simply select any text in the Flash animation, press Ctrl+B to break up the text into letters, and then press Ctrl+B again to break up the letters into shapes. Then group the shapes or make into symbols as you want.

READY TO RENDER

When you do the export, let the machine do the video rendering and leave it alone — don't try to do other work on the machine. Don't tempt it to crash. Don't even look at it funny.

SUMMARY

You've seen that there are three options for exporting from Flash to output to video (QuickTime, AVI, and image sequences). Remember to create the original Flash project at a 4:3 aspect ratio. Using a frame-rate that is at or is a divisor of your target video frame-rate is also helpful. If you follow the checklist before exporting, the process should go smoothly, and you'll have clean, high-quality files to import into your video-editing program or to bring to a postproduction house.

Audio for DVD

If you are going to DVD, ultimately sound needs to be 48 kHz, and your MPEG-2 encoder should be able to convert the audio. If it can't, usually you can use a video-editing application to export a 44 kHz sound file at 48 kHz.

For example, if you open up a QuickTime or AVI file on a Mac using QuickTime Pro with the MPEG export option that is installed by DVD Studio Pro, when you export into MPEG-2 format, the audio will come out at 48 kHz. But if you end up in a situation where you have separate video and audio files that you want to import into a DVD authoring application, they will most likely be rejected if they are at 44 kHz, so you may need to convert to 48 kHz before importing, using a sound editing application.

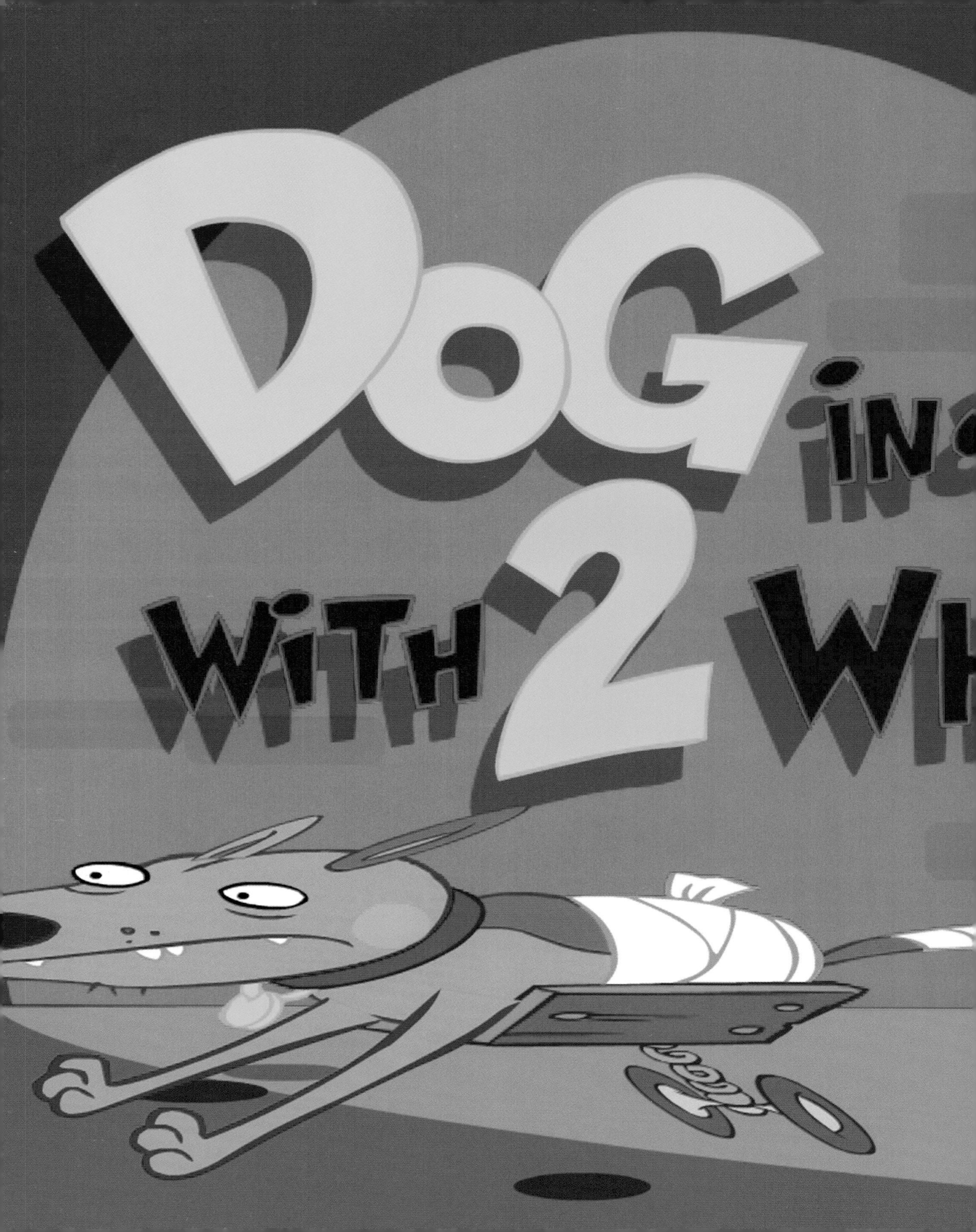
DOG
WITH 2

Titles, Fades, and Credits

Special thanks to Chad Fahs for primary development of this chapter.

One of the best reasons to use a video editor with Flash is for the creation of text and titles.

Most animation, video, and film projects use credits and titles of some sort. While it's easy to create titles and credits in Flash, there are issues particular to video displays and computer graphics that make them difficult to reproduce effectively when they're transferred to video. In this chapter, we discuss working with and repurposing titles from Flash itself, and we introduce how to create titles using separate video editing applications.

WORKING WITH TITLES AND CREDITS IN FLASH

Basic text titles and credits can be created in Flash by fading keyframes in and out (or popping them on and off) over black, or another background. For scrolling titles, you can create a symbol that contains all the text, set the starting and ending positions of the text in keyframes, and tween to get the text to scroll at your preferred speed.

As mentioned in Chapter 3, "Working with Television Display," it's important to use text that is at least 18 points high, and you should avoid fonts with serifs. If you are doing a text scroll, the speed at which the text scrolls will affect how the titles look on video. If it goes too slowly, the edges of the letters may seem to wiggle, and if it goes too fast, the text may appear to blink in and out as it moves. With titles done in Flash, it's important to test your output before doing a final render.

If your original Flash titles use white as a background color, modify that and use a light gray or other off-white color instead, before going out to video. In general, white on black text works better.

Probably the biggest issue with doing titles and credits in Flash is the framerate. If your original animation was created at a low framerate for the Web or mobile device, any tweens used to create fades, scrolling, or flying text will look very chunky, even after converting to 30 fps in your video editor after rendering in Flash. This is because when you convert the Flash-rendered sequence to 30 fps (or 25 fps for PAL), the NLE doesn't add any in-between frames — it just repeats the frames you have. In an animated sequence with characters, this is often acceptable, but it can be very noticeable with titles and credits.

Because of this, if your original titles are under 30 fps, consider cutting them off and pasting them in a separate Flash movie at 30 fps (25 fps for PAL). Adjust the titles as needed to work correctly at the higher framerate, and render the title sequence separately to be combined with the main animation later in the video editor.

With these caveats in mind, you can successfully generate titles and credits in Flash that render out to video with good results.

FADES IN FLASH

If your original animation is under 30 fps (or 25 fps for PAL), and you have fades and other transitions in the body of the animation, we recommend rendering out the whole animation, but cutting out the fades in your video editor and re-doing them there so the fades run at a true 30 fps (not simply 15 fps with repeated frames). This is the best way to get superior quality in your final product; you'd be surprised what a difference nice, smooth fades make once your project is in video — it's worth the trouble. That said, if you don't need to have a perfectly polished final product, leaving the fades that were rendered from Flash at a lower framerate works fine — it just looks a little less professional.

[N O T E]

Before exporting a movie from Flash, make certain that you account for the framerates required for video, particularly if you are planning to combine your Flash-originated material with other video content. This means that you should also be aware of whether you need to use standard progressive frames produced for computer-based video, or whether you need to account for the interlaced frames that you may be combining with your Flash animations. If you are combining progressive Flash animations with other interlaced video, you should try de-interlacing your video content with a plug-in provided by your NLE.

FLASH-BASED TEXT EFFECTS: SWFX AND SWISH

Anyone who is generating animation or video in Flash may wish to consider using one of the third-party tools such as SWfX or Swish to generate text — both are available in fully-functional demo versions for download.

Generating advanced text effects in Flash can be a time-consuming and complex process, and a few tools have evolved to automate the process.

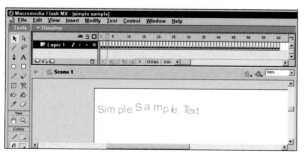

● 13.1

Essentially they give you the ability to choose a pre-set text effect, you type in your text, customize the size and other settings, and you end up with an SWF file that you can import into a Flash project, (13.1) where all of the individual keyframes and instance effects have been automatically created for you for each letter, in each frame, making complex effects doable.

SWfX

Wildform's SWfX application is available for both Mac and Windows, and runs about $60.00 in the United States. It is downloadable from the Wildform site at www.wildform.com.

The SWfX interface is streamlined in a simple main window (13.2) with a separate floating preview window (13.3,13.4) making it very simple to type in text, choose a size, adjust settings, and save into SWF

● 13.2

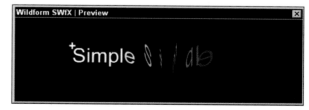

● 13.3

● 13.4

format. There are over 300 individual effects to choose from.

Because of the way that the SWf X effects are saved and the limitations of Flash 4, only 123 of the effects will import directly into Flash (the ones based on Flash 3 technology). The rest of them, based on Flash 4 technology, can be used with Web-based Flash delivery through the Load Movie functionality of ActionScript, but cannot be imported in a way that will render out to video.

SWISH

Swishzone's SWf X application is available for Windows only, and runs about $30.00 in the United States It is downloadable from the Swishzone site at `www.swishzone.com`.

Swish's approach is closer in look and feel to the actual Flash interface (13.5). There are less overall preset effects, but there is a greater degree of customization available (13.6). Swish will also allow direct output to .AVI video format.

CONCLUSION

For the cost-conscious and those who like to tinker, both of these programs are worth investigating. Video-editing applications and plug-ins have a host of titling and text generation capabilities and options that are specifically designed for video, but some may find that Flash-based text capability can be a doable alternative on a budget. Furthermore, it may be a simple way to begin exploring the concept of text in motion.

PROCESSING AND EDITING VIDEO

While video generated in Flash can produce great results on its own, there are elements of the process that are sometimes better suited to video-specific applications like Final Cut Pro or Avid. By using one of these NLEs for titles and credits, the text and motion graphics you create will be guaranteed to look good on TV, which is not always the case with Flash text. Many animators prefer to render the body of their animation in Flash, but leave the titles and credits to do in postproduction. This tag-team approach is the best method in many situations.

Once you understand the benefits of using a video editor in conjunction with Flash, it is time to take a look at a few applications that can be of use. While there are a number of software titles available that can produce great results, the following sections discuss applications that are widely used and which many of you may already own as part of your multimedia studio. It is important to choose an application that

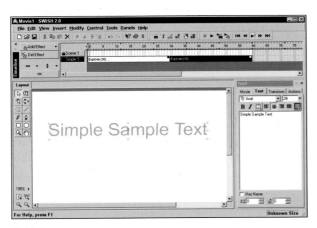

● 13.5

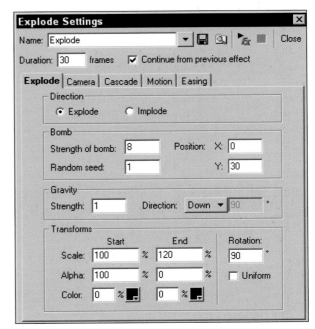

● 13.6

contributes to your workflow, which modern NLEs do very well by combining traditional editing functionality with image processing, effects, and text capabilities. It is with these applications that you can edit and process standard video material together with your Flash-based projects. You may also use them to prepare material with color-correction tools and other image enhancements prior to exporting your final movie (see Chapter 14, "Polishing and Delivering Flash Video," for more information on color-correction tools). Whichever software you choose for the job, you should be able to adapt many of the techniques discussed in this chapter as a starting point.

USING FINAL CUT PRO

Apple's Final Cut Pro is a terrific video-editing application for Macintosh computers, which allows you to work with video material that ranges in quality from standard DV to High Definition resolutions, with the option to add the capability to edit film as well.

● 13.7

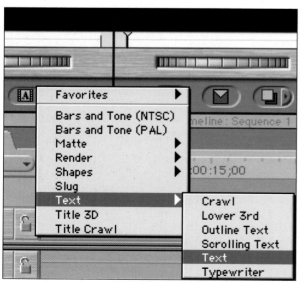

● 13.8

Of course, like most video editors, Final Cut Pro includes tools for adding text to your program and adding transitions between clips. In the following sections, we discuss common methods for creating titles, fades, and credits for the video programs you created in Flash.

Creating Titles

After you have assembled and edited your video, you can add titles to your movie. You can insert titles at any time and modify them to accommodate any changes made later to the length or content of your program. The title generators included with Final Cut Pro are capable of producing great results using the TrueType fonts available on your system.

[N O T E]

When using text for video, it is best to select a larger font without many fine lines to avoid problems caused by interlacing of video fields. For example, sans serif fonts size 18 or larger work well.

Titles can be generated for your video by using the simple titling tools in Final Cut Pro. To create a title, follow these steps:

1. Click the text icon in the lower-right corner of the Viewer window (13.7).
2. Choose Text→Text from the drop-down menu. When you have made the selection, you should see "Sample Text" in the Viewer window. This indicates that there is text to be modified for a new clip, which is later composited over your video (13.8).
3. Click the Controls tab at the top of the Viewer window. A window should open with several options for adjusting the text for this clip (13.9).
4. Click in the Text box and type a new title.
5. Adjust the Font, Size, Style, and Alignment for your title. Although you can only select Left, Center, or Right for the placement of your text, you can choose a new origin point if you want the text to be centered around a new location. You can also make advanced adjustments for your text, including Tracking, Leading, and Aspect, and Kerning, all of which should be familiar to users of Illustrator or other design and layout applications. If you want to make other modifications, like adding

drop shadows or varying opacities, use the Filters tab at the top of the Viewer window.

6. When you are finished making adjustments to the text, click the Video tab to return to the main Viewer window (13.10).

7. Next, you want to adjust the time for the new text clip by marking in and out points in the Viewer window or by dragging the end point of your clip after it's in the Timeline to create a new duration (13.11).

8. Add the text clip to your Timeline as you would any other clip, by dragging it directly into the sequence, dropping it onto the Canvas window, or by using one of the insert or over-write buttons. Add it to one of the upper video tracks for it to remain visible over your video. You should see your title composited on top of your main video track (13.12).

After you have created a single title, you may want to create more clips, which can transition between each other through the use of fades or other dissolves.

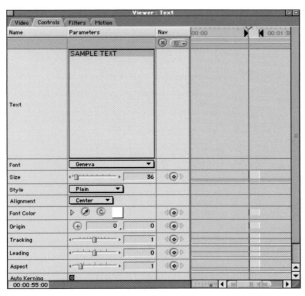

● 13.9

● 13.11

● 13.10

● 13.12

Fades

Transitions are commonplace in any movie or video program and are often used to smooth over an edit, to suggest a change of location, or to indicate the passage of time. Although video generated with Flash may be able to use transitions, such as fades without the need for an NLE, the result you can achieve by using an application such as Final Cut Pro are superior in quality and more customizable than what you find in Flash. Final Cut Pro includes several types of transitions that you can use, including fades and dissolves, some of which are capable of real-time playback. With Final Cut Pro 3, the real-time capabilities of the application have improved, however, a special hardware card may add even more transitions that can be played without rendering first.

Adding a fade to clips in a sequence is accomplished by working in the Timeline:

1. With your sequence open in the Timeline window, highlight a point between two clips

● 13.13

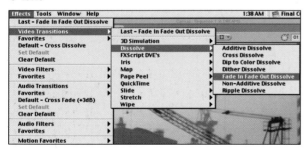

● 13.14

● 13.15

by clicking between them with the default Selection tool (13.13).

2. When a point has been selected, choose Effect→Video Transitions→Dissolve→Fade In Fade Out Dissolve to designate a fade between the two clips (13.14).

3. Double-click the transition in the Timeline (13.15) to open a box for modifying the properties of the effect.

4. A window should open in the Viewer where you can specify the exact start and end point and the amount of the effect, as well as the overall duration (13.16). Remember, you may need to render the transition before previewing it.

Now that you are familiar with the creation of titles and the uses of fades in your video program, consider making credits that you can add to the end of your finished program.

Credits

Using the Scrolling Text option, you can create text that scrolls vertically up the screen, simulating the effect of credits that play at the end of a movie. This is one of the most common ways to display credits, although you can always place names on the screen as you have done with your titles and fade between them to create transitions.

Follow the steps below to create centered, scrolling credits for your movie in Final Cut Pro. You may

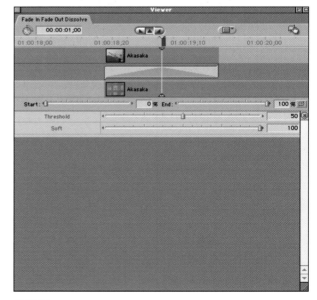

● 13.16

want to have a sequence already open in the Timeline window, or you can create credits over a black background.

1. Click the text icon in the lower-right corner of the Viewer window.
2. Choose Text→Scrolling Text from the drop-down window (13.17).
3. Click the Controls tab in the Viewer to open a window where you can modify the text for the clip.
4. Enter the text that you want to scroll in the Text box. If you want to include a title and name on the same line that is centered and separated by a space (a common method for creating scrolling credits), then you need to enter an asterisk (★) between the words to be separated (13.18).
5. Adjust properties for your text, including the direction that it should travel (either up or down).
6. When you are finished making adjustments to the text, click the Video tab to return to the main Viewer window.
7. Next, adjust the time that it takes your text to scroll up the screen by marking in and out points in the Viewer window or by dragging the end point of your clip after it's in the Timeline to create a new duration (13.19).

Although Final Cut Pro is one of the best video-editing applications available today, there are other popular and powerful applications to choose from, each with a similar interface for working with clips and adding text to a project. On the PC side, Avid Xpress DV is becoming a popular choice for professional and semiprofessional users, particularly those working with DV footage in a busy studio environment.

USING AVID XPRESS DV 3

Avid Xpress DV 3 is the first software-only video-editing application offered by Avid and is positioned to compete with Final Cut Pro. Finally, in the Avid environment, you can work with DV footage on a laptop or at home while easily moving projects back and forth between a high-end studio without the need for translating information or rendering an incomplete EDL (edit decision list). It is available for both PC and Mac.

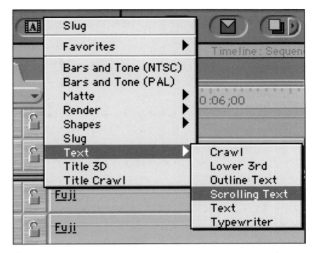

● 13.17

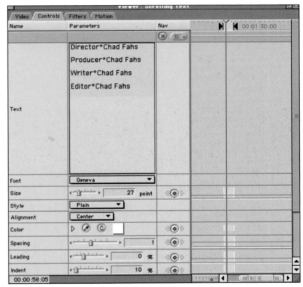

● 13.18

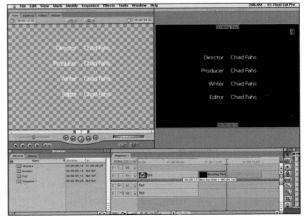

● 13.19

[NOTE]

At the time of writing, Avid announced Xpress DV 3.5, which is shipping for Mac OS X and Windows XP Professional — and you get both versions in the same box. 3.5 introduces several new features, including advanced color correction tools, and over 100 customizable, real-time effects.

Creating Titles

Working with Titles in Avid Xpress DV is a little different than working in Final Cut Pro. The most obvious difference is the Title tool that is used to work with text. Also, after a title is created with the Title tool, it is saved as a separate clip in your bin for addition to your sequence.

The following steps demonstrate how to create a title using Avid Xpress DV's built-in tools:

1. With your project open in the Timeline, you may select a clip or sequence to use as a reference.
2. Choose Tools→Title Tool to launch the Title Tool window (13.20).
3. With the Title Tool window open, begin typing your title at the desired location, using your background as a reference for placement. Notice that the title safe markers indicate the safest areas for placement of your text (13.21).
4. Adjust the title using the tools provided at the bottom of the Title Tool window. This includes the use of the standard text tools along with film, shadow, and border colors, and opacity settings. Also, the various selection tools allow you to draw an invisible bounding box for your text in which you can precisely align the text while referring to your video background. The Title Tool window serves as a great tool for accurately producing titles (13.22).

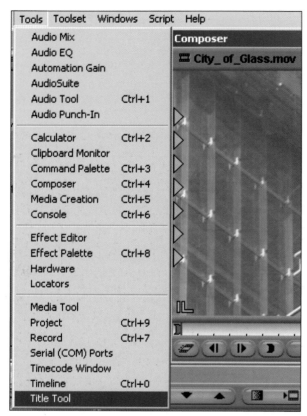

● 13.20

● 13.21

● 13.22

Chapter 13 *Titles, Fades, and Credits*   169

5. After you have created your title, save it by choosing File➔Save Title and selecting a location (13.23).

6. The new title is placed as a clip in your project bin. You can drag this clip onto the Timeline window above the clip you want to use as a background (13.24).

Fades

Creating Fades with Avid Xpress DV is just as simple as you might expect. After you have familiarized yourself with the Timeline interface and some of the menus, this task should be a breeze. However, you can accomplish the same task in different ways,

which may be a little confusing for a new user. In the following example, you learn how to use the Quick Transition feature to create a fade between clips. This is one of the easiest methods to make a transition.

1. Click a point between two clips in the Timeline or draw a selection box around the point to select it. The transition point should now be highlighted in the Timeline (13.25).

2. Click the Quick Transition button located at the top of the Timeline window (13.26).

● 13.23

● 13.25

● 13.24

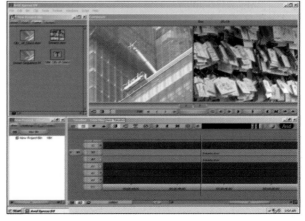

● 13.26

3. In the Quick Transition window that appears, select the appropriate options for your transition (13.27). Potential settings include the type of dissolve or fade and the position and duration of the effect. Make certain that the proper location is selected to save the effect.

4. After you modify the effect, click Add. With Avid Xpress DV, you can see a preview of your transition without needing to render it first.

Credits

Although Avid Xpress DV includes great tools for creating titles, you may primarily rely on other applications, such as Boris Graffiti Ltd. (included as a plug-in), to handle more complex text animation duties. This is essentially another application (13.28). With this tool, you can create moving text, similar to what you can create in Final Cut Pro, while modifying its properties as you would with the Text tool.

Boris Graffiti Ltd. is added by dropping the effect onto a clip from the Effects palette. With the Effect Editor open (13.29), you can access the detailed Boris Graffiti interface. If you choose to create scrolling credits with Boris Graffiti, take some time to become familiar with it its functionality. If you are familiar with After Effects, you should not have a problem using this plug-in, because it relies on similar keyframing techniques to create motion.

SUMMARY

In this chapter, you learned about creating titles, fades, and credits with Final Cut Pro and Avid Xpress DV. You should have a pretty good understanding of the options that are available in today's popular NLEs for smoothly integrating text and transitions into your Flash-for-video projects.

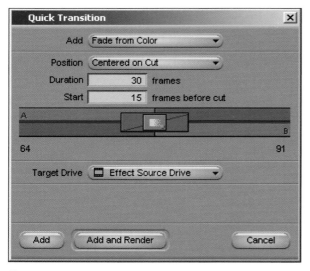

● 13.27

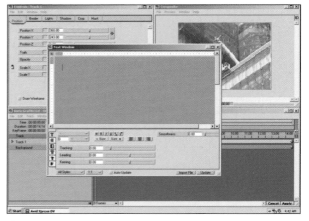

● 13.28

13.29

Chapter 14

Polishing and Delivering Flash Video

Special thanks to Chad Fahs for primary development of this chapter.

A desktop video suite can be a powerful tool for taking video exported from Flash and generating a broadcast-quality master.

Video post-production is a complex undertaking, requiring knowledge of video formats, editing, hardware, and recording equipment. If you're new to working with video, this chapter won't cover everything you need to know to get professional results on your own. For example, we assume that you are familiar with some video-editing basics, including importing video, images, or sound. However, our goal is to give a good overview of the issues, the equipment needed, an overview of the steps in printing to video, and to provide a basis for more learning and experimentation. We focus on tools and methods that would be at a budget and skill level of a smaller studio or an independent animator.

POLISHING AND DELIVERING FLASH VIDEO

If you've got a gig creating content that will be broadcast on TV and requires professional results, then you should consider working with a professional postproduction house for this final step. Beyond the equipment and hardware, professional postproduction technicians provide the wisdom, intuition, and experience that can put extra shine on a project and can make sure that the video meets all the required specifications. In that case, reading this chapter can provide you with enough knowledge to speak intelligently with the post house and can hopefully save you some money.

But if you're going to video or DVD for a smaller project, or if the project doesn't require professional-grade video, then by all means, dive in and do it on your own. You can get great quality on less expensive systems by using "above average" video stock, which is fine for DVD, demo reels, local broadcast, and other uses.

CONVERTING FRAMERATES

Before you go very far with postproduction and tweaks with video, your video needs to be at the correct framerate. If your Flash project is not set to a framerate that will match the intended delivery format for television (NTSC — 30 fps, PAL — 25 fps), the first step after you export from Flash to video is to convert the framerate.

Converting the framerate of video generated from Flash is handled with a video-editing application, such as Final Cut Pro, Avid Xpress DV for Premiere, or a compositing tool, such as After Effects. It is often simply a matter of using a default setting when creating a new project in the video application, and importing the video file that has been exported from Flash, applying edits/effects as part of the postproduction process, and then exporting — in this kind of situation the framerate conversion is often handled more or less transparently.

For example, if you take a video file that was exported from a Flash project where the project was at 15 frames per second, the video file might be imported into a new Final Cut Pro project where the framerate of the project is set to 30 frames per second.

FRAMERATES AND DIVISIBILITY

In an ideal world, you either generate the original Flash project at a framerate that matches your final delivery method, or you develop the original project at a framerate that is half the final delivery format's framerate. For example, if you are going out to NTSC television, which is 30 fps, you can develop your Flash project at 15 frames per second. The conversion process is smoother if you are converting framerates that evenly divide the final framerate (for example, $2 \times 15 = 30$).

On the other hand, say you have a project that was developed at 12 frames per second. You can still export to video and convert to 30 fps (NTSC), but it may not appear as smooth in the final delivery format as if the project had been developed at 15 fps. See our discussion of framerates and pulldown in Chapter 3, "Working with Television Display."

PROCESSING VIDEO

After you have completed a Flash animation, rendered it to a video format, and edited it to your satisfaction (including any effects work or compositing that needed to be done), it's time to consider any additional "tweaks" that can enhance the quality before finally outputting to tape or disc.

REMOVING FLICKER

Some studios and postproduction houses recommend using the "reduce interlace flicker" or "de-interlace frames" option in your NLE, even though content generated in Flash on a computer does not have the same interlacing issues that captured analog video would have. Erik Utter, from Flying Spot (a postproduction house in Seattle), explains it this way:

"A graphic element that consists of a single horizontal line that looks fine on a PC will flicker on a TV monitor. This is because the TV signal is interlaced.

The picture is first drawn with odd lines, then a second pass is made with the even lines. Each pass is referred to as a field. Two fields make up an entire frame. If there is a graphic that consists of just one line, it will only be drawn on a single field (half of the frame) of the TV display. This results in an "on time" of only 50 percent of the frame, which creates the flickering artifact. If the image is filtered to display single-line elements on both fields, the flickering effect will stop. This is usually a desirable option to use."

This applies to any images that have sharp, thin lines, which is often the case in animation.

[TIP]

Bob Cesca, President of Camp Chaos, has an additional tip when working with de-interlacing filters: "I also discovered that once I've de-interlaced my animation, I add a 'Sharpen' filter (in Vegas 3.0, I set the Sharpen filter to 0.60) to compensate for the slight drop in resolution from the flicker reduction. The results are amazing."

Look at the documentation for your video-editing software, and experiment with de-interlacing or flicker reduction filters to see if this technique helps your animation look smoother on a TV monitor.

COLOR CORRECTION

Processing video, particularly as it pertains to color, is an important step for maintaining or enhancing the most basic, yet most readily perceptible, elements of your project. The manipulation that you do at this point may be subtle, reducing variations between scenes, or dramatic, by creating new looks and tonal schemes for a project.

For video and film projects, correcting colors is an important final step before a project can be shown. However, when working solely with Flash vector images, this may not be as much of an issue, because you are already working from a chosen set of colors, which you necessarily define for every element in your animation. This negates much of the need to correct aberrations in color levels between scenes, because each element is drawn from a library and remains exactly the same as before. Of course, it is still important to make sure that the overall color levels are video safe, which can be accomplished by restricting the range of colors that you are working with from the beginning of a project or by applying a filter in applications like After Effects before final output.

If you have incorporated bit-mapped images into your Flash animations by importing JPEGs and other raster images, you need to consider colors more carefully than if you were only working with vector images using a predefined color palette. Bit-mapped images, such as photos, can introduce a wide range of colors that may not have been originally chosen for an animation. In this case, you may need to consider the consequences of using particular bitmaps more carefully.

First of all, make sure that the images you import into Flash are as close to ideal as possible before starting to work with them as part of your animation. Consider whether the colors they use mesh well with the vector-based images that you are mixing with them. Apart from that, carefully consider how everything should look when output for display on a television monitor. Bit-mapped images, particularly those taken from photos, may be problematic for TV if they are not adjusted first.

Whether accomplished through the use of special filters or adjusting simple parameters for a clip, there are many ways to correct or change the colors for your video. In fact, color adjustment and correction tools are one of the hottest features of many new software releases. For example, the latest version of Final Cut Pro includes color-correction tools similar to those that were once only found on expensive systems, such as DaVinci. Even though there are many new capabilities available to us, it is important to understand the basic parameters that we can affect regardless of the particular system we are working on.

ADJUSTING COLORS

For anyone who wants to adjust colors in their video, there are a few simple settings that can do a lot with very little work required. These include settings that are most relevant for video that's already been captured or is generated as a QuickTime or AVI file. Because this is the case with any project created in

Flash and imported into a nonlinear editor (NLE) or effects program, these are the types of adjustments we are going to cover. Of course, you can make other settings and adjustments when importing video through the log and capture features of an application, such as Final Cut Pro or Premiere. However, these capture considerations are more specific to matching footage shot in a camera to the analog inputs on a computer system. If you are working with DV footage imported through FireWire or graphic footage generated as a QuickTime/AVI file, then those log and capture considerations do not apply.

There are a few parameters, usually adjusted by moving sliders on the screen, that can significantly affect the look of an image. Depending on the software you are using, the names for these settings may be slightly different.

Final Cut Pro 3

Apple's Final Cut Pro is a great application for adjusting and correcting colors for video. Although it contains many of the same features and parameters discussed for Premiere, it also includes new color-correction abilities that allow the user to make precise adjustments. These new tools are similar in many ways to those used by professional studios and post houses. Included with these new tools are professional scopes and displays that give an editor accurate feedback on the adjustments they are making. Spend a little time learning these new tools, as the investment of time can result in a significant improvement in the quality of your output.

Whether you have improperly white-balanced your camera or simply want footage from different sources to match better, Final Cut Pro 3 offers many useful features for correcting colors in a video clip. These include tools for monitoring and accurately judging image quality, as well as filters and effects for making adjustments. By using these tools as you refer to clips in your project, you can achieve an overall color and tonal quality that remains consistent throughout an entire program. Of course, if you are primarily working with Flash-generated content, then continuity should not be as much of an issue unless you are also incorporating raster images or other video sources in your project. In most cases, the benefits of using color correction are best realized once you have finished editing and are nearly ready to export.

Simple results can be achieved by using the Color Corrector filter (14.1) located in the Effects menu. With this filter, you can adjust values for a clip that include balance and hue as well as fine-tune whites, mids, blacks, and saturation. Many of these settings should be familiar if you have worked in an application, such as Photoshop. Professional colorists should be at home here too, because the color correction parameters in Final Cut Pro 3 are similar in many ways to the more expensive tools used in high-end studios for film and broadcast production work.

To activate the filter, you first need to select your clip in the timeline, choose Effects➔Video Filters➔Color Correction➔Color Corrector, and activate the filters tab for your clip to view the settings. If you want to work with the visual interface, click the Visual button next to the title of your effect in the Filters tab or simply select the Color Corrector tab at the top of the clip's Viewer window (14.2). After you

open the visual interface, you can drag within the different color wheels to change the settings and move the indicator for a particular value. The placement of colors on the wheel is matched by the corresponding value on the vectorscope tool that is available in the Final Cut Pro 3 Tool Bench, which includes professional video scopes for gauging important properties of a video clip. Choose Tools➔ Video Scopes to check levels on a clip.

If you desire a more visual interface and subtle controls for adjusting your clips, Final Cut Pro 3 offers a 3-way color corrector filter, which displays blacks, mids, and whites on their own separate wheels (14.3).

The steps below demonstrate a typical use of the color correction tools in Final Cut Pro 3:

1. Locate a clip in the timeline that you want to apply color correction to and click on the clip to select it.
2. Choose Effects➔Video Filters➔Color Correction➔Color Corrector 3-Way to activate the color correction effect for that particular clip.
3. Double-click the clip so that it appears in the Viewer window and select the Color Corrector 3-Way tab.
4. Choose Window➔Arrange➔Three Up to make the video scopes visible while you adjust the clip (14.4).
5. Click the Auto Contrast button to automatically adjust your clip to an acceptable level, based on

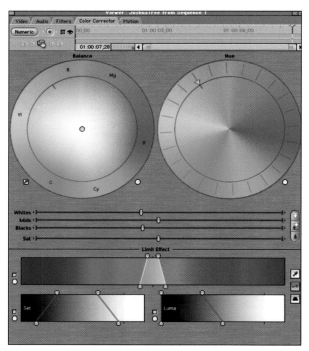

● 14.1

● 14.2

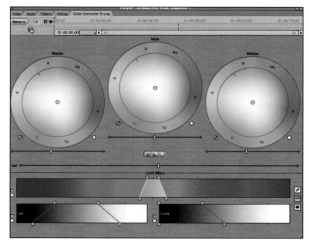

● 14.3

the luminance levels registered for your video (14.5).

6. If your image was under or overexposed, adjust the sliders for blacks, mids, and whites as appropriate.

7. Adjust the white values in your image using the auto-balance controls by clicking on the Eyedropper tool (14.6) next to the Whites color wheel and selecting a spot in your video clip that is supposed to be white, such as a white wall. This tells the controls to set this color as your new white value and adjusts the clip accordingly.

8. Next, you want to adjust the black colors in your video by clicking on the Eyedropper next to the Blacks color wheel and choosing a part of the image that is supposed to be pure black.

9. When you are finished with the auto-balance controls for white and black, you can adjust the controls manually to achieve precise results.

Adobe Premiere

Adobe's video editing software offers many effects for adjusting the color in an image or clip. After you have added a clip to the timeline, you can apply changes by selecting Adjust or Image Control from the Effects palette (14.7). Expand the list of available effects by clicking on the selection triangle and dragging one of the choices onto the clip you want to work with.

Useful choices include: Brightness and Contrast, Color Balance, Color Balance HLS, Channel Mixer,

● 14.4

● 14.5

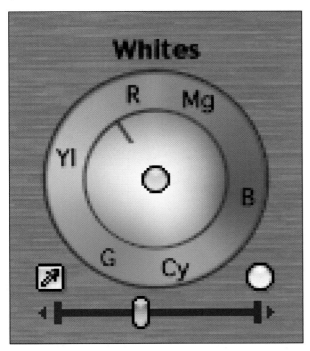

● 14.6

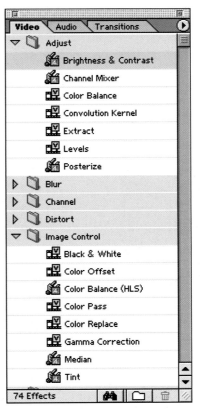

● 14.7

Levels, and Gamma Correction. Each of these choices includes parameters that you can adjust to alter the look of an image. By playing with the sliders, you can instantly test the effect and see the results on the computer screen or an external monitor:

- **Brightness** alters the radiance of an image by making the entire image lighter or darker. *Contrast* adjusts the intensity of colors in an image (14.8).
- **Color Balance** enables you to alter the amount of each red, green, and blue (RGB) channel in your image. When mixing color values, you will probably use this method fairly often (14.9).
- **Color Balance HLS** is a slightly different form of color adjustment, allowing you to change Hue, Lightness, and Saturation (14.10).
- **Color Balance HLS — Hue** changes the chroma values in an image, creating a new set of colors and often a significantly different look (14.11). This value can be adjusted in small increments to compensate for differences in

colors between scenes, or it may be changed dramatically to create more unique color schemes, tints, or otherworldly appearances. White and black levels do not change, but individual colors move up and down on the chart.

- **Color Balance HLS — Lightness** adjusts the overall brightness of an image, making it lighter or darker without respect for a particular tonal range. This setting affects dark and light areas

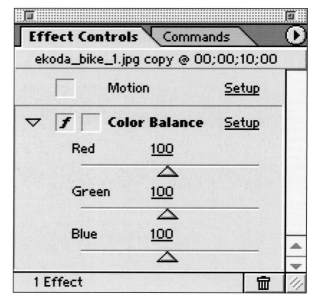

● 14.9

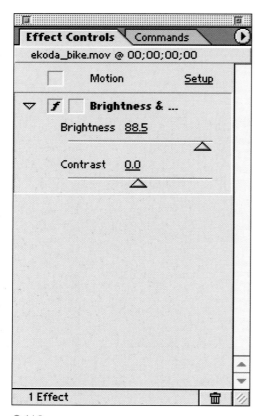

● 14.8

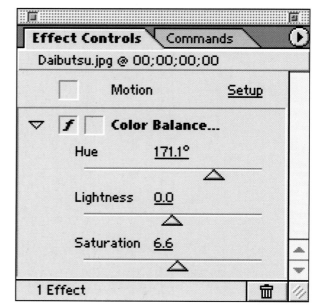

● 14.10

alike and, therefore, is not as precise as gamma correction or other tools that you may use.

- **Color Balance HLS — Saturation** adjusts the amount of color in an image. A large amount of saturation creates a very high contrast picture with a posterized effect, and a low amount creates a black and white image devoid of color.
- **Channel Mixer** effect offers more precise control over color (14.12).
- **Levels** in Premiere are basically the same as in Photoshop. You can set the range for your black and white values so that you can adjust the dynamic range for your clip (14.13).

- **Gamma Correction** allows you to lighten or darken an image, while only significantly affecting the midtone values and not the shadow and highlight portions of an image. This setting is good for adjusting a clip if images seem to be a little too dark or too light, but you do not want to significantly alter the entire image. In addition to a standard slider control, Premiere gives you a preview window that you can use to zoom into an image, in order to get an idea of what effect gamma correction may have on a particular region of the video (14.14). You can use this feature to make certain that details are not lost or obscured by the effect.

● 14.11

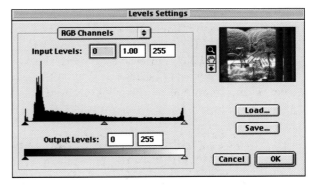

● 14.13

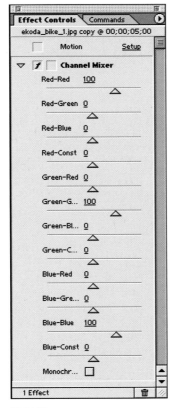

● 14.12

● 14.14

Although Premiere is one application for editing video and adjusting colors, there are many other NLEs (nonlinear editors) and applications built specifically for the purpose of professional color correction. Choose an application that fits your budget and project workflow. For example, most people are going to find it easier to do all their editing and color adjustments within the same application. However, there are those individuals in a professional studio environment who find certain tools work better and offer more precise control than those offered as part of a complete package. Of course, as software and hardware matures, more powerful capabilities are being integrated into the programs that you might use today.

SOUND

As with color, sound is an important consideration to keep in mind when reviewing an overall video program. Whether you are working with a postproduction studio or working entirely in-house, there are a few of issues and options involved in sound processing that you will probably want to become familiar with.

Mixdown

If you have been recording audio on multiple tracks, a postproduction studio can help you to develop a professional mixdown, where all the tracks are combined into a single stereo track. You can certainly learn how to create a mixdown on your own, but an experienced sound engineer can help ensure individual levels and placement (such as where a sound "appears" in a *stereo mix* — a combination of volume, EQ, and panning somewhere in the left to right spectrum).

Effects

After the basic sounds are tracked, whether you are doing sound within Flash or within a separate application, you can work with an engineer (or a plug-in in your favorite audio application) to "sweeten" the sound, adding reverb or other effects to enhance the sound presentation. If you were working with sounds in Flash in different tracks, you won't be able to export multiple tracks. For this reason, you may want to consider working with sound in another application, such as Sound Forge (Win) or Peak/Deck (Mac), where you have more control over sound effects.

Another way to get sound out of Flash in a way that could make it easier to apply specific effects to individual tracks/layers, is to save a copy of your Flash project, delete every layer except the one you want to export, get it out of Flash, and repeat as necessary; then bring all of them to the production studio or sound application and re-assemble them in an environment where you have more control.

Mastering/EQ

When you end up with a single stereo file that will form the basis of your project, mastering and overall EQ can serve as a final tweak to maximize the overall sound quality. Prior to mastering, in the multitrack mixdown stage, you might adjust the individual levels character voices or music, whereas in mastering you are affecting the overall sound and tweaking to perfection to get the best possible audio quality.

Sync

Verifying that all the sound, music, and dialogue in your project is properly synced to the animation is very important. This step is often done in a video application or audio application, which gives you the ability to make minute adjustments to the soundtrack. Certain kinds of sync, such as when sound effects are triggered, are probably easier to fix when you have multiple tracks of sound, before all the tracks have been combined into one.

You can also do this kind of sync adjustment within Flash itself, but then you may need to readjust a bit in final video editing. Even if syncing seems perfect in Flash, there are often minor sync problems after exporting to video due to differences between the 30 fps of the exported Flash animation and the true NTSC 29.97 fps. Unfortunately, Flash does not yet support *SMPTE* time code, which is the standard by which video keeps time.

Overall, sync should be verified and reviewed across the entire program so that you don't start out with dialogue perfectly aligned to the video and wind up with the situation out of whack by the end of the program. Whether it's you or an engineer checking the situation, it's an important factor.

PREVIEWING VIDEO

To properly gauge how your video should look, including any adjustments that may need to be made, you need to use an external monitor that is representative of what your audience is going to see. A computer monitor can differ significantly from a television monitor, because it is designed for working in RGB space with millions of colors at high resolution. A TV is designed for lower resolutions with a more limited color palette. Also, peculiarities exist between video standards NTSC and PAL, and you also find minor variations even within the displays for countries that use the same standards. For example, the black levels for an NTSC television signal in Japan differ slightly from the same signal in the United States. For these reasons and others, using an external monitor or TV for previewing your video is vital in the creation of a professional production.

To hook up an external monitor to your computer, you need a video card that is capable of outputting a video signal. Several cards are on the market that can accomplish this, including popular cards by Matrox, such as the RTMac or the RT2500. Other options include Canopus, Pinnacle, and Digital Voodoo. The majority of cards available today provide output from editing software like Final Cut Pro or Premiere, but there are some cards (such as Digital Voodoo) that can provide an external preview while working in applications such as After Effects or Photoshop. When shopping for a new card, consider your options carefully.

For example, one of the benefits added to some of these cards is the ability to work with multiple computer screens in addition to a separate TV monitor. If you are not already working with a dual monitor setup, you are missing out on the advantages of increased workspace provided by an expanded desktop. This is particularly useful when working with video and graphic applications, which require a lot of space for palettes, bins, and preview windows.

After you have a computer card in place for attaching a separate NTSC or PAL monitor, you need to start looking for a good display to go with it. Sony makes some of the best displays for previewing video. Many of their professional models allow you to adjust a wide number of settings on the monitor, without the need for confusing menus. Also, they add features like the ability to instantly switch between multiple inputs or to display images with or without the overscan being visible (this feature is great for seeing how much of the original image you would lose on a standard TV).

If you cannot afford one of the moderately priced Sony monitors (typically around $1,000 in the United States), consider attaching an ordinary TV purchased specifically to use as a monitor. You can also use a set that you may already have around the house. Although an ordinary consumer TV does not include the same number of adjustable parameters and features of a professional monitor, it can be useful if you want to see what your video is going to "really" look like in conditions that aren't always perfect. This option is also good if you want to show a client what a project looks like on a large-screen TV or when using a portable projector. Whichever option you choose, make sure to calibrate your monitor using color bars, which can be generated through most NLEs or even a video camera. Doing this should insure that what you see on the TV is actually matching what you are getting from the original video signal.

[N O T E]

Some links are provided at the end of the book for investigating various manufacturers more thoroughly.

PRINTING TO VIDEO

When you have finished a video project to your satisfaction, you need to output that information to a format that can be viewed by your target audience or archived for broadcast purposes and duplication. Any editing system should have this capability, although the particular system you are using may be limited in its abilities to work with certain formats. Make certain that you have the proper setup for delivering a project at the best possible quality you can manage. For example, a basic computer setup with a FireWire connection is capable of editing DV right out of the box. However, you need special hardware cards to work with analog video or high-quality digital formats. Make sure to consider the delivery format you require when choosing your system, whether it's in your home or in a professional edit suite.

THE SYSTEM

A typical video-editing system, including the necessary components to edit output video, is comprised of the following:

- Basic CPU (with as much RAM, hard drive space, and processor speed as possible).
- One or more computer monitors for working on the project as shown in Figure 14.15 (multiple monitors are ideal because you can have more windows open to make adjustments as you are working on a project).
- NTSC or PAL preview monitor, which shows you a fairly accurate representation of what your project will look like on television. This is an important part of post-production — especially in adjusting colors, because a computer monitor and television display color differently.
- Speaker setup for previewing sound. A sound setup could include an external mixing that gives you the ability to connect the sound between cameras/decks and the computer and have hands-on capability to adjust sound with knobs (as opposed to doing so strictly in software).
- Some kind of video deck, whether VHS, Mini-DV, or a higher-end broadcast format. Although using your camera as a "deck" is possible if you connect it directly to your computer for recording and playback, many prefer to have a deck dedicated to capture and mastering. This setup can help to preserve the life of the camera; it also is more convenient as you can leave everything connected all the time.
- DVD burner if you are developing DVD projects. A DLT drive (Digital Linear Tape) drive may also be necessary if you are manufacturing DVD projects and your DVD manufacturer

requires a DLT master. Many accept DVD-R discs, but the most common format for submitting projects is still DLT, and if you need to use DVD copy protection, the only way to submit the master is on DLT.

Using the typical system that we describe, you can do anything from generating your own VHS tapes to generating broadcast-quality masters. You can also connect a device, such as a Mini-DV camera/deck and generate a Mini-DV tape that you can send off to serve as a master tape for duplicating VHS tapes. You can also convert it to a broadcast format. Keep in mind that some tape formats (such as Mini-DV) are compressed, so that you may be better off turning in the video files to a postproduction studio directly as digital files (such as on a FireWire hard drive), rather than exporting to a tape format that causes you to lose some image quality.

THE PROCESS

Printing to video is often as simple as connecting your video deck and choosing the Print to Video export option in your video editing application (14.16). If you are using a controllable deck or camera (such as one controlled through FireWire), this function can automatically jump to a certain spot on the tape and set the record/stop functions automatically for you. If

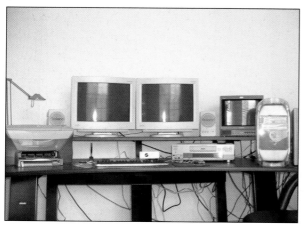

● 14.15

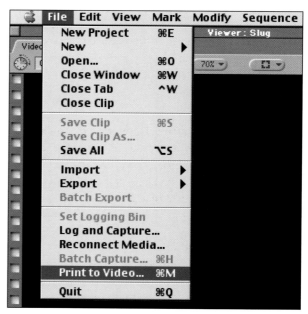

● 14.16

you are printing directly to VHS, you can set the VCR to record and then trigger the print to video functionality, and the VCR will record in real-time.

In a digital environment, if you are going to a digital deck through FireWire or another interface, such as the high-end Serial Digital, the tape deck stores each frame of the video successively in digital format on the tape. With higher-end analog decks, such as Betacam SP, they record with frame accuracy with the right connection, a feature that enables exact time length and synchronization. In either analog or digital realms, the material is recorded to tape in real-time.

Audio can be handled automatically through a digital interface, such as FireWire, or, depending on your system, you may be able to connect the audio outputs directly on a video card directly to the video deck. (If you are outputting to VHS, you need to have a video card that has analog video and audio outputs that you can connect to the VCR using standard RCA-type connectors.)

You can use additional features, such as adding *X* seconds of black to the beginning of a tape that can be activated, depending on your final output. Adding color bars (which allow a studio/duplicator to have a reference point for adjusting colors) or black space at the beginning of a tape master is known as a *leader* and adding black at the end is known as a *trailer* (14.17).

If you are developing copies for yourself, you can adjust the print to video settings to make the tapes appear how you like — but if you are developing a master tape for duplication or broadcast, check with the studio to make sure how the beginning and end of a video segment need to be prepared.

[T I P]

You can find helpful information on example configurations for desktop video and a lot of other information about digital video in the DV Primer, a free PDF document available for download from Adobe: www.adobe.com/products/dvcoll/main.html.

VIDEO DELIVERY FORMATS

Several considerations affect the type of media or format on which you choose to deliver your project. Although the details and situations for each project differ, you should carefully consider any elements

that may dramatically impact the output of your material.

First, consider what level of image and sound quality are important to achieve for your project. Although in many cases, this choice may appear transparent to the end-user, due to the generally high-quality formats that we use today, it is still crucial that sufficient quality is established and maintained throughout the creation of your project. Certain formats hold up better to the demands of editing, including the back-and-forth inputting and outputting of video to an NLE and the constant shutting and playback of a tape mechanism (especially with A/B editing). In addition, each format has benefits or limitations for color, resolution, and audio. Although we do not discuss the differences between video standards in this chapter (refer to Chapter 3, "Working with Television Display," for a discussion of NTSC versus PAL and SECAM), it is important to consider the differences between resolutions within a particular system, such as NTSC.

Secondly, you should think about how and where the material will be shown. This includes determining what effects a particular environment is going to have on your presentation and what format would work best under those conditions. For example, if your video is going to be played on a plasma screen display in a hotel lobby or corporate office, you need to consider the ability to loop the video, while presenting high-quality footage that best represents the client's image. Also, in this type of a situation, the

● 14.17

video needs to be manageable so that almost anyone can maintain it, and it should also be resilient to repeated usage.

Another situation may involve large screen projection for a concert or other live event. Consider whether the video format displays a lot of noise or noticeable image dropouts. Just remember, regardless of which format you choose, make sure that it can be played back by your end-user. Do they have the right kind of player to view your material? This is a very important question that should be asked from the beginning of any project. Of course, you may choose to initially output your project onto a better, less accessible format and then dupe it to a more widely available standard. This is a typical method, where you work initially with a high-quality master format, and then dupe to a lower quality format.

Lastly, consider the budget for a project when choosing a delivery format. Each format has certain costs associated with it. This includes everything from the cost for a deck and tapes, to the system required to work with it. Although many high-quality formats are within the reach of many video producers at all levels, some formats are too expensive and impractical to work with for many people. Depending on how much you (or your client) are willing to spend, you should use the format that provides the best quality and flexibility for the amount you can afford. Is the project going to be archived? If so, you may want to spend a little more on a better format and think of the cost as contributing to long-term insurance for your project.

ANALOG FORMATS

Analog video formats produce images and sound that are carried by a magnetic tape. These formats are the oldest type of format. They create video and audio using electronic methods that read wave patterns and not a set of "1s" and "0s" like digital formats. This format is the oldest and is still the most widely used format for consumers. Anyone who uses a VCR to record their favorite television program uses analog equipment and tapes.

Aside from their questionable quality (which is not so much of an issue with professional formats, such as Betacam SP), consumer-level analog formats are less resilient than digital formats and degrade over time and through repeated use. This is a significant problem if you intend to use it as an archival format or

one that is used for editing and re-recording of material, such as dubbing from one tape to another. Every time you play or record an analog tape, a little quality is lost. Some formats are less susceptible to this loss of quality, but issues such as generation loss are obvious with others.

[N O T E]

For links to more information on analog formats, including manufacturers and suppliers, see the Formats section of Appendix D.

Betacam SP

This format has been the format of choice amongst many postproduction facilities for several years. Although it is not the highest-quality format available, its ubiquitous presence in most studios and its all-around outstanding performance have guaranteed it lasting success. There are two different tape sizes for Betacam SP, the larger of which can hold longer record times.

Betacam is a component format, meaning it handles the elements of an RGB signal separately, which improves the sharpness and colors of an image. Originally released as, simply, Betacam, the format was later updated to SP with better frequency response and signal-to-noise ratio, along with improvements in audio performance. It relays color information at a perceived 4:2:2, over the sampling of DV's 4:1:1. Therefore, Betacam can technically display a wider range of colors over standard DV (however, the difference is negligible, if non-existent, when viewed side by side).

This format is great to use for duping copies of a program or for sending out copies of a project for broadcast, because almost every studio has a deck. Still, Betacam SP decks are relatively expensive for small studios or home use, even following the release of Sony's competitively priced UVM series of playback and recording decks, which can cost between $5,000 and $8,000. Also, to properly edit Betacam material, you should use a system with a good video input card and hard drives fast enough to capture and display motion JPEGs at approximately 30–32MB per second. A simple FireWire setup does not suffice for this format. Also, using component inputs and outputs is a must if you want to achieve the best quality from your source material, because using the

S-video or composite connections cause some information to be lost.

U-Matic

Also known as ¾-inch tape, this was once the standard in every editing studio until the superior Betacam usurped its position as the format of choice. Developed by Sony as one of the first videocassette formats, U-Matic was widely in use during the 1970s. Like Betacam, it also has an SP variation, which in this case improves the brightness and color frequencies. There are many studios that still have a U-Matic machine to play back archive materials. The U-Matic format is no longer practical for many production tasks, although it is technically superior to S-VHS in quality and usability. Many advertising agencies still work with ¾-inch tape, and some even prefer it.

VHS

VHS is a composite-only format and is present in nearly every home, making it a perfect low-quality format for delivering video programs. In fact, VHS (forgive us Betamax) is the format that transformed our movie viewing habits and introduced Blockbuster into our collective unconscious. However, at about 250 lines of resolution, the quality of VHS is significantly lower than any digital format you may use. It introduces many frustrations for content creators, including colors that bleed and significant noise and drop-outs that may distract viewers from the quality of the source material. This is not a good format for archiving material, due to its low resolution and generation loss when copied. Also, like any analog format you work with, you need a video card that can output an analog signal (composite in this case) if you want to print to tape.

VHS is a great format for delivering demo reels, especially to industries or businesses that haven't yet embraced the digital world, such as advertising agencies or companies outside the tech industry. This is beginning to change, but many companies prefer VHS tape to CD-ROM or DVD. And with VHS, you don't have to worry about which operating system or Web browser your audience has — the tape can be played in any standard VHS machine, and they'll be watching it on a TV, not a computer.

S-VHS

S-VHS, or "Super" VHS, is a clear improvement over its predecessor, offering about 400 lines of resolution over the standard 250 for VHS. Unfortunately, S-VHS tapes do not play back in regular VHS machines, limiting its compatibility and usefulness as a distribution medium. Also, even though its resolution and color represents an improvement over standard VHS (it separates luminance from chroma information), it cannot compete with the quality of the digital video formats that are now available. Mini-DV can actually be cheaper and easier to edit with than S-VHS, producing quality that is clearly superior, without the same sort of noise and dropouts associated with analog tapes.

DIGITAL FORMATS

Digital video formats differ from analog formats by using binary code instead of physical, waveform information by storing video and audio as data, similar to a computer's hard drive. The main benefit of digital formats is that they do not degrade over time and maintain perfect quality, without generation loss, even when transferring from one tape to another. To fit a large amount of data onto a small tape, these formats use compression to squeeze the data to a manageable size. Compression ratios vary according to the particular format, with the higher-quality formats, like Digital Betacam, using less compression to capture and transfer video information. Another consideration that arises with digital formats is the sampling (or quantization) that occurs for luminance and chrominance picture information (this topic is discussed in Chapter 3, "Working with Television Display"). Choose the digital format that works best for your project and remember that some situations (blue and green screen work) require better color sampling and lower compression ratios than others.

[N O T E]

For links to more information on digital formats, including manufacturers and suppliers, see the Formats section of Appendix D.

Digital Betacam

This is the format of choice for archiving and "upconverting" from other digital formats. It is a rather expensive format (the digital successor to Betacam SP) that provides 4:2:2 *quantization* with either 8- or 10-bit color information and a low 2.3:1 compression ratio. Compression artifacts are virtually nonexistent when working solely with this format. The signal-to-noise ratio is also superior to virtually any other standard definition digital format.

For these reasons, Digital Betacam is used for any standard definition video program that requires the highest quality when budget is not so much of a concern. This format requires a costly deck and an editing system with serial digital inputs and a fast array of hard drives. Because the system requirements are too steep for most home studios, Digital Betacam is usually reserved for situations where you can afford studio time to record and edit your program. Also, Digital Betacam decks can play back analog Betacam SP tapes but cannot record to them.

Mini-DV

The mini-DV format is one of the most popular consumer formats available today, particularly for users of home video cameras. Using 5:1 compression that transfers approximately 25 mbps (also known as DV-25), DV produces extraordinary image and audio that can rival Betacam SP, even though DV only uses 4:1:1 sampling. This reduced amount of color information is hardly noticeable in most situations, however, it becomes important when attempting to manipulate the video for compositing work. DV is still an excellent, inexpensive medium for capturing, recording, and playing back video programs. It can be easily edited through popular software applications, such as Final Cut Pro or Premiere and captured with a simple FireWire connection on your computer. The storage and speed demands are much less than those of uncompressed analog formats, such as Betacam SP, reducing the transfer rates from around 30MB/sec to less than 4MB/sec. Storage space is approximately 12GB for every hour of mini-DV footage.

[N O T E]

You'll also find a consumer format called Digital-8 present in lower-end camcorders produced by Sony. This format is different than Mini-DV, even though you can connect such a camera through a digital connector (Sony calls it iLink — but it's basically FireWire). The Digital-8 format is similar to Mini-DV but not as popular. Allegedly, over time, Digital-8 has more of a tendency to degrade in quality with regular playback than a Mini-DV tape. A Mini-DV tape is also a much more widely accepted format in the digital video community.

But don't despair if you have a Digital-8 camera; they can be fairly useful and can also be a nice way to capture footage from older analog 8mm or Hi8 tapes through FireWire.

DVCAM

Sony's professional upgrade to the consumer Mini-DV format, DVCAM offers more features that appeal to professionals working with DV-25 footage. Although the basic specifications are identical to Mini-DV (it also uses 4:1:1 sampling and a 5:1 compression ratio), the biggest differences are with the tapes, which are wider and stronger, produce fewer dropouts, and have longer record times. They move a little faster than mini-DV, capturing information over a greater length of tape and improving the reliability of information.

Also, DVCAM offers the ability to manually set time code that corresponds to "real" SMPTE time code numbers, which is required if you want to use DVCAM tapes to edit film projects offline. DVCAM is a great format for archiving your projects. Although not as good as Digital Betacam, it provides a relatively inexpensive professional format for producing stable, nearly flawless video, with no degradation.

DVCPRO

Panasonic's answer to Sony's DVCAM format, DVCPRO is similar in its specifications to DVCAM, although the two formats are not always compatible with each other. Although most DVCPRO decks are capable of playing back DVCAM tapes, DVCAM decks do not play DVCPRO tapes. This fact is important to consider when choosing between the two formats, because you may run into incompatibility issues between your studio and another post house.

Although it may seem that Sony has the advantage in the arena of consumer and prosumer digital formats (it is more widely used and accepted in some sectors), Panasonic's offering has slightly better specifications for its tapes, even though the basic DV-25 compression scheme remains identical to Sony's. In fact, the biggest difference with DVCPRO tapes is the resilience of the media, the quality of the mechanism, and the speed of the tape (nearly double that of Mini-DV and slightly faster than DVCAM). Also,

DVCPRO uses better metal particle tape, however, DVCAM uses the same metal evaporated tapes as DV.

Like DVCAM, DVCPRO is also superior to Mini-DV because it allows for more "pro" features such as real-time code, wider track pitch, and longer recording times per tape. The length of tapes is particularly important if you are recording long programs, such as movies or concerts that exceed one hour. DVCPRO tapes are available in a wide range of recording times.

Currently, DVCPRO is divided into two main formats, the standard DVCPRO and DVCPRO 50. The standard DVCPRO format uses the same DV25 compression scheme as the Mini-DV and DVCAM format, while DVCPRO 50 uses a lower compression ratio, to deliver pictures at nearly twice the data rate, along with improvements in color reproduction. This puts DVCPRO 50 in line with other professional digital formats, such as Digital Betacam.

DVD/DVD-R

DVD as a form of *playable* digital video is the fastest growing consumer video format ever created, and, thanks to a new line of internal and external DVD-R recorders, it is now one of the newest *recordable* formats that we have available for outputting our video projects.

January of 2001 signaled the release of the SuperDrive with high-end G4 Macs (about 4 grand), at a price including the computer that was less than the previous generation of DVD burners (about 4 grand). The Apple/Pioneer SuperDrive was released at the same time as iDVD, a consumer level DVD application, and DVD Studio Pro, a professional powerhouse DVD program.

Soon thereafter, the first external FireWire-based DVD burner was released by all4DVD (www.all4dvd.com) (14.18), based on the mechanism

● 14.18

that Pioneer had developed and licensed to Apple. This made portable DVD authoring possible, and eventually a number of manufacturers began to include DVD burners as an added feature on desktop systems, and several companies released external DVD burners.

Initially the price of media was very high with limited availability (except directly from Apple or Pioneer), but now the price of recordable discs is dropping significantly and you can find them increasingly at consumer retail outlets — at the time of writing, you could very well walk into CompUSA and pick up a 5-pack for $20 in the United States, or buy a spindle of a 100 from a direct supplier for much cheaper. (Chapter 16, "Cross-Purposing Flash for Web, TV, and DVD," covers DVD in more detail — and for more information on the SuperDrive and DVD Studio Pro, check out the DVD Studio Pro Bible at www.dvdspa.com).

Unlike the other digital formats mentioned, DVD is a disc-based medium that uses a special MPEG-2 compression algorithm to store picture information. Using temporal compression techniques to store only the information that changes between frames, MPEG-2 provides the DVD format with an efficient method for storing large amounts of high-quality, broadcast video information (it samples at about 4:2:0). Also, the DVD specifications allow for interactive features to be added to a disc, making the random access of video and supplemental information possible.

This makes DVD a great delivery format, especially when you want to provide a way to navigate through a diverse amount of material. Added to these capabilities are features like 5.1 surround sound audio, subtitles, multiple angles, and multiple audio tracks, making DVD extremely versatile and fun to use. Ultimately, DVDs surpass Laserdiscs and virtually every other consumer format in quality, finally providing a way to deliver movies and other material as they are meant to be shown.

Although DVD is a great format for delivering video to consumers, its *lossy* MPEG compression makes it less than ideal for archival purposes. However, the difference in quality between a DVD video and the studio master can be almost unnoticeable if professional hardware encoders are used to convert your video to MPEG-2 for DVD. (For more discussion on hardware encoding, check out *DVD Demystified*, by Jim Taylor, or visit `www.dvddemystified.com/dvdfaq.html#5.3.1` for a list of encoding tools.) Still, make sure that you keep a high-quality master of your program on a format such as Digital Betacam and use DVD primarily for delivering the content to a wider consumer audience.

Video-CD

Video-CDs (VCDs) are similar in some ways to DVD, with the exceptions that they are stored on CD media, use MPEG-1 compression, and do not have the same level of interactivity. The quality of a VCD is roughly equivalent to VHS, although this digital format does not degrade with multiple viewings. This format is popular in countries throughout Asia, where it has practically replaced the VCR.

If you have a CD-R burner on your computer (which comes standard on most computers sold today), then you have a way to burn inexpensive copies of a video program as a VCD using the lower-quality MPEG-1 format, which is approximately half the resolution of DVDs MPEG-2. The difference in quality is noticeable, and may be extremely distracting at points in complex or high motion portions of your video, which can cause extreme pixelation and blockiness of the image. For these reasons, VCD is a terrible broadcast or archival format, although it can still be great for cheaply delivering a video program for use with computer software players or in many set-top DVD players, many of which also play VCDs.

We have seen that a desktop video suite can be a powerful tool for taking video exported from Flash and generating a broadcast-quality master. If you are just beginning to develop experience with video, you will probably want to work with a postproduction studio and take advantage of their expertise — however, with the right tools and experience, you can accomplish everything on your own.

SUMMARY

In this chapter, we discussed several considerations for finishing and delivering your Flash-to-video production. After your video has been exported and any necessary editing has been done, additional steps, such as color correction and audio tweaking, can serve as the next to last (and often necessary) steps in ensuring broadcast quality. The final occurs when you print to video and develop your master tape (or DVD!).

Chapter 15

Creating Sizzle with After Effects

Special thanks to Chad Fahs for primary development of this chapter.

Flash animators can now import and export the SWF format to or from After Effects. This is good news for those who cross-purpose a lot of content for both video and the Web.

Anyone working with video and motion graphics today has probably used After Effects (15.1) at some point in the course of their production career. Of course, many people rely on After Effects as a part of their daily routine. After all, it is an industry standard application for animation, effects, and compositing. As a universal production tool, After Effects appeals to a wide range of users, including editors, animators, film producers, and even Web designers.

With the release of After Effects Version 5.5, Flash animators can import and export the SWF format to or from After Effects. This is good news for those who cross-purpose a lot of content for both video and the Web. In this chapter, we cover some After Effects basics, as well as the capabilities After Effects has for dealing with Flash content.

AFTER EFFECTS CAPABILITY

The methods for creating any project in After Effects, whether they are destined for a television set or the Internet, are essentially the same, with only a few minor notes for optimizing the output of a project to the Flash SWF format. Therefore, learning the basics

Adobe® After Effects® 5.5

● 15.1

of After Effects is essential, regardless of how you are planning to use the material.

If you have never used an application similar to After Effects before, you may feel a bit intimidated. The many tools and capabilities built into After Effects increases the complexity of fully learning the application. However, as long as you understand the basic principles and techniques for creating compositions, then you should have enough to accomplish a great deal with this software. For those of you who are already experienced Flash animators, many of the principles we are going to discuss should be somewhat familiar. Just remember that working with images for video and television requires special treatment that is not always necessary for Web imagery.

UNDERSTANDING COMPOSITING

Compositing is the art of combining layers of graphics on top of each other, to create compositions that are composed of multiple images. In many instances, the graphics you are compositing are going to have transparent and opaque areas, which allow certain parts to show through and others to remain visible. This is accomplished through the use of alpha channels, which can be added or created for graphics and video clips in a nonlinear editing application (NLE), Photoshop, Illustrator, or other graphic's software. After Effects works with alpha channels, along with standard video and graphic layers, in a manner that is nearly identical to Photoshop. This consistency between applications makes for a simple transition from one to the other, because the skills you have from one familiar interface will translate easily. However, the only major difference is After Effects deals with the added dimension of time (15.2). This offers many more possibilities and complexities for your images.

In addition to working with graphics that have already been created in an application, such as Photoshop, After Effects is great for compositing layers of video where only certain elements need to remain visible. For the most part, the best way to accomplish this form of compositing is to use video material that was originally shot using a properly lit blue or green screen as a background. This technique allows the use of After Effects' "keying" feature, which removes a narrow range of colors (that you define) and creates a transparent alpha channel in its place. By doing this, you can drop out the background behind your primary subject (for example, an interview subject sitting in front of a blue background) and composite only the desired foreground element onto your composition.

Remember that the better your source footage is, the better your keying results are going to be. This is especially true when working with video that uses a lossy compression scheme, such as DV. Sometimes getting a good blue screen image when using DV is difficult (which removes some important blue values and produces slightly jaggy edges as shown in Figure 15.3). However, the better your lighting is, the more likely you are to achieve acceptable results. If you are using DV, you may want to consider importing it as an analog signal using a special capture device, such as the one included with many of the Matrox video cards. This may actually soften the image a bit and eliminate some of the jagged edges in the process. If you can use a 4:2:2 color image, such as those produced with Betacam SP or DigiBeta cameras, then you can achieve even better results.

Of course, you find many instances, even in professional productions, where you do not have the luxury of shooting against a special backdrop. In these cases, you can use After Effects; masking tools along with the other keying effects designed to eliminate unwanted elements from your composite. Among the many tools available for keying are the Color Difference Key, Color Key, Color Range Key, Difference Matte, Extract, Inner Outer Key, Linear Color Key, Luma Key, and the Spill Suppressor. Depending on which version of After Effects you are using and whether you are working with the Standard After Effects or Production Bundle, some of these options may not be available.

- **Color Difference Key** divides an image into two separate mattes. One matte (Matte Partial B) creates a transparency for your layer that is based on a color, which you specify, eliminating that color from the image. The second matte (Matte Partial A) adds transparency to specific areas of the image, based on a selected color, so that the areas that *do not* contain the color are transparent. These two mattes are then combined into a single matte, or alpha matte, with the combined transparency values. This technique works well for properly lit material, and it even works for footage that contains fine details, such as smoke, shadows, and hair.

- **Color Key** (15.4) is the most basic keying method, which "keys" out all the pixels with colors that are similar to the color value that you specify. You can adjust the tolerance level to determine how severe the effect should be, which broadens the range of pixel values that need to be excluded. In addition, you can use

● 15.2

● 15.3

the feather controls to adjust the smoothness of pixels around the keyed out areas for that layer. This method is often imprecise, but it is great for quick keying effects, especially those that are shot against blue or green backgrounds.

- **Color Range Key** makes specified parts of an image transparent by using the Lab, YUV, or RGB color space. This key is particularly useful for inconsistent blue and green screen shots that have not been properly lit, or for footage that contains more than one color or different shades of the same color.

- **Difference Matte** (15.5) uses a source image to key out any pixels that match identical pixels in your target layer. This keying tool is great for eliminating a static background with a moving image in front of it, such as a static shot of a wall with someone walking in front of it. By using a reference shot of the wall without your subject (before it enters the scene) and combining it with your motion footage using a difference matte, you can replace the original background with something else. Of course, this only works if you are using shots with a stationary camera.

- **Extract** removes any pixels within a specified brightness range using the provided histogram. This works better for images that are shot against backgrounds with a drastic difference in brightness from the elements you want to keep, including black and white walls or shadows.

- **Inner Outer Key** (15.6) isolates any foreground objects from the images background, including hard to define elements like hair or other subjects with fine detail. To make this work, begin by creating a rough mask for the elements you want to remain opaque, which defines the approximate inner and outer edges of the objects. This can be done by drawing a closed path around the border of an object and adjusting the mask highlight radius. You may also choose to create separate inner and outer paths that enclose all the potential components of the object. Set the feather and threshold values and then adjust the amount you want it to blend with the original image layer.

- **Linear Color Key** creates transparencies by using RGB, hue, or chroma information that relates to a color that you have specified. By adjusting the effect's tolerance and softness using the thumbnail windows as a reference (the left thumbnail is the unaltered source, and the right is your new preview), you can often achieve better results than if you use a basic color key.

- **Luma Key** makes areas of a specified brightness, or luminance, transparent. This works best for

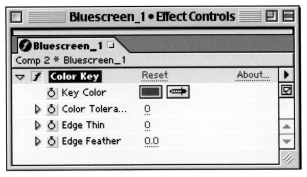

● 15.4

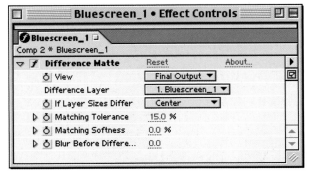

● 15.5

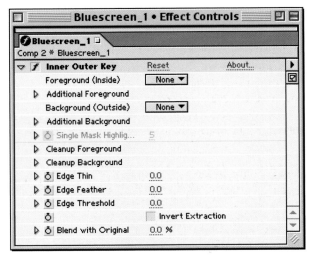

● 15.6

backgrounds that differ significantly in brightness from the foreground objects, such as a black object against a white background.

- **Spill Suppressor** works on images that have already been keyed, to remove additional "spills" of any key color that may remain in the image. This eliminates many of the unwanted pixel colors, which results from light that often reflects off a blue/green screen onto a subject. To prevent this problem when shooting your source footage, make sure to provide adequate distance between your subjects and the background. In addition, a strong key light that separates backgrounds and foregrounds should help (some of which are typically placed overhead and angled slightly forward).

There are also different views in After Effects that allow you to see the alpha channels as you work with them. When working in the alpha channel view (15.7), you can easily see where your layer transparencies are located to assist in keying and placement of different elements.

In addition to keying tools, you can use the masking features of After Effects to easily select areas of interest in your composition. The masking features can assist in producing cleaner edges for your keys, or for eliminating traces of other unwanted elements. Masks can then be animated and moved to track an object or to allow for other special effects. Using mask modes, multiple masks can be combined based on the interaction of elements, such as Add, Subtract, Intersect, and Difference modes that are somewhat similar to what you would fine in other graphic applications like Photoshop and Flash. You may also use the traditional Masking tool to draw boxes around specific areas of your composition or you can use one of the other special mask tools provided by

After Effects in the Production Bundle, including Simple Choker, Matte Choker (15.8), and Alpha Levels.

- **Simple Choker** adjusts the edges of a matte in small increments to either shrink or expand the area included in the mask. Using this feature is a great way to gradually adjust a matte, and it can be used in conjunction with other techniques, such as the Color Difference Key, to eliminate more traces of color from the edges of an image.
- **Matte Choker** preserves the shape of a matte while filling sporadic transparencies that may occur in opaque regions of an image. Use softness values to adjust the spread of pixels added to an image and choke controls to determine the spread of the matte overall (negative values spread the matte, while positive values "choke" it — preventing it from expanding). Thus, you can close unwanted holes in a matte.
- **Alpha Levels** increase or decrease the transparency by changing the values defined for pure black or white areas of a matte. Using this tool, you can make areas that were previously gray or semitransparent into ones that are more or less black and white (transparent or opaque).

To make your compositing efforts worthwhile, you need to have multiple images that can be arranged in defined orders, or layers, one on top of the other.

UNDERSTANDING LAYERS

Working with layers in After Effects is similar to working with layers in an NLE, such as Final Cut Pro, Premiere, or Avid. By stacking layers in the Timeline, you can composite elements or join graphics into a composition, adding animations and effects over time.

Show only ALPHA channel (Shift: unmultiplied color channels)

● 15.7

Matte Tools	▶	**Matte Choker**
Paint	▶	**Simple Choker**
Perspective	▶	

● 15.8

In After Effects, you choose to create five different types of layers (15.9). By choosing to create one of these layers, you are also selecting the type of properties you want available for that layer and, in some cases, interactions that affect multiple layers in your composition. By choosing Layer→New from the top menu, you can create a Solid, Light, Camera, Null Object, or Adjustment Layer.

The first, and most common, type of layer you can create is a *solid*. You use this layer type the most, because all your graphics fall into this category. When you begin a project and import your graphics, each of these images is going to create its own solid layer when added to the Timeline. All of your solid layers contain the same set of properties that can be modified, such as position, scale, rotation, and opacity, and each of these layers may also have effects applied to them. The dialog box that opens when you create a new solid layer (Layer→New→Solid) allows you to specify the Width, Height, Units (pixels, inches, millimeter, or % or composition), and color for the layer. You may also simply click the Make Comp Size button to automatically create a layer that is the same dimensions as the composition in which you are working.

Solids may be either two-dimensional or three-dimensional, depending on the needs for your composition and the effects you want to apply to them. By clicking on the 3D layer icon (15.10) in the Timeline properties (which looks like a cube), you can create a layer that is capable of being oriented in 3D space, adding the X, Y, and Z positions that allow

for the application of camera moves and lighting. You will probably use this feature often to add depth and complexity to your animations.

Layers that are specified as a *light* contain a set of properties different than solids. In fact, they are primarily created to affect the amount of luminance applied to solid layers. They may be applied to one layer, or to several layers at once, including your entire composition in the case of global lighting. However, they must always be applied to solids that are specified as 3D layers (15.11). This is important if lights are to be effective, because they are primarily used to create shadows and depth, which can only be created if an image with more than two dimensions is present. Otherwise, it cannot interpolate the dimensions and relative depth of a flat image with only horizontal and vertical space.

Lights can be used to create unique atmospheres for a composition or to adjust the luminosity of certain

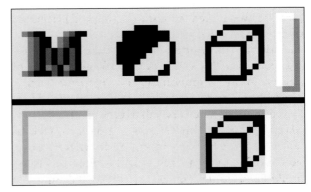

● 15.10

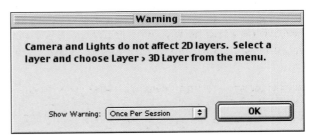

● 15.11

Solid...   ⌘Y
Light...   ⌥⇧⌘L
Camera...   ⌥⇧⌘C
Null Object   ⌥⇧⌘Y
Adjustment Layer

● 15.9

elements and graphics that need to stand out more than others (15.12). The possibilities that lighting makes available for your composition are virtually limitless. You may even think of it as similar to lighting a movie set, where the placement of each light dramatically influences the look and feel of a picture.

After you have chosen Layer→Light, the Light Settings dialog box appears (15.13), asking you to

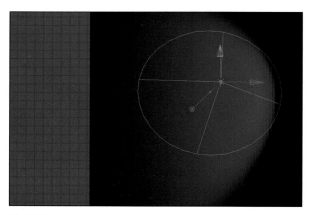

● 15.12

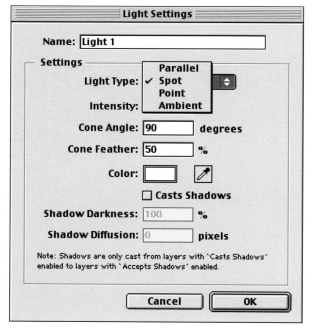

● 15.13

choose certain properties for the light you are creating. The first of these is Light Type, which is the most basic property that you can choose for a light. It determines the other properties that are available, by "graying out" those options in the dialog box that do not apply. The choices include Spot (default), Parallel, Point, and Ambient. You might guess from the name what kind of lighting each of these represents. *Spot* creates a directed beam of light, similar to a spotlight thrown onto a stage performer in a theater. *Parallel* creates a directional beam from a source that has infinite distance, which is different than a spot light that has a movable source. *Point* shines an omni-directional light from a single source, similar to a light bulb. *Ambient* light shines a light over the entire scene, changing the overall brightness without casting shadows.

Next, you can choose the intensity, cone angle, and cone feather. These affect the brightness level, spread of the beam, and softness of the edges, respectively. Added to this are the Shadow Darkness and Shadow Diffusion options, which are relevant to light layers that are not ambient and have the "cast shadows" check box selected. Opening the Options tab for your light layer reveals these choices if you want to make modifications at a later time (15.14).

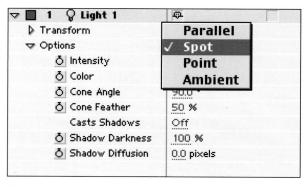

● 15.14

One of the new features added to After Effects 5.5 is the ability to create color shadows that cast colored light onto another layer, often creating a stained-glass effect. This can be done by adjusting the Light Transmission property for a solid layer that sets the percentage of light capable of shining through it. By placing a light behind the layer and turning on the light's Cast Shadows option, a unique effect can be achieved.

Camera is another type of layer you can use in After Effects (15.15), which can be used to view 3D layers with the angle and distance of a particular lens. They can also be animated to move around a scene or incorporate camera data from an application like Maya. When you create a new camera (Layer→New→Camera), you can select a number of presets or specify many properties that affect the ways you view a scene, including the Film Size, Zoom, Angle of View, Focal Length, Focus Distance, Aperture, F-Stop, and Blur Level, in addition to selecting special units of measurement. Cameras are great for compositing with several 3D layers, and you may want to try them out as your experience with the application grows.

The next type of layer that can be created is a null object. These are invisible layers with all the properties of an ordinary layer (except opacity), which can be used as a "parent" to other layers. By creating a null object and adjusting its properties, you can manipulate the attributes of other layers that are associated with it. For example, you can create a null object that would allow you to change the position of several layers at one time, by linking them to the null object and then changing its position. Because the null object is invisible, the only changes are going to be seen with the visible layers.

The last layer type is an *adjustment* layer (15.16), which is essentially the same as an adjustment layer in Photoshop. In fact, you can import adjustment layers into After Effects from Photoshop. The benefit of an adjustment layer is that you can apply effects or changes directly to it, affecting all layers beneath it in the composition. Because the layer is invisible, adding an effect or other adjustment is only seen in layers that have already been created. Adjustment layers are great for making changes to several layers at once, and there are going to be many instances where you can benefit from using them. Properties for an adjustment layer can be animated like other layers to provide precise control over changes.

In addition to the layers and properties mentioned, images composited in After Effects as solids may also

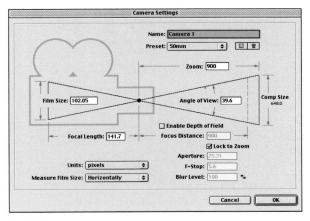

● 15.15

Layer Effect Animation View Window Help

New	▶	Solid...	⌘Y
Layer Settings...	⇧⌘Y	Light...	⌥⇧⌘L
Open Layer Window		Camera...	⌥⇧⌘C
Open Source Window		Null Object	⌥⇧⌘Y
Mask	▶	Adjustment Layer	
Quality	▶		

● 15.16

contain layer modes (15.17), similar to Photoshop, that alter the way layers interact with each other. The best way to determine the results of a particular mode is to use trial and error, testing each of the modes that sound interesting to you. A few of the more popular options available for you to choose include:

- **Normal** (default) composites the layer on top of the one beneath it.
- **Dissolve** uses layer transparency to replace colors from the layer on top with the one beneath it.
- **Darken** displays the darker of two pixel values when comparing layers.
- **Multiply** multiplies the color values of the two layers and then divides them by either an 8- or 16-bit pixel value (based on the mode you are working in), creating altered colors that are not brighter than your source.
- **Add** combines the color values of the selected layer with the one beneath it, creating lighter colors, which do not change the values of pure black or pure white.
- **Lighten** compares the pixel color values of the two layers and displays the lightest ones.
- **Screen** multiplies the opposite brightness values for your layers and displays a result that looks like you have superimposed two photo negatives, although the result is not darker than the original source image.
- **Overlay** mixes the colors of each layer together.
- **Soft Light** actually darkens or lightens an image depending on the grayscale values of an image, similar in principal to adding a diffused spotlight on the layer.
- **Hard Light** is similar to shining a hard spotlight on a layer, which either multiplies or screens the colors based on their relative grayscale values.
- **Difference** subtracts the color values of the layers.
- **Hue** creates colors with luminance and saturation values of the combined layers, while maintaining the original hue.
- **Saturation** creates colors with the luminance and hue of the combined layers, while maintaining the original saturation.

✓ **Normal**
Dissolve
Dancing Dissolve

Darken
Multiply
Linear Burn
Color Burn
Classic Color Burn

Add
Lighten
Screen
Linear Dodge
Color Dodge
Classic Color Dodge

Overlay
Soft Light
Hard Light
Linear Light
Vivid Light
Pin Light

Difference
Classic Difference
Exclusion

Hue
Saturation
Color
Luminosity

Stencil Alpha
Stencil Luma
Silhouette Alpha
Silhouette Luma

Alpha Add
Luminescent Premul

● 15.17

- **Color** preserves the luminance of underlying layers while combining the hue and saturation.
- **Luminosity** creates colors with the luminance values of the layers, while preserving the hue and saturation, the opposite of the Color option.

In addition to stacking layers, creating links between objects, and moving graphics across the screen using keyframes, another major advantage of After Effects is the ability to animate specific properties for each layer. This includes using keyframes to vary the amount of transparency, or adjusting the scale and rotation of an object over time (15.18). It also includes the use of new features such as parenting and expressions.

The parent-child relationship between layers allows you to make adjustments (or animations) for one layer that cause the designated child layer to move relative to its parent (15.19). This parent-child relationship is great for animations that require objects to be joined to each other, such as an animation of a walking figure that has graphics composing its jointed limbs. By using a parent layer that moves and assigning child relationships with other layers, these graphics can be grouped together and moved simultaneously, without the need for more keyframes and adjustments, which could take a considerable amount of time to animate. Timesaving features such as these make After Effects an efficient tool for animation.

In addition to the use of parent layers, the most powerful feature of After Effects has to be expressions. *Expressions* are scripts that define a relationship between two elements in a composition. Using a form of JavaScript, expressions can create complex associations, such as causing one property to adjust automatically as another changes. If you want to work with expressions, you should refer to the After Effects expression language guide for more information on working with the language. Another technique that you can try in After Effects is the use of the "pick whip," where you can automatically create expressions that link properties by dragging the pick whip from one property onto another. When you do this, an expression is generated to define that relationship. For example, linking the rotation property of one object to the opacity of another using this drag and drop method automatically creates a relationship, in which opacity changes for one object changes with the rotation of another object. If you understand the special JavaScript language used to define it, you could make more complex modifications to this expression.

AFTER EFFECTS: FLASH CAPABILITY

With the advent of After Effects 5, Flash export capabilities were added to the application. This was a major addition for many artists, who now saw After Effects as a tool for creating animations for video and the Web. Another great feature of After Effects is its ability to export links added to markers on your layers that can activate Web links, making After Effects capable of creating interactive Flash animations. Recently, import capabilities were also added to After Effects, expanding its possibilities as a tool for creating Flash work.

Flash Versions and Import/Export Capability

The following applies to both Mac and PC versions of After Effects:

- **Import:** After Effects 5.5 supports import through QuickTime, so the import is dependent on how QuickTime supports Flash. QuickTime 5 and later support Flash (and QuickTime 4 may support it as well in this context). Note that version 5 of After Effects does **not** support Flash import.
- **Export:** After Effects 5 and 5.5 support Flash version 4 SWF export. Theoretically, Flash 5 and Flash MX players should still support playing AE

○	Anchor Point	360.0 , 240.0
○	Position	360.0 , 240.0
○	Scale	⊠ 100.0 , 100.0 %
○	Rotation	0 × +0.0 °
○	Opacity	100 %

● 15.18

● 15.19

Flash export because they are backwards compatible with Flash 4 content. Keep an eye on file sizes if they are an issue for your project—it may be that when generating Flash content in AE, the file size could be different (larger) than otherwise would have been the case if it had been developed in Flash.

Adding Layer Marker Web Links

Using layer markers, you can add interactive jumps to URLs within your Flash animations. You accomplish this by adding a link to a marker that you have created at a specific point in the Timeline, automatically launching HTML information from your animation.

Creating a Web link for your Flash animation using layer markers is simple. Just follow these steps:

1. With your composition open, select a point in your Timeline where you want to place the marker. This is where the action that launches the URL is going to occur.
2. Next, choose Layer→Add Marker (15.20).
3. Double-click the marker in your Timeline, which opens a new Marker dialog box.

4. In this box (15.21), enter information for your Web links, including the URL and Frame Target. Some frame targets may include: _blank, _parent, _self, _top, _level0, and _level1.

The effects of your Web links can be seen when you play the animation with an active Internet connection on your computer.

Importing Flash

With the release of After Effects 5.5, you are now capable of importing native SWF Flash files. Importing a Flash file is similar to importing any other graphic or video clip. However, when working with a Flash file, you are only able to modify the stand-alone SWF file and not the original project, with layers and keyframes still in place.

To import an SWF Flash file, follow the steps below:

1. Open the After Effects application by clicking on the appropriate icon.
2. Choose File→Import→File (15.22) and select an SWF file.
3. Make sure that "Import As: Footage" is selected.
4. Click Import to bring the file into After Effects.

Although you do not have many options for manipulating a pre-existing Flash file, many more options are available when exporting the file.

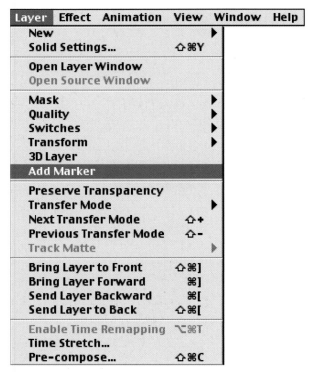

● 15.20

● 15.21

● 15.22

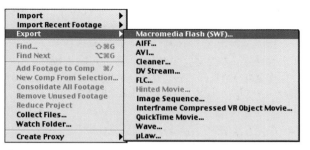

Exporting Flash

Any of your compositions can be exported to the SWF Flash format. However, remember that not all graphics and effects are capable of being vectorized, and the composition you export to SWF may not perform well if you plan to go out to the Web. On the other hand, anything you create specifically for broadcast video is not restricted by the same bandwidth constraints as files that are destined for the Internet. If at some point you want to cross-purpose your After Effects composition for Web and video, it's a good idea to keep the trade-offs between fancy effects and bandwidth in mind.

If you want to keep the file size for your Flash animation down to a manageable size for the Web, make sure that you prepare elements before working with them in After Effects. Therefore, create as many of your graphics as possible, utilizing vector images, either from Photoshop, Illustrator, Freehand, or another application. This includes graphics created in After Effects, which works with its own native vectors for creating solids and other shapes. If you do not create images that can be vectorized (such as bitmap, raster graphics, and motion blur effects), After Effects requires the remaining images to be rasterized using JPEG compression. This adds significantly to the final file size, and in many cases can make it unmanageable for the Web. While exporting, you may also choose to ignore those elements that are not capable of being properly vectorized. In addition, all your audio is exported as MP3 files, which is the same format used by the Flash application. If your video is intended for broadcast, make certain to select the highest output settings for your Flash file. You can always come back later and re-export the composition for use on the Web.

To export an animation as an SWF Flash file, follow the steps below.

1. After you have chosen the composition you want to export, select File→Export→ Macromedia Flash (SWF) (15.23).
2. Choose a name and location for the file you want to create.
3. Click the Save button (15.24).
4. In the SWF Settings window (15.25), specify the options you want for your Flash animation. If you are exporting your animation for video, you should choose the highest quality settings

● 15.23

● 15.24

● 15.25

possible for the file. For JPEG Quality, choose "10" (with Maximum in the drop-down list) and set audio to stereo 44.1 kHz at the highest bit rate (if your project includes audio).

5. Click OK to complete the settings and create the SWF file.

You are asked to specify several options for your SWF settings. The general categories include Images, Audio, and Options, with a few options beneath each one:

- **JPEG Quality** is a number that indicates the image quality of the rasterized graphics in your composition. You can either type a number or move the slider to the desired setting. This setting is only pertinent if you have chosen the *Rasterize* option from the Unsupported Features drop-down list. The *Ignore* option takes all the frames and effects that cannot be vectorized and excludes them from the final Flash composition.
- **Audio** (15.26) specifies quality settings for the MP3 file generated in the SWF. This includes settings for *Sample Rate* (11.025, 22.050, or 44.100 — "CD" quality), *Channels* (Mono or Stereo), and *Bit Rate*. The default for Bit Rate is Auto, although there is a wide range of choices beginning at 24 Kbps to 56 Kbps. Leaving the default setting (Auto) is often best because this setting optimizes the file for the smallest size, given the current Sample Rate and Channel settings.
- **Loop Continuously** specifies whether you want the Flash animation to loop continuously as it plays back. Make sure to check this box if you

are going to create HTML that tells your flash animation to loop.

- **Prevent Import** is an option that prevents someone from importing the SWF file into an editing application like After Effects or Macromedia Flash.
- **Include Object Names** creates layers, masks, and effects in your SWF file that have the same names as those in your After Effect's composition. This is useful for any future editing you may want to do with the animation.
- **Include Layer Marker Web Links** specifies that you want the layer markers you created to link to URLs on the Web.
- **Flatten Illustrator Artwork** specifies that you want vector images created in Illustrator to be flattened and simplified for export as Flash vectors, to reduce file sizes.

In the next section, we discuss basic considerations for putting together a new composition in After Effects.

STEP BY STEP: WORKING WITH COMPOSITIONS

A new composition is required for each new animation sequence that you create. It consists of a Preview window and a corresponding Timeline that holds all your layers. Before you can start work on a new composition, you need to select a few important settings, which are often determined by the graphics and video material you are working with.

SETTING PREFERENCES

After launching the After Effects application, you need to create a new Composition and specify some settings before you are able to create a new animation:

1. Open the After Effects application.
2. Choose Composition→New Composition, which launches the Composition Settings window.

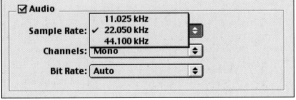

● 15.26

3. Type a name for your composition at the top of the window (15.27).

4. You may select a preset canvas size for your composition using the Preset drop-down list, or you can type in the exact dimensions using the Width and Height fields provided. Select the check box "Lock Aspect Ratio to 3:2" if you want your dimensions to always be compatible with the standard ratio for television images. If you select a preset from the drop-down list (15.28), all the settings (with the exception of the quality and durations) are selected for you.

5. For the Pixel Aspect Ratio drop-down list (15.29), select the setting appropriate to your output format. Doing this ensures that all square and non-square pixel elements are compensated for, prior to output to your destination format. For example, if you are creating an animation that is intended for D1/DV NTSC, select that option. If you choose square pixels, it is assumed that the animations you create are intended solely for a computer monitor. Otherwise, you are going to see visible distortion when viewed on a television, because of the difference between pixel ratios (discussed in Chapter 3, "Working with Television Display").

6. Choose a Frame Rate that is appropriate for your output format. The default is sometimes set to 30 frames per second, however, you may

Custom

Small, 160 x 120
Medium, 320 x 240

NTSC, 640 x 480
NTSC, 648 x 486
✓ NTSC DV, 720 x 480
NTSC DV Widescreen, 720 x 480
NTSC D1, 720 x 486
NTSC D1 Square Pix, 720 x 540
PAL D1/DV, 720 x 576
PAL D1/DV Square Pix, 768 x 576
PAL D1/DV Widescreen, 720 x 576

HDTV, 1280 x 720
D4, 1440 x 1024
Cineon Half, 1828 x 1332
HDTV, 1920 x 1080
Film (2K), 2048 x 1536
D16, 2880 x 2048
Cineon Full, 3656 x 2664

● 15.28

Composition Settings

Composition Name: AE_Comp

Basic / Advanced

Preset: NTSC DV, 720 x 480
Width: 720
Height: 480   ☑ Lock Aspect Ratio to 3:2
Pixel Aspect Ratio: D1/DV NTSC (0.9)   Frame Aspect Ratio 27:20
Frame Rate: 29.97 Frames per second

Resolution: Full   720 x 480, 1.3M per 8bpc frame
Start Timecode: 0;00;00;00   Base 30drop
Duration: 0;00;10;00   is 0;00; 10;00 Base 30drop

Cancel   OK

● 15.27

Square Pixels

✓ D1/DV NTSC (0.9)
D1/DV NTSC Widescreen (1.2)
D1/DV PAL (1.07)
D1/DV PAL Widescreen (1.42)
Anamorphic 2:1 (2)
D4/D16 Standard (0.95)
D4/D16 Anamorphic (1.9)

● 15.29

want to select a different value if your output is intended for television or for the Web. For example, if you are producing animations for television, you should select 29.97 fps, which is a drop-frame value that allows proper synchronization between images and audio that are intended for broadcast with an NTSC signal.

7. Choose a Resolution to determine the output and preview quality of your animation. By choosing Full (15.30), you are selecting the best quality, which also requires more memory and rendering time. If you have limited memory available on your computer, you may choose to work at a lower resolution (such as Half, Third, or Quarter) and then increase the resolution when you finally output your project. You may also specify a Custom setting if you know the exact needs for working at a particular resolution.

8. Next, specify a Start Timecode if it is different than 0:00:00:00. This is particularly important if you are working with feet and frames for film, but for most projects, you are going to start at 0.

9. The last setting you need to make is the Duration of your Timeline for the composition. This is the overall duration for your project, although you may choose to specify only a particular portion of the duration when you

output your final project. Select a time that you think is long enough for your project.

10. When you are finished making settings for your composition, click OK.

Next, you need to import any files you want to work with in your composition.

IMPORTING FILES

Importing files with After Effects is simple if you have used other graphics and video applications. Just follow these steps:

1. Choose File→Import.
2. Choose the File option in this menu if you want to import only one item at a time, choose Multiple Files if you have several items to import, or choose Placeholder if you want to use graphic or video files to be replaced at a later time.
3. After you have located the file or files you want to import (15.31), you should choose the correct Import As setting, whether you are importing footage (such as a video or graphic file) or a project, which is an After Effect's composition that has its layers.
4. When you are finished selecting files, click Import to bring them into the Project window,

● 15.30

● 15.31

which is located on the upper-left-hand side of the screen.

INSERTING IN THE TIMELINE

After you have imported files for your project, you are ready to begin constructing animations using the Timeline (15.32). The Timeline is where all your graphics and video files are arranged and keyframes are added. It is where you are going to be doing most of your work in conjunction with the Preview window. Adding items to your Timeline may be accomplished in a few ways. Two of the most common methods are listed below.

Method 1

1. Drag a file from the Project window onto the Timeline window at the bottom of the screen (15.33). Be sure that the starting point for your

graphic or clip is at the desired point (which is usually at 0 when beginning a new project). If you have moved the player head to a different position, this is where the item is then added to the Timeline. Use the player controls to jump to the beginning of the Timeline if you are not already there.

2. Position items in the Timeline by modifying the position attribute in the Transform drop-down list for that particular layer, or by dragging it around the preview window.

3. Continue adding layers as you have just done.

Method 2

1. Drag and drop a file from the Project window directly over the Preview window to add another layer to the Timeline. By dragging the item around the window, it should snap to the invisible lines defined for that window (15.34). If you drop the item first, you should be able to move it around freely. If you hold down the Shift key while moving the object, you can move it in smaller increments.

2. Continue adding items to your Timeline using the Preview window.

After you have added and animated projects in your Timeline, you should preview the results.

PREVIEWING PROJECTS

After you have created a project in your Timeline, you'll want to view your project as it will appear in its finished form. Of course, rendering some animations takes longer than rendering others, so seeing a

● 15.32

● 15.33

● 15.34

complete animation as you are working on it is not always practical or possible. However, if you activate the RAM Preview Options in After Effects (15.35), you can view your animations by rendering portions of your sequence and storing them in your available system RAM. The more RAM you have available, the more of your animation you are able to view. To activate this option, simply press 0 on your numeric keypad. After you have done this, After Effects starts to render each frame into RAM. The amount of time it takes to render each frame depends on the speed of your computer and on the quality settings for your composition. When the rendering is done, your animation should play back in real-time. Again, the amount of your animation that plays depends on how much RAM you have available.

In addition to viewing your project on a computer monitor, you may also want to consider a third-party hardware card that allows you to preview your project on an external monitor. Having the ability to preview on an external monitor is important if your project is destined for television and video, because there are many discrepancies between color and composition on a TV and computer monitor that are difficult to spot unless you can preview them. For anyone producing animations for broadcast, this is an essential tool that helps avoid problems like "hot" colors or the exclusion of important sections of an animation that may fall outside the action and title safe ranges.

BUILT-IN SPECIAL EFFECTS PLUG-INS

After Effects comes stocked with many powerful and useful plug-ins for creating special effects that can be added to your compositions. Depending on whether you are using the Standard or Production Bundle version of After Effects, some of the effects may be unavailable to you. For the most part, the only major difference you might see is with the keying and compositing tools that are added to the Production Bundle. In either case, you could spend hours playing with the many fun and exciting effects that are available.

In addition to the standard effects that alter basic settings for elements like color, contrast, text, and audio, there are many other, perhaps less practical, effects that can add a great deal of interest to your animations:

- **Distort** creates a variety of warping effects on an image, which can simulate waves, mirrors, or other materials with bending properties (15.36).
- **Paint** adds a unique vector-painting tool to After Effects, which allows you to draw directly over individual frames of video in a non-destructive manner (15.37). It adds traditional animation tools, such as onion skinning, to make animating your lines easier. In addition to using

RAM Preview Options

Frame Rate: (29.97) ▾

Skip Frames: 0

Resolution: Auto ▾

☐ From Current Time

☐ Full Screen

● 15.35

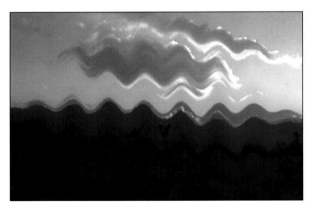

● 15.36

this effect for traditional drawn effects, you can also create traveling mattes for your composition. This effect is great to work with if you have a Wacom pen and drawing tablet.

- **Render** creates a variety of objects and atmospheric effects that you can use in your composition. It includes grids, lens flares (15.38), lightning, radio waves, and a multitude of other items that can be used for backgrounds or for adding details to your project. Try out each of the effects by playing with the attributes for each one to see the type of images you can create without the

need for manually creating textures, shapes, and other designs in Photoshop or Illustrator. This can be a great place to start if you need ideas for your composition.

- **Simulation** is a particle effects generator, which simulates the movement of small elements in different shapes and patterns. One of the typical effects that can be created is the shattering of a video image (15.39). Particle Playground handles the broader animation of the individual pieces automatically, eliminating the need to keyframe every element and creating a natural, random motion.
- **Stylize** adds many of the effects you have come to know through Photoshop. With this effect, you can simulate the look of brush strokes and embossing, or create mosaic and tile patterns from your images. These are effects that require a suitable justification for being effective. When overused (like many of the other effects mentioned), these effects can look amateurish, so make sure to apply these with moderation.

Although the effects mentioned above are capable of a great deal of variety and sophistication, other effects may work better for your project. You may be

● 15.37

● 15.38

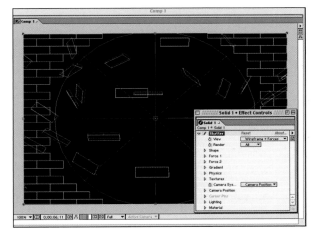

● 15.39

trying to achieve a particular effect that cannot be accomplished satisfactorily by using After Effects. In this case, you should think about expanding the After Effects palette with third-party plug-ins.

THIRD-PARTY SPECIAL EFFECTS PLUG-INS

There are a number of third-party special effects plug-ins available for After Effects.

Delirium

Digieffects (www.digieffects.com) has a nice selection of plug-ins for After Effects, including a set called Delirium, which is representative of the wide array of third-party effects that are available for use with After Effects (15.40). By selecting one of these filters and adding it to your composition, you can achieve extraordinary results that range from simulations of natural environmental effects to the creation of completely unreal designs. Within each of these effects are incredibly precise controls, which affect attributes like the size and generation of elements.

The following are only a few examples of the effects available with the set of Delirium plug-ins.

Bubbles are a unique effect that can be subtle, when used sparingly in a water scene for example, or overwhelming when applied as a transition between scenes (15.41, 15.42). It is best to use this in places where the transparency can be seen, such as against a darker backdrop.

Electrical Arcs can produce that sci-fi look that can be seen in movies, such as *Star Wars*, or to simulate a more terrestrial version of a natural phenomena (15.43, 15.44).

Fairy Dust can be applied as an otherworldly touch for a scene (15.45, 15.46). Like the other effects

DE Bubbles
DE Camera Shake
DE Channel Delay
DE COP Blur
DE Day for Night
DE Electrical Arcs
DE Fairy Dust
DE Film Flash
DE Fire
DE FireWorks
DE Flicker And Strobe
DE Flow Motion
DE Fog Factory
DE Framing Gradients
DE Glower
DE Grayscaler
DE HLS Displace
DE HyperHarmonizer
DE Lens Flares
DE LooseSprocket
DE MultiGradient
DE Muzzle Flash
DE Nexus
DE Puffy Clouds
DE RainFall
DE Retinal Bloom
DE Schematic Grids
DE ShowChannels
DE Sketchist
DE Smoke
DE SnowStorm
DE Solarize
DE Sparks
DE Specular Lighting
DE Thermograph
DE Turbulent Noise
DE VideoMalfunction
DE Visual Harmonizer
DE Wave Displace
TILT Camera
TILT Far Light
TILT File Obj

● 15.40

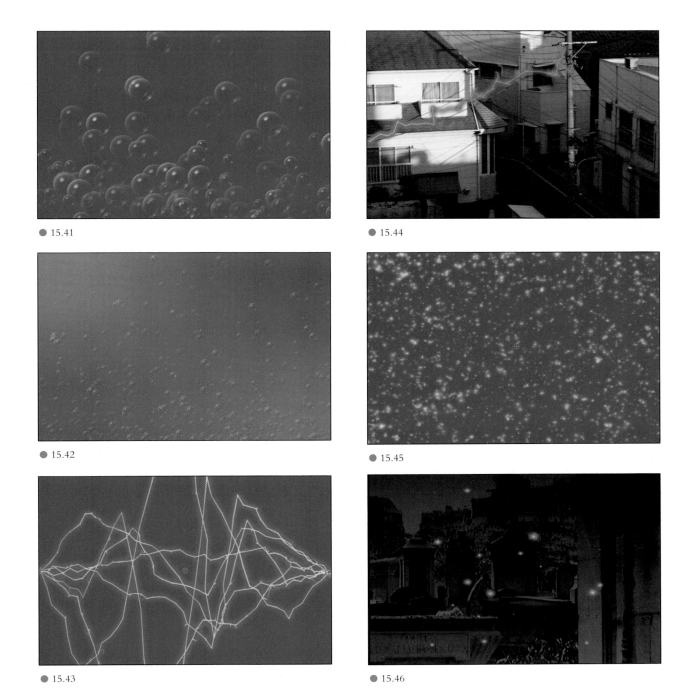

● 15.41

● 15.44

● 15.42

● 15.45

● 15.43

● 15.46

mentioned, it can be made to originate from a single point, like a wand, or it can move around the screen to follow an object.

Fire simulates a natural effect very well and, as an effect, is more useful than stock footage of fire, because you can fine-tune the look, speed, and amount of flames to fit your needs (15.47 and 15.48).

Puffy Clouds can add unique sky effects or atmospheres to a scene when applied properly (15.49 and 15.50).

RainFall can turn a sunny day into a virtual downpour (15.51). This effect can be great for matching footage that was shot on days of differing weather.

SnowStorm is capable of creating a light downfall or a heavy blizzard (15.52). The wind speed can be varied to make it drift, or it can be made to pile up on other graphic layers.

● 15.47

● 15.49

● 15.48

● 15.50

Thermograph creates the look of scientific footage or futuristic spy movies by creating the appearance of video images based on the heat (in this case, light) given off by an object (15.53).

Cinelook

Another useful third-party plug-in is called Cinelook, also from DigiEffects (15.54).

With this set of filters, you can make your video clips take on the look and attributes of various film stocks

● 15.53

● 15.51

● 15.52

● 15.54

(15.55). Cinelook is great for merging video with material that originated on film, or for achieving a more theatrical look for your DV footage. Cinelook provides a good way of testing out new tones and colors for your video footage and expanding the mood and atmosphere for your project. Also, it can add the appearance of film motion to video, using an effect that blurs movement slightly between frames, simulating the 3:2 pull-down effect that is used when transferring film to video.

Cinelook includes the ability to include film "damage" with your video. This creates the look of old or abused film prints, simulated with scratches, dirt, or stains that would ordinarily appear after years of mistreatment (15.56).

This section has only been a brief look at the many plug-ins that are available for you to purchase and add to your After Effects arsenal. Just remember to keep the theme of your project in mind when using them and avoid going crazy with effects and aesthetics that do not complement your material.

SUMMARY

Although we have attempted to cover a wide range of After Effects' capabilities in the course of a single chapter, many more features are out there to be explored. After you have made the leap into using this powerful application, you may find it difficult to tear yourself loose. Like Flash and Photoshop, After Effects offers incredible possibilities for a creative mind.

● 15.55

● 15.56

int Royale's

CD/12" Cover

VHS Cover

game.co.uk

MICROSITE

MINTY
H: 11"   W: 13kg
SPEED: 200 Mph

Complete your collection of 43 cards
when you play the Mint Royale Star
Island web game at:

www.mintroyalegame.co.uk

"SHOW ME"

PLAY THE GAME

Play Online   Send Message   Buy Toys   Banners   Play Video

Download Game

PLAY THE VIDEO GAME... Mint Royale's
AND SEE THEM ALL!

SCORE PAGE

VIDEOGAME

Arcade game.
Contains hidden card game.

Data Capture

Cheats

CARDGAME

43 cards to download and print.

MINTY
70

Print Cards

Rules

Card Case

MINISAURUS
50

Chapter 16

Cross-Purposing Flash for Web, TV, and DVD

Cross-media delivery is an excellent motivation for incorporating Flash into the production process —
elements from the TV job can be used online in e-cards, site design, screensavers, mobile devices, and so on.

MARK SIMPSON, SIXTY40

Increasing numbers of developers, authors, and animators are discovering that Flash is very powerful for developing content in a variety of directions.

One of the most interesting directions you can go with video generated from Flash is DVD, because a new crop of powerful, affordable DVD tools are increasingly giving DVD authoring capability to a wide variety of studios and individual artists. In this chapter, we'll introduce some DVD basics and authoring techniques, and then look at other concurrent delivery methods, such as Web-based games.

BENEFITS OF CROSS-PURPOSING

For the purposes of this chapter, we define *cross-purposing* content as the process of designing a project from the ground up with a variety of delivery options in mind.

When considering the possibilities of cross-purposing content, a variety of benefits become apparent, depending on your original goals:

Maximizing budget and resources: Whether you're an ad agency or an individual artist, Flash enables you to deliver on the Web, TV, and DVD by utilizing content from one starting point, without having to start completely from scratch for each new medium. If you're competing for business on a tight budget, having the ability to offer more delivery options for less than they would cost separately can be advantageous.

Reaching a wider audience: With the same essential content, Flash gives you the flexibility of reaching a wider audience than if you were developing for only one medium. You have a suite of options for the client to consider, where they can pick and choose which mediums to deliver to without necessarily having a big impact on the bottom line. They come in the door wanting to do a 30 second television spot, and the same file could be adjusted and delivered on the Web — at a better quality than if traditional video had been used for Web delivery.

New promotional/revenue opportunities: When your starting point is Flash, the medium is an ideal way of setting the stage for promotions. For example, your primary goal may be delivering an animated segment on television or on the Web. But you could also take the video and develop a DVD for fans, or a portfolio DVD to showcase the studio's offerings. The promotional potential of content developed with Flash is a publicist's dream, because it can go in so many directions — even if it's just being given away at conventions on business card CDs.

DVD DELIVERY FAQ

Here we address some frequently asked questions about DVD authoring.

Q: Is it difficult to go from Flash to DVD?

A: No. After exporting the video, you encode the video into MPEG-2 format and use a DVD authoring application to create menus that link to the video content.

• TABLE 16.1: CAPACITIES OF VARIOUS DVD FORMATS

FORMAT	APPROX. CAPACITY	# OF SIDES	# OF LAYERS
DVD-5	4.7 gigabytes	1	1
DVD-9	9 gigabytes	2	1
DVD-10	9 gigabytes	1	2
DVD-18	18 gigabytes	2	2

DVD used to be limited to Hollywood production studios with large budgets, but new tools are making it an affordable possibility for many. A new generation of independent DVD authors are using tools, such as DVD Studio Pro, and releasing professional DVD titles. Unique DVD features, such as subtitles or multiple camera angles, can drive some of the interest in the medium. For example, a content provider could expand their reach into new markets by adding multiple-language content to their DVDs.

Q: How is DVD different than regular video?

A: In a sense, DVD is regular video, but it's compressed. To fit two hours of video on one side of a disc, DVD pioneers developed the compression to get maximum quality with minimal file size. DVDs also allow you to add interactive choices, which set it farther apart — and with the rise of DVD movie rentals, people are starting to appreciate and expect interactivity. You can make a DVD that would behave literally like a VHS tape — you put in, press play, and see the video. But one of the first things that make DVD fun (and powerful) is the DVD menu, where you get to add in all the extra options that the audience can choose. Some of the "special" offerings of DVD include the ability to switch between multiple camera angles, multiple audio tracks, subtitles, and other features.

Q: Can this all be done in-house?

A: Yes, all of it or at least most of it depending on the quality you need for your end result. It might be good to outsource certain aspects of a DVD project, such as a video interview, for example, with a production company. Theoretically, you can hook up a Mini-DV camcorder and do it in the conference room, but if you're going for higher quality, you probably want to get the video with professional lighting, and so on. You may also want to outsource the video encoding. When you deliver video on DVD, it needs to be in MPEG-2 format — which is actually often used to deliver broadcast television signals via satellite. As an example, the encoder that comes with DVD Studio Pro is okay, but for the highest possible quality, you could outsource the encoding and end up with better quality and take up less space on the DVD, if you run into space issues.

Q: How much video can you fit on a DVD?

A: In general, with the current generation of DVD players, you can fit about two hours of video on a DVD. When you start adding multiple video tracks and other features, it can start filling up. Out in Hollywood, the encoders they use to develop movie release DVDs are optimized, so they can generate the highest possible quality in the least amount of space. This allows them to pack as much as they can on the DVD. There are also double-sided and dual-layered DVDs, which offer additional storage capacity (Table 16.1).

Q: What are multiple tracks?

A: Multiple video or audio tracks on Hollywood DVDs are usually special features that allow you to put interesting material running simultaneously — like while you're watching a movie, they might have a director's commentary track that you could switch to. The multiple audio tracks can also allow you to have dialog recorded in different languages. You can also have subtitles as well as the language choices.

Q: What are the options for prototyping during development?

A: If you've already been developing video files of the animation, you could just burn recordable DVDs (DVD-Rs). Another option is to make an mDVD or "Micro" DVD, using Flash to simulate the DVD interface and integrating all the video files in a self-sufficient, standalone Flash MX file (for example, `www.microdvds.net`).

Keep in mind that the recordable DVDs you can burn in-house aren't 100 percent compatible with DVD players, so if the clients have the right DVD player, you're fine, but if they have an older one, the DVD may not work. In that case, you could also provide a VHS tape. If the client doesn't need to see the full screen video and just wants to have a sense of how things are going, Flash-based "micro-DVD" prototypes would be 100 percent compatible, require no plug-ins, and could be viewed online.

Q: How does the manufacturing cost of DVDs compare to CDs?

A: It's more expensive than CDs, but not that much more. A typical run of CDs can be manufactured for around $2.00 in the United States per CD (including covers), and a similar run of DVDs might cost about the same, perhaps a little bit more, depending on the packaging you choose. To start exploring the idea of manufacturing a DVD, visit a DVD manufacturer's Web site and talk to them about manufacturing and packaging options (for example, `www.emvusa.com`).

FROM FLASH TO DVD

In this section, we'll take a quick visual tour through some of the techniques and applications that would be used in a typical scenario of going from Flash to DVD using DVD Studio Pro, which is a great choice for DVD authoring on a Mac.

First, we make the assumption that you have a Flash-based video segment to work with. Then, the overall DVD process becomes a matter of encoding the video, designing a DVD menu, and authoring the DVD.

In most cases, with any DVD project, you spend the most time developing the DVD project elements outside of the DVD authoring application. A DVD authoring program is an *authoring* environment, where you put everything together, however, you can't create graphics or edit video in a program such as DVD Studio Pro — you do that in other applications (16.1).

ENCODING VIDEO

As we mentioned earlier, it's possible to take a video segment exported from Flash and encode it for DVD without ever bringing it into a video application. You simply take the exported video file and run it through your favorite MPEG-2 encoder. But when you're working with Flash video for DVD, you'll probably want to use a video editor, such as Final Cut Pro, for all the reasons we've covered in earlier chapters.

The following sequence of events resulted in a DVD-compliant MPEG-2 video, generated from a Flash file.

1. Video was exported from Flash as QuickTime video (16.2).
2. QuickTime animation compression with millions of colors was used to provide high video quality. Using the Animation codec set to maximum quality is fairly standard (16.3).

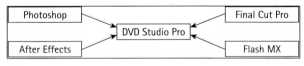

● 16.1

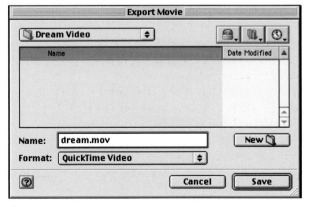

● 16.2

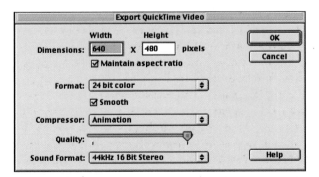

● 16.3

3. The QuickTime file was opened in QuickTime Pro (16.4) and encoded with QuickTime MPEG Encoder (16.5). (Purchasing DVD Studio Pro is currently the only way to get the MPEG encoder plug-in for QuickTime Pro.)

4. The file was exported from QuickTime Pro. Video was saved as MPEG-2 with an .m2v file extension (16.6). In general, MPEG-2 export audio is saved separately by QuickTime Pro at the DVD-compliant 48 kHz sample rate. With

this project, the CD audio was converted directly and used instead of the audio from the Flash file.

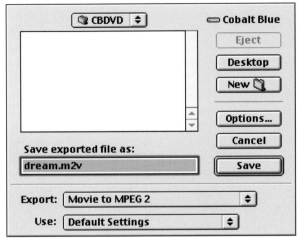

● 16.6

● 16.4

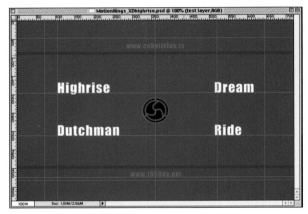

● 16.7

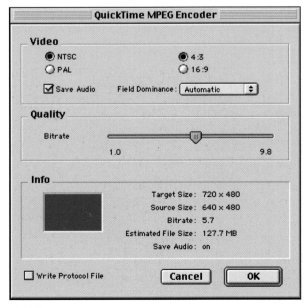

● 16.5

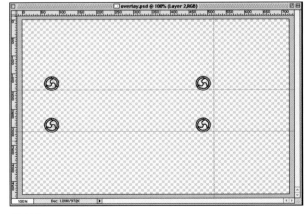

● 16.8

DVD MENU DESIGN PHASE: MOTION MENU

One of the exciting features of DVD is that you can create a DVD motion menu, which, simply put, is a DVD menu screen with video or animation in the background. To get a sense of how motion menus are used in DVD, get yourself a DVD player (or use the DVD-ROM drive in a computer), rent out a few DVDs from Blockbuster, and study the possibilities.

Motion menus involve:

- The preparation of a Photoshop file for the menu design.
- Combining the foreground menu with an underlying animation or video, usually in a compositing program, such as After Effects.
- Putting the motion menu together in a DVD authoring program.

Here is a step-by-step example of a motion menu:

1. A multilayered Photoshop file is created as the basis of the DVD menu design (16.7).

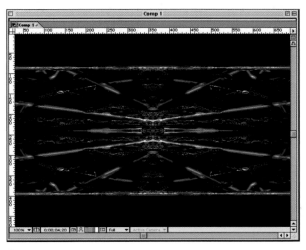

● 16.9

● 16.10

2. A separate 1-bit overlay file is created, which tells the DVD player what graphic to use to indicate DVD menu selection (16.8).

[N O T E]

Using a graphic as a button choice is an advanced alternative to the standard DVD "highlight," which often consists of semi-transparent rectangles that sit over text and indicate menu selection.

3. In After Effects, the background animation (16.9) is inserted underneath the Photoshop file in a separate layer on the timeline (16.10).
4. The Photoshop file and animation are then combined ("composited") into a single video clip (16.11). The static foreground elements form the menu choices, and the animation runs in the background.

The combined clip is exported in QuickTime and then encoded into MPEG-2. It is ready to import for use as a motion menu in DVD Studio Pro. (*Note:* Not all DVD authoring software supports motion menus. Be sure to research the tools to see if they support what you want to do. For more information, check out the Resources appendix or visit www.dvdspa.com.)

DVD AUTHORING PHASE: DVD STUDIO PRO

In DVD authoring, the goal is to import project elements such as video and then create the interactive links between a DVD menu and the content on your

● 16.11

DVD (16.12). This allows the audience to use the DVD menu to choose what they want to see on the DVD. In our example, the main menu links to four separate music videos, including a Flash-based music video. All the video clips look the same to the DVD authoring program; it doesn't care where the video came from, as long as it is encoded into MPEG-2 format.

In DVD Studio Pro, interactive links are created in the Menu Editor (16.13). The underlying motion menu clip is loaded in, and we use the overlay that we showed previously in Figure 16.8 for the button graphics.

You use the Menu editor to define button *regions*, sort of like hotspots in a Web page, but in this case it's just telling the DVD player where to show the button graphic.

Before outputting the entire project, you can preview a project. You get a simulated DVD remote control, and you can see how the DVD menu works as if you were looking at it on a television (16.14, 16.15).

After the elements are assembled and working correctly from the main menu, the content is burned to a DVD and tested. For more information on the DVD mentioned in this example, visit either production company Web site at www.cobaltblue.tv or www.1950da.net.

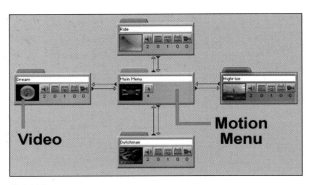

● 16.12

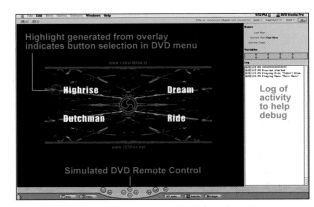

● 16.14

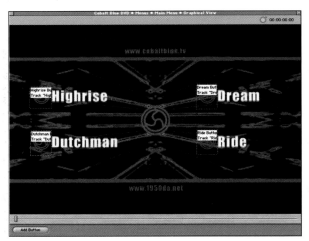

● 16.13

● 16.15

EXAMPLE: CAMP CHAOS DVD

The Camp Chaos "Best of the Web #2" DVD is a nice example of content drawn from a Web-based creative property and developed for DVD (`www.campchaos.com`). The look and feel of the project is consistent between the packaging (16.16) and the DVD menu (16.17).

The DVD menu allows the audience to interactively experience the DVD:

- **Play All Toons:** This DVD button plays all cartoons automatically, one after the other.
- **Chapter Menu:** This button leads to a screen where the audience can choose a particular cartoon to watch.

- **Special Features:** This button allows the audience to access the special features, such as alternate versions of some of the cartoons and extra videos.

The cartoons on the DVD came directly from the Web versions in Flash. They were exported as image sequences with separate sound, assembled in Vegas Video, and exported to MPEG-2. The DVD manufacturing was provided by Multimedia 2000, Inc. (`http://www.m-2k.com`).

These cartoons were all created with Flash vector art, so they scaled easily and look crisp on DVD, even on a big home theater (as professed by director Bob Cesca). The DVD is a showcase of Camp Chaos fan favorites, including such series as *Monkey for President* (16.18) and the satirical and infamous *Napster Bad*,

● 16.17

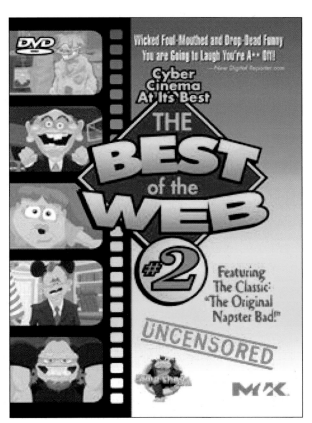

● 16.16

● 16.18

which pokes fun at Metallica's James Hetfield and Lars Ulrich (16.19–16.22).

APPROACHES TO CROSS-MEDIA DELIVERY

Say you know ahead of time that you want your Flash animation to be delivered on the Web, TV/video, and DVD. Which comes first — the small Web version or the big video version?

Although it's true you can build a Web-only Flash animation at 8 fps with a document size of 320x240 pixels and get it to scale up to video size, it's likely not going to be great quality. Likewise, if you make a solid broadcast-quality animation with lots of frame-by-frame animation at 24 fps and lots of pans and zooms, no matter what you do, it will play back a bit chunkily on most computers when you deliver it on the Web.

CROSS-PURPOSING PRINCIPLES

Cross-purposing is always a compromise. The more you compromise, the less you will need to modify in order to deliver on each medium. You have no hard and fast rules to follow, but here are some principles to keep in mind:

- Decide which medium is the most important for your project, and let the considerations for that medium drive your animation methods and technical decisions for the *base* version. Adapt the other versions from the base version.
- No matter what your medium, use the best animation and art techniques you can muster. There's no reason Flash animation has to look cheap.
- Consider creating the animation at video resolution at a framerate that is a factor of your target video framerate (for example, 720x540, or

● 16.19

● 16.20

● 16.21

● 16.22

• TABLE 16.2: CROSS-PURPOSING FLASH CONTENT

DELIVERY METHOD	FRAME-RATE	DELIVERY SCREEN SIZE	FILE SIZE	COMMENTS
Web	15 fps	640x480	1.4 megabytes	High level of compression. Interactive Link at end leading back to Web site.
E-mail	15 fps	640x480	1.4 megabytes	Standalone Projector file requiring no plug-in. Interactive link.
Floppy	15 fps	640x480	1.4 megabytes	Standalone Projector, Interactive link. Vast majority of PCs still have floppy drives, cheap delivery medium.
CD-ROM/ DVD-ROM	15 fps	640x480	1.4 megabytes or higher depending on available space	With increased space afforded by CD-ROM and DVD-ROM, audio MP3 compression levels and JPG compression in Flash file can be increased.
DVD	29.97 fps	720x480	175 megabytes	MPEG-2 video. Video exported from Flash as QuickTime animation compression, millions of colors, 640x480, exported from DVD Studio Pro version of QuickTime Pro as MPEG-2. *Note:* Original CD audio track converted to 48 kHz and used along with MPEG-2 video, rather than MP3 audio from Flash file.
TV	29.97 fps	720x480	N/A	Generate raw video file and convert to broadcast tape format for submission to music video television shows.

640x480, at 15 fps). Then, when you deliver on the Web, simply embed the movie in a Web page, and use HTML tags to set the window size to a smaller, more computer-friendly size, such as 320x240. Compress the sound by using MP3 as desired. If you use this technique, you'll find that you can really compress bitmap graphics in the Flash animation (try JPEG = 10 even), and they'll still look good at the smaller window size.

- It's always harder to scale up than to scale down, but it can be done.
- If you've used lots of fancy camera techniques in the TV version of your Flash animation, consider making a separate version for the Web and edit out the zooms and pans — be creative about cutting. Those camera moves won't play back well on most computers. Alternatively, you can export to a video format with a small window size. This way works best if you've done a lot of effects in postproduction.

- Being organized with your backgrounds, character art, and props makes it a lot easier to throw those assets into a Flash or Shockwave game, should you choose to go that route.

POTENTIAL DELIVERY OPTIONS

Let's look at an example of a project that stretches the boundaries of cross-purposing Flash content (Table 16.2). Cobalt Blue's "Dream" video was developed simultaneously for delivery on the Web, e-mail, full broadcast-quality, and DVD delivery. Initially, a shortened version of the video was developed to allow more quality relative to the intended file size for being able to e-mail it. E-mail and floppy versions had significant MP3 and JPEG compression, but the visual quality was still very nice because a lot of vector art was used.

With the Dream video, it was decided as an experiment to use a single Flash file for development of all delivery methods, rather than having different files for each delivery method (16.23). A compromise was made, setting the framerate at 15 fps, developing at 640x480 pixels. A standalone version weighing out at less than 1.4 megabytes was delivered via e-mail and floppy disk, with interactive promotional links at the end of the video (16.24), also suitable for CD-ROM or DVD-ROM content.

The fact that content can be squeezed onto a single floppy disk and also perform well on a DVD is an example of the enormous power of Flash. Thanks Macromedia!

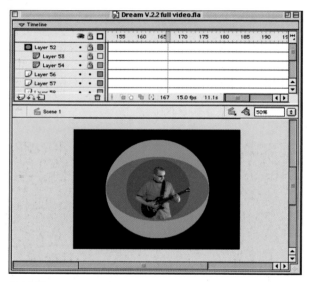

● 16.23

● 16.24

GERBIL LIBERATION FRONT

The Gerbil Liberation Front project is another example of the entire spectrum of Flash, demonstrating the extreme flexibility of the medium. The ability to cross-purpose can result in a significant savings of time and money. It allows maximum exposure with efficient use of resources, as in this example, where the same Flash project file that was used to generate the large television-ready video files was also encoded and compressed into MPEG-2 for DVD delivery, as well as in SWF format for the Web (16.25–16.27).

Beyond these familiar extremes of file size, standalone Flash files with music video and streaming MP3 were fit onto floppy disks, and given away as a

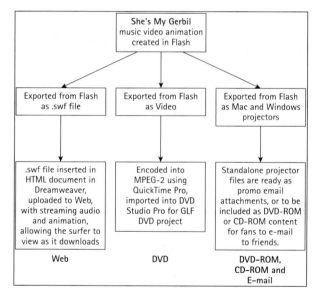

● 16.25

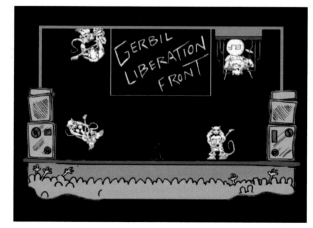

● 16.26

successful, inexpensive promotional item at record stores (16.28). The standalone version of the music video includes links at the end to jump straight to the band site (16.29) (`www.gerbilfront.com`), where fans can inquire about purchasing the DVD (16.30), and thus come full circle to the broadcast-quality version of the video.

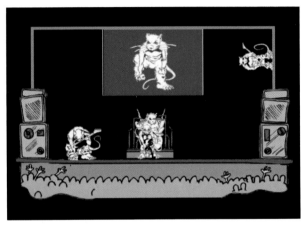

● 16.27

● 16.28

CROSS-PURPOSING AND GAMES

Consider the spectrum of cross-delivery, from Web to television broadcast, to methods of disc delivery, such as CD or DVD. In all these mediums, Flash can certainly deliver a *linear* animation, where you watch a sequence from beginning to end, such as a cartoon or promotional segment. When developing for video and TV, it is natural and desirable to plan content that has some kind of unfolding story.

But Flash also has the obvious appeal as a means of delivering interactive video games. Even if the primary delivery method for your content is something like television broadcast, a Flash-based game may be a way of enhancing the delivery of the same content in another medium. Games utilizing Flash can be delivered in a variety of mediums, as long as the mediums support Flash interactivity. Examples include the Web as well as interactive TV, mobile devices, and Sony PlayStation 2.

● 16.29

● 16.30

There are many examples of Flash projects that have been developed for television and games; it's often a natural extension of a music video or even a TV series.

EXAMPLE: MISS MUFFY — BULLSEYE ART

Miss Muffy is a Flash-based cartoon series originally developed for the Web by Bullseye Art (www. bullseyeart.com). It is destined to be a multi-part series broadcast on television.

The Web version of the cartoon opens with an episode introduction (16.31) and features a game the audience can play while the Flash file is downloading (16.32). The game occurs as introduction/preload, before the episode starts playing, and when the game is loaded, the audience is notified, and the episode can begin (16.33).

The screen size of the Web version is significantly smaller than the full broadcast version, but the same look and feel is preserved throughout the Web and TV (16.34).

EXAMPLE: CLINIC GAME — unit9 Ltd.

Animation and Web development studio unit9 Ltd. (www.unit9.com) created a suite of Flash-based content for client Domino records, which serves as a good example of the convergence of Flash, video, and games.

unit9 created a music video for the band Clinic's single "The Second Line," and the Flash-based game was designed to correspond closely to the video. The video was shown on MTV in Germany (mentioned in Chapter 1, "Flash: Breaking Out of the Web"), and the games were hosted at a unique URL specifically related to the name of the song (www.thesecondline. com) (16.35).

At the Web site, fans are given a choice to play the online version of the game (SWF loading through the browser), to download the game, or to see a QuickTime version of the video.

The downloadable version of the game is a stand-alone projector file exported from Flash in Mac and

● 16.31

● 16.33

● 16.32

● 16.34

PC format, which has an introductory screen with instructions (16.36) and then goes on to successive games screens where you can guide a character through a number of obstacles as the song plays in the background (16.37).

SIMULATING DVD IN FLASH

Over the years, as Flash has become successively more powerful, and DVD has become more familiar as a medium, it was inevitable that DVD would end up being simulated in Flash. The Macworld DVD Studio Pro Bible introduced the concept from the perspective of DVD authoring, offering Flash as a way to simulate and promote a DVD. From the other side of the spectrum, simulating DVD in Flash has become a hot discussion at the popular Flash designer's site, Flashkit (www.flashkit.com).

The arrival of Flash MX and Sorenson Squeeze has brought even more video capability and is ideal for simulating just about anything you can do with DVD, including video and interactivity.

An example of a studio doing DVD simulation is 1950da (www.1950da.net), a production company that specializes in authoring music video DVDs. They also explore utilizing Flash to offer additional promotional services to clients, including Minivids (www.minivids.com), for floppy or e-mail attachment delivery of Flash-based music videos. More recently, they have been developing a MicroDVD format, or "mDVD" for short (www.microdvds.net).

mDVD is specifically designed to allow a client to have a Flash-based version of their DVD, *even if none of the DVD content originates in Flash*. An mDVD goes beyond simulation of DVD and actually represents a scenario where DVD content can be *repurposed* and delivered as a standalone Flash file.

Our example is the Cobalt Blue mDVD, representing DVD content mentioned earlier in this chapter, repurposed into an mDVD. The original broadcast-quality music videos and full-sized menu design are reformatted, compressed, and integrated into a single Flash file (16.38).

● 16.37

Copyright © 2001 Domino Records.

● 16.35

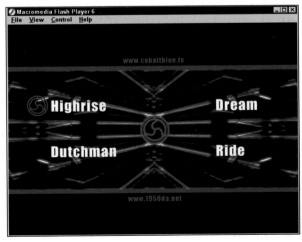

● 16.36　　　Copyright © 2001 Domino Records.

● 16.38

The original Photoshop file was used to create a 640x480 Flash interface design, which closely simulates the look and feel of the DVD menu, allowing fans to experience the music videos and get a taste of what the DVD is like.

The videos are delivered within the framework of an overall picture, making the small screen size more acceptable (16.39), and the audience can click a Return button in the lower-right corner of the screen to get back to the main menu. (The return button in the Flash project functions like the Return or Menu button on a DVD, bringing the viewer back to the main screen, Frame 1 of the Flash project.)

Just as with other forms of Flash, mDVDs can be created according to the file size and features desired by a client by adjusting compression of audio and graphics, and so on. For example, the main Cobalt Blue mDVD contains four entire music videos, representing approximately 12 minutes of video content — the screen size is small (160x120), the framerate is very low (6 fps), and the audio quality minimal (11 kHz), but the desire was to be able to e-mail a DVD. The PC projector file is 4 megabytes, about the size of an MP3 file. A higher-quality version of the mDVD was created where the video is at 240x180, each video is excerpted for 60 seconds, and subtitles were added containing the song lyrics (16.40). (To download the mDVD or for more information on Cobalt Blue, visit `www.cobaltblue.tv`).

SUMMARY

In this chapter, we've taken a quick tour of cross-purposing content, touching upon the benefits, DVD basics, cross-purposing principles, and examples of other ways that Flash can be the cornerstone for projects that get delivered in a variety of media. Starting with Flash, anyone with the right tools and approach can simultaneously deliver content through the Web, e-mail, CD, DVD, VHS, TV, you name it — even floppy disk!

● 16.39

● 16.40

Manufacturing a DVD: Overview

If you plan on releasing your video project on DVD, at some point you will probably want to consider sending a project off for manufacturing; it allows your project to have a more professional appearance, with 4-color printing available directly on the disc, and a variety of packaging options, and it could simply be a matter of quantity. Even with the dropping prices of blank DVD-R, DVD-RW, and DVD+RW media, at a certain point it will be cheaper per unit (and take a lot less time) to have the discs manufactured.

PREMANUFACTURING ISSUES

As you can see in the following section, you need to think about the differences between making your own DVDs and getting them manufactured. A third option is to make a single DVD-R of your own, but then have someone else make copies for you. And as with CDs, you can get special duplicators and printers that can print in four colors on specially prepared blank DVD media (www.primera.com). The question of which method of delivery may depend on how important the appearance of the final disc is.

In general, having a DVD manufactured results in the highest quality. Here are several issues to consider about the process:

- **Encoding:** Even though you can do your own MPEG-2 encoding, you may want to consider having a studio encode it for you. In general, a

high-end hardware-based encoder is capable of squeezing out a higher amount of quality at the same file size. But check to see if they're using anything special — they may be using the same tools you are! We suggest that if you have a chance, hire out your encoding, have the studio give it their best shot on a test sequence and make you a reference DVD-R, and compare it to your own in-house capability.

- **Submission format:** When you want to send a project off for manufacturing, traditionally DVD projects are burned to DLT tape (Digital Linear Tape), and generally, on Type III DLT media. A DVD authoring program, such as DVD Studio Pro or DVDit, will have the ability to burn directly to DLT tape, and DLT drives typically require a SCSI connection.

- **Compatibility:** A big reason that many people wind up getting DVDs manufactured is that manufactured DVDs are 100 percent compatible with DVD players. If you burn your own DVDs, they are less compatible (roughly speaking DVD-R discs are 90 percent compatible, DVD-RW are compatible with about 80 percent of players, and DVD+RW discs are more in the range of 70 percent compatible — these numbers will improve as more new players come out and as more people buy the DVD+RW-compatible DVD players from Sony, Philips, and others).

- **DVD burners:** Even if you plan on submitting projects via DLT tape, having a DVD-R drive can be helpful. A DVD-R drive can allow you to burn discs and test them on DVD players, and is also an easy way to back up large amounts of data and transfer your digital video files and DVD project elements from one computer to another.

If you are shopping for a drive, make sure that you get a DVD-R drive, also known as a DVD "minus" R (although salespeople may not initially know what you're talking about if you use the minus word). Some of the DVD-R drives can also write to DVD-RW discs, which is convenient for testing. (*Note:* A DVD-RW drive will also write to DVD-R discs.)

There is a format known as DVD+RW, but for the near future, DVD+RW discs are not as compatible as DVD-R discs, so it is advised that you get a DVD-R drive. All the different formats can get a bit confusing, and if you want to dig in deeper, try visiting Jim Taylor's excellent DVD FAQ at `www.dvddemystified.com/dvdfaq.html#4.3` — even though the site is an excellent source for reference information, no one can completely make up for the confusing compatibility situation created by manufacturers of competing formats.

But if you want a simple solution, stick with DVD "minus" R drives, and it doesn't hurt to have a good, fast hard drive either. A good choice for digital video in general and DVD in particular are high-speed regular (A.1) or miniature (A.2) bus-powered hard drives. You can get the miniature bus-powered drives in capacities as low as 10 or as high as 60 gigabytes at the time of writing, and with the right one you can even capture video to it. Bus-powered drives do not require you to plug in a power supply, they draw power from the FireWire connection — they are great for sending projects, and for working with digital video or DVD authoring on a laptop.

All4DVD is a good source for Mac or PC-formatted versions of the drives that were mentioned previously, as well as for internal or external FireWire DVD burners (A.3) and various types of DVD-R media (A.4). Their drives feature the Oxford 911 chipset, which is helpful for data throughput, and are encased in an enclosure that helps air to circulate to avoid overheating in demanding situations. These are the folks that came out with the first external FireWire DVD burner; Apple has certified the external hard drives for use with Final Cut Pro (`www.all4dvd.com`).

● A.2

● A.3

● A.1

MANUFACTURING ISSUES

When you get a DVD manufactured, there are several things that you need to deal with, and the issues are similar to CD manufacturing, including packaging and disc art.

BASIC RESEARCH

It's a good idea to do as much research as you can, in order to understand the manufacturing process better. A good place to start is to visit a DVD manufacturer's Web page, where they will often have information about submission standards and packaging options, and they usually have some way to request a quote. DVD manufacturers often include direct access to downloadable templates for disc art, usually in Illustrator, Freehand, raw EPS, or even PDF format (A.5).

DISC ART

Disc art can be as simple or as complex as you want to get. As with CD manufacturing, you can choose how many colors you need to use. (In 4-color printing, 4-color or CMYK printing is "full color" whereas 2- or 3-color printing is designed to allow you to have specific background and foreground colors. The more colors you have, the more sheets of film you have to generate. Begin by talking to the manufacturer and asking them about the various options.)

You may want to download a template, develop your own art, and then have the manufacturer check it over and give you a proof before the disc is run. Unless you really know what you're doing, it is probably a good idea to arrange for a printed proof, to make sure you are looking at exactly how the color will turn out. (You can't trust colors on the screen to represent printed colors.)

In the following example, a template provided by a DVD manufacturer (EMV USA — `www.emvusa.com`) has been loaded into Illustrator (A.6). The template in this case is for a "micro" DVD, die-cut from the regular sized DVD, so the template has an indication that the cutting size is 80mm and provides a guideline for placing art.

The art was sent off to the manufacturer, and the art was checked to make sure that everything is okay.

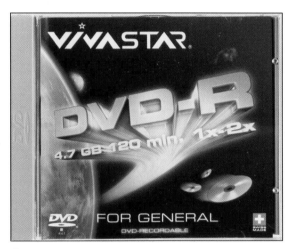

● A.4

● A.5

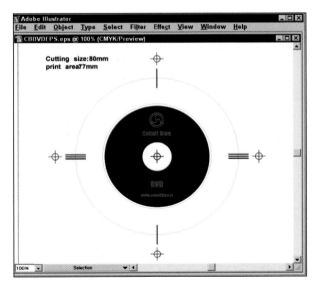

● A.6

[N O T E]

In general, it is a good idea to convert (or make) any text into outlines so that the document you are submitting is not reliant upon fonts, in case the manufacturer doesn't have the font you are using. When you convert text to outlines, it takes the editable text and converts it to letters as if you had drawn them natively.

A proof was provided in PDF format (A.7), and ultimately a Pantone booklet was consulted, so that a specific Pantone color number could be given to the manufacturer for the solid blue color, instead of waiting for a print proof, because it was a simple two-color job.

DISC PACKAGING

You can choose from a host of DVD packaging options, but the most common delivery format is a standard black Video Case (A.8), which gives you an inside clasp if you want to include a booklet. The standard case also includes a transparent sleeve on the outside, which you can either develop yourself or have printed.

Templates are also available for this art from some manufacturers, or you can make your own — a standard insert for the outside DVD cover is 10¾x7⁷⁄₁₆ inches. If you have access to a good laser/color laser printer and have some familiarity with desktop publishing, it's fairly easy to do. You can even do "full-bleed" printing (printing solid colors to the edge of

a design) as in the example below of a DVD cover insert where the 8½-x-14 inch area of a legal sized sheet is being used to place the insert design, along with cut marks (A.9).

You can fit a DVD cover insert design on an 8½-x-11 inch piece of paper if you put it up to the edge, but most inkjet and laser printers will not print to the edge of the page, or allow you enough room to place cut marks that serve as a guide for cutting.

It is probably a good idea to find a graphic designer within your company or to outsource the creation of graphics for disc art and disc packaging, but as we have seen, if you want to, it is possible to do yourself, even to the point of printing and cutting your own inserts.

DISC FORMAT

Table A.1 lists several DVD disc formats, including single sided (DVD-5), single sided/dual layer (DVD-9),

● A.8

● A.9

● A.7

and so on. This is another area in which you should spend some time talking to a manufacturer and reading up to learn about the various possibilities. If you really want to know what's going on, pick up a copy of *DVD Demystified* by Jim Taylor (McGraw-Hill). This book is an awesome reference — and you can also use its voluminous aggregate page weight for exercise purposes. (Sorry, Jim, couldn't resist.)

[NOTE]

There is a difference between the way data is stored on a hard drive and the way that it is stored on a DVD. Consequently, you may have a DVD project that is a bit less than 4.7 gigabytes on your hard drive, but it won't fit on a DVD-R or manufactured DVD. The difference has to do with the various ways of storing data/rounding off numbers, and so on. Practically speaking, if you stay below 4.5 gigabytes on your hard drive, you should be fine.

• TABLE A.1: DVD DISC FORMATS

DISC FORMAT	NUMBER OF SIDES	NUMBER OF LAYERS	CAPACITY
DVD-5	1	1	4.7 gigabytes
DVD-9	1	2	9 gigabytes
DVD-10	2	1	9 gigabytes
DVD-18	2	2	18 gigabytes

Video-Editing Suites

If you want to develop Flash for broadcast, you can do just about every step of the project in-house when you have the right equipment. You can expand your current system to include the necessary components, or you may want to build a system from scratch.

This appendix is designed to give you a brief look at some of the specific components in a representative system. We start with a Mac-based system, and then touch upon a rough PC equivalent. In this context, we are looking at systems built around DV, where the assumption is that there is not a need to work with uncompressed video. If you need to work with uncompressed video, you will need additional hardware specifically designed to support the advanced storage and throughput requirements. For professional, knowledgeable advice, try contacting Promax, a reseller that can build customized systems on a Mac or PC. This type of company can help you put together a system suited to the needs of digital video including any configuration of hardware and software you may need as well as being available for recommendations (www.promax.com).

If you have not taken sides in the Mac versus PC controversy but are looking for direction, the official author's recommendation would be to go for a Mac-based system, preferably with Final Cut Pro as a video-editing application and DVD Studio Pro for authoring DVDs. Macs are ideally suited for digital video editing and pack an incredible amount of power, quality, and usability for the price in a situation where you want to develop broadcast-quality video.

In a studio environment, if you have someone who can configure and troubleshoot, you may find it preferable to work with PCs in order to save money, especially if there are a lot of PCs there already that are being used for general office work — then the support people will only have one operating system to deal with.

But the individual or small studio user will probably be happier with Macs. With Macs, the operating system and drivers are straightforward — you don't have to deal with as many possible hardware and software combinations when installing, upgrading, or configuring systems. (You can also keep a token PC around if you need to run a PC application.) Macs are not perfect, but in the end, they are easier to deal with, and you will probably have more fun on a Mac.

MAC-BASED VIDEO-EDITING SUITE

Macs are an excellent choice for setting up a video-editing suite. Apple invented FireWire, and the FireWire interface can serve as a flexible way of capturing, storing, and delivering video. In addition to the FireWire system, you can get special capture boards that allow access to additional broadcast quality connects and decks, such as the component video connectors that you would need to connect to a Betacam SP deck.

But for many purposes, without investing heavily in high-end equipment, a capable system can be built that allows you a lot of flexibility for working with video, and you can start out with a format like Mini-DV or DV-CAM, and have material converted or send off your FireWire hard drives for direct conversion to appropriate broadcast media. At some point, you may find that the revenue coming in may justify the purchase of more advanced equipment.

THE SYSTEM

This particular Macintosh system is composed of the following hardware (B.1):

- Power Mac G4 Dual 500 MHz with 40GB and 100GB internal hard drives and 512GB of RAM (www.apple.com)
- 7200 rpm VST 75GB external FireWire hard drive, for video storage (www.vsttech.com)
- Pioneer A03 DVD-R/DVD-RW recorder, for backing up files and duplication of DVDs (www.all4dvd.com)
- Compaq DLT2000 connected via Adaptec SCSI card, for creation of DVD masters for replication (old model obtained from www.ebay.com)
- Matrox RTMac for Final Cut Pro, providing composite and S-Video analog inputs and output to external monitor (www.matrox.com)
- Sony 14" NTSC studio monitor, for previewing video from Final Cut Pro (http://bpgprod.sel.sony.com/)
- Two 21-inch Mitsubishi monitors connected through standard video card and Matrox RTMac (www.mitsubishi-monitors.com/)

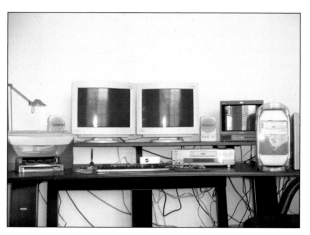

● B.1

- Sony DSR-30 DVCAM deck, for capture, record, and playback of DV and DVCAM material (www.sonyusadvcam.com/)
- Roland studio monitors, for listening to audio (www.rolandus.com/)
- Contour Shuttlepro multimedia controller, for easy navigation and editing of video in Final Cut Pro (www.contourdesign.com)
- HP Scanjet, printer, and scanner for general office duties including graphic capture, copying, and client correspondence (www.hp.com)
- Winsted studio desk, which provides the ideal amount of space and support for video systems (www.winsted.com)

RECOMMENDED SOFTWARE

We recommend the following software:

- Final Cut Pro (www.apple.com) for video editing, (includes Peak DV for sound editing)
- Adobe After Effects for postproduction (www.adobe.com)

PC-BASED VIDEO–EDITING SUITE

Upgrading or putting together a PC-based video system is certainly possible; it can be a bit trickier than working with Macs, getting the different OS versions and drivers running smoothly. But, PCs are a viable option. The determining factor in finding the ideal operating system may be determined by the video-editing software — for example, the PC version of Avid Xpress DV 3.5 requires Windows XP Professional.

Limit software installation to only what you need to do your video editing and/or DVD authoring. Don't make your video-editing system your Internet computer or general-purpose computer if you can at all avoid it. And make sure to keep a separate drive for capturing video — take a look at the drive optimization tools that allow you to optimize and defragment at regular intervals. You may be able to get away with using a computer that includes pre-installed software of all different varieties, but it's easier to deal with problems down the road if you only need to re-install exactly what you need for video editing.

Another good idea is to work with external FireWire drives for everything outside of the applications. This way, if the computer crashes, you have everything you need, safe and convenient, on an external drive that you can take to another computer if you're in a time-intensive situation.

A number of these principles apply to Macs as well, but it's probably even more important in a PC situation, with the number of potential bugs in the operating system itself, the higher frequency of viruses, and so on. Keeping any system as simple as possible in terms of installing only what is required helps you stay free from headaches. One option to consider is getting a generic custom-built PC with no "extra" pre-installed software so that you're starting from scratch.

Try to take some of these principles into account while managing your system, and also consider the idea of learning about "partitions" on your hard drive, where you can set aside the space, and have a separate installation of the operating system. Partitions can allow you to have a "fresh" installation and needed applications, and keep it separate for particular uses, and still have your original system in place as is. (But keep in mind that it is best to still have an entirely separate hard drive for capturing and editing video for optimal performance — a separate partition on the main computer hard drive is still sharing access time with the applications, operating system, and so forth.) To look further into partitions, check out Partition Magic (`www.powerquest.com/partitionmagic/`), a program that can allow you to create new partitions on an existing system.

Also, if you are using a system that comes with a lot of pre-installed software, if you don't do partitions, you may at least want to learn about everything that is installed, spend some time with tech support, and de-install as much of the software as possible to avoid potential conflicts.

THE SYSTEM

Here is a typical PC-based "starter" system that would be appropriate for running Avid Xpress DV 3.5, available from a supplier such as ProMax (`www.promax.com`).

- Pentium 4 — 2000MHz Single Processor desktop, 512MB RAM, 40 gigabyte "boot" drive
- Seagate 80GB EIDE Ultra ATA/100 7200rpm, floppy drive
- 24x10x40 CD-Rewritable Drive
- Windows XP Professional
- Matrox Millennium G-450 AGP Dual 32MB Card
- Sony 14" NTSC studio monitor, for previewing video
- 19 inch RGB black monitor
- Altec Lansing 621 3Pc. Speaker System
- Logitech Cordless Mouseman Optical Black
- Avid Xpress DV Black Keyboard

RECOMMENDED SOFTWARE

We recommend the following software:

- Avid Xpress DV 3.5 (`www.avid.com`) or Adobe Premiere (`www.adobe.com`) for video editing
- Sound Forge XP for sound editing (`www.sonicfoundry.com`)
- Adobe After Effects for postproduction (`www.adobe.com`)

TIPS

It is possible when ordering online to customize a system with extra hard drive space, a particular operating system, and other options.

In general, when putting a system together, the faster the processor, the more hard drive space, and the more RAM, the better. With a desktop system, you may want to get as fast a processor as you can and then get extra ram and hard drive space other than from the manufacturer (a way to save money). For example, you could get the desktop, then go to 18004MEMORY for the RAM and pick up external FireWire hard drives for extra space. (5400 rpm FireWire drives are okay for storage, but you'll want 7200 rpm for capturing DV, preferably with a Oxford 911 chipset for optimal throughput, such as drives from All4DVD.)

Glossary of Cinematographic, Postproduction, and Animation Terms

AC-3: Multichannel audio with up to 5.1 channels of discrete audio. Also referred to as Dolby Digital.

A/D converter (Analog/digital converter): Audio hardware that converts analog signals to digital signals.

Aliasing: Also known as "the jaggies," the undesired blocky or stair-stepping edge that can sometimes occur in digital imagery, usually the result of displaying a lower resolution image in a higher resolution than it was intended to be viewed in.

Anamorphic: Widescreen video squeezed to fit into the space of a standard-size video signal.

Animatic (Boardamatic, Story reel): A composition in Flash, film, or other animation format of the storyboards combined with the rough voice bed or music, so the director can preview how the action and shot sequence will work before refining the animation.

Anticipation: The movement a character or object makes before it executes an action. For example, before throwing a ball, the thrower needs to anticipate the throw by pulling an arm back. Or a baby may have a puzzled hesitation, then take a deep breath before bursting out crying.

Anti-aliasing: The attempt through software filters to soften jagged edges of digital imagery/video. See also Aliasing.

Aspect ratio: Relative horizontal and vertical screen sizes for a video or film image.

Assets: The individual elements that make up a project. In the context of DVD, this includes graphic, video, and audio assets that are combined to make the final project.

AVI (Audio/Video Interleaved): The most common file format for digital video on the Windows platform.

CBR (Constant bit rate encoding): Sets a fixed data rate for MPEG or other video codecs.

Cel animation (frame-by-frame): A traditional, non-digital form of animation where individual frames are hand drawn, usually some form of plastic such as acetate. The individual cels are then loaded into machinery that records them onto film in succession.

CGI (computer generated images): Generally 3D animation used to superimpose special effects or used as standalone visual content. Typical applications include Maya, Lightwave, and 3D Studio Max. Also known as CG for short (computer graphics/computer generated). May also be used in the context of creating CG titles in video postproduction.

Chrominance: The portion of a video signal that comprises hue and saturation. Chrominance does not include brightness (luminance) information.

Codec (Contraction Of Compression/ Decompression Algorithm): Codecs (for example, Cinepak, Sorenson) are unique methods of compressing video that are used with digital video at the editing or viewing stage. When you work with digital video, you can choose a particular codec that will have unique characteristics, such as the relative amount of quality relative to file size, and so on.

Component video (connectors): Component video connectors have a ubiquitous three-prong connector, used commonly in higher-end video cameras and decks, such as Betacam SP.

Compositing: The process of combining several layers of video or graphics into a flattened image or video clip. Typical application: Adobe After Effects.

Compression: Processing a graphic, audio, or video clip to reduce the file size while attempting to preserve the original quality as much as possible.

Compression ratio: The amount of compression applied to a particular file format, which reduces the amount of information relative to the original source material/signal to minimize file sizes and make the transfer of data more efficient. For example, the 5:1 compression used for DV.

Condenser mic: A microphone that generates sound by vibrating one electrically charged surface next to another.

Crosstalk (aka Bleedthrough): In audio, when sounds from one channel can be heard in the other channel — the sounds bleed through.

CSS (Contents Scrambling System): CSS is a form of copy protection used in DVD to prevent unauthorized duplication.

Cycle: A series of frames in an animation that is repeated to show movement that is cyclic in nature, for example, a walk cycle.

D1: Standard size video frame measuring 720x486 rectangular pixels for NTSC and 720x576 rectangular pixels for PAL.

Data rate: Also known as the data transfer rate, the amount of data that is transferred over a certain period of time. On the Web, it is often measured in kilobytes per second, on a hard drive. It is often measured in megabytes per second.

DCT (Discrete Cosine Transformation): The algorithm applied to compress a graphic or video frame, such as those used in JPEG files and MPEG video.

De-interlacing: The process of fixing visual leftovers that come from interlaced video.

Digital puppet: A character done in Flash or other computer animation tool. Composed of parts that are moved (like a marionette), rather than redrawing each frame to move the character.

Dissolve: A type of transition in which the last frame of one scene blends into the first frame of the next scene. There are many ways to dissolve from one scene to another.

Dolby Digital: Multichannel audio with up to 5.1 channels. Also referred to as AC-3.

Dope sheet: A sheet that keeps track of the cels that make up each frame of an animation. Also tracks dialog per frame and camera instructions.

DV: Digital video format used in the latest breed of consumer and pro-sumer cameras and decks, which contains video frames that measure 720x480 pixels for NTSC or 720x576 pixels for PAL, and data that can be transferred via Firewire for use with nonlinear video editors like Final Cut Pro or Premiere.

Ease in and ease out: Animated motion that starts out slow and gets faster (easing in), or starts out fast and slows down (easing out). This is important for most motion, which is rarely the same speed throughout the motion.

EQ Module: An audio device that enables the boosting of particular parts of the audio, such as bass, midrange, or treble.

Exposure sheet: See Dope Sheet.

Fields: Separate, interlaced portions of a frame that combine to create a complete picture.

Field dominance: A characteristic of *interlaced* digital video where either the upper field or lower field is displayed first.

Frame: An individual picture in a successive series of images in video or film, which can deliver animation or the illusion or realistic motion when displayed in rapid succession.

Framerate (FPS/Frames Per Second): The rate of how many individual frames are displayed in a second. Film is 24 fps; NTSC video is 29.97.

Gain: The volume control of a sound.

In-betweens: In-betweens are portions of a traditional cel animation that are drawn to simulate motion between significant frames. Original cels (keyframes) are given to animators who specialize in drawing the in-betweens. For example, two frames are drawn where a character is in two different spots — the in-betweens are illustrated so that the character gradually goes from one spot to another, and when the film is viewed, the motion is simulated.

Interframe compression: Video compression process in which the compression takes place *between* the frames. It focuses on what information is changing from frame to frame.

Interlaced: Video that has two fields per second, where successive *fields* are displayed rather than a full frame at a time. Each field displays alternating horizontal lines that make up half a frame.

Intraframe compression: Video compression in which the compression takes place *within* each frame. Also used for still images.

Iris out/iris in: A specific type of transition in which the scene is overtaken by blackness leaving a diminishing circle of the scene in the center, shrinking to complete blackness. The opposite transition is iris in.

Keyframe: A frame in an animation that is a key pose or point in the motion. Used as a reference point for other surrounding frames, and as a basis for timing.

Keyframing: The process of assigning points (keyframes) within an animation or video sequence where settings can be adjusted, or the process of animating by keyframes.

Letterbox: Widescreen video that appears on a standard television with black bars on the top and bottom of the screen in order to display a wider aspect ratio.

Limiting: In audio editing, when the gain of a signal is controlled so it does not go over a desired limit.

Luminance: The portion of a video signal that represents brightness.

Macrovision: A form of copy protection used in VHS and DVD to prohibit unauthorized duplication (www.macrovision.com).

Menus (DVD): Screens in a DVD where the audience is given interactive choices that allow them to jump to specific parts of a DVD.

Mixer: Audio hardware that allows sounds from multiple sources to be controlled independently from one device.

MPEG (Moving Picture Experts Group): A family of video compression standards (MPEG-1, MPEG-2, and MPEG-4) that are used for numerous video applications including DVD, CD-ROM, and the Web.

Multipass VBR: Variable bit rate encoding that is created by processing information in multiple passes, including analysis of the image before encoding to produce the best possible quality.

NLE (Non Linear Editor): A video-editing system that allows the user to adjust and reposition clips on a timeline, with the ability to preview and finalize individual adjustments at any time (for example, Final Cut Pro, Adobe Premiere, Avid). Older (linear) systems required all adjustments to be made in order, from the beginning to end of a tape.

Non-square pixels (rectangular pixels): Rectangular pixel size used by standard definition television signals, in contrast to the square pixel sizes used by graphic applications and computer monitors.

NTSC (National Television Standards Committee): Video standard used in the United States and Japan, with a framerate of 29.97 fps and a typical screen size of 720x486 pixels for standard video.

Onion-skinning: A feature in Flash that allows the user to see frames on either side of the current frame for aid in animating motion or adjusting position.

Overscan: The area of a video image that is cut off and resides outside the display area of a television set.

PAL (Phase-Alternating Line): Video standard used in the majority of western Europe, China, South America, and Australia with a framerate of 25 fps and a typical frame size of 720x576 pixels for standard video.

Pan and Scan: Widescreen video and film images that are made to fit onto standard-size video (4:3) by selecting a single part of the frame or panning over areas of the original widescreen image. For example, a movie is filmed with the long rectangular 16:9 aspect ratio, which will not fit into the 4:3 space, but as a compromise, viewers are shown various portions of the original 16:9 image, generally the center.

Panning: A cinematographic term that refers to pivoting a stationary camera from side to side or up/down across a scene.

Pitch shift: The process of changing the pitch of a sound up or down. Pitching up makes the sound seem higher, pitching down makes it sound lower.

Plosive: A sound made by the mouth and lips in which the air is completely blocked, as in *p*, *b*, or *t*.

Postproduction: The point in the evolution of a film or digital project where all the individual elements are combined and additional material is added, such as credits, titles, fades, or special effects.

Preproduction: The planning stage of a project that occurs before *production*.

Pull-down (3:2 pull-down): The process of converting 24 fps to 29.97 fps in NSTC video, as with film to tape transfer. Also known as *telecine*.

QuickTime: A common file format developed by Apple for playback and delivery of video from the

Web, disc, or hard drive. Characterized by the .mov file extension. (www.apple.com/quicktime)

Rasterize: The process of converting an image to a pixel-based format.

Rectangular pixels (Non-Square Pixels): Rectangular pixel size used by standard definition television signals, in contrast to the square pixel sizes used by graphic applications and computer monitors.

Refresh rate: The rate at which a display screen can be redrawn per second.

Region codes: Special coding applied to a DVD that specifies the regions in which the disc can be played. The world is divided into numbered regions and a region-coded DVD from region 1 (USA) will not play in another region (such as Europe). Region coding is an option determined by a DVD producer; it is not on all DVDs but is on most, if not all, Hollywood releases. There are also region-free DVD players that will play multiple region codes, but generally DVD players have one region code.

Scan lines: The individual horizontal lines that make up a video signal and comprise the overall displayed image.

Scan rate: The amount of time it takes to draw lines of information on the screen.

Scrubbing: The activity of moving an audio playhead back and forth over a timeline to hear details in a waveform.

SDI (connectors): Serial Digital Interface; a form connection for digital video that is used on high-end cameras, recording/playback devices, and capture cards.

SECAM (Système Electronique Couleur Avec Memoire): Video standard similar to PAL that is used primarily in France, as well as in portions of eastern Europe and Africa, with a framerate of 25 fps and a typical frame size of 720x625 pixels for standard video.

Secondary action: The animation principle that states complex objects are composed of parts that have their own momentum and need to be treated that way. For example, a dog's long ears will flap behind him when he's running.

Square pixels: Pixel ratio used in the creation and display of graphics on a computer. A computer monitor displays images with square pixels, while a television displays images with rectangular pixels.

Squash & stretch: The animation principle that states it's good to emphasize (or over-emphasize)

motion or emotion by stretching or squashing the object in question. The volume of the object must be preserved for the effect to work. Often used with a bouncing ball, or sudden movements. This is an application of a secondary action to a single object.

Storyboarding: The process of using a storyboard as a tool for planning the shooting or development of a film, video, or multimedia project. Individual pictures on a storyboard are rough sketches or ideas that represent flow from one scene to another, or one screen to another, accompanied by descriptions of the motion to be applied in each shot.

Subtitles: Text that is typically placed at the bottom of a video or film image, which contains language translation or information about a scene. It is possible with certain DVD applications, such as DVD Studio Pro, to create your own subtitles for a DVD project.

Sweetening: The process of improving the appeal/quality of audio in a project with the use of digital audio postproduction tools. This often involves the use of such effects as reverb and equalization.

Sync: Using a digital video or audio application to synchronize recorded audio, dialog, and sound effects with an animation or video sequence.

Transients: Waveforms that jump out of the preferred recording range and cause distortion. They typically occur in a recording environment due to the way people talk, for example, if they accidentally hit a mic.

Transition: A way to move from one scene to another, such as a fade, a dissolve, or cut.

Truck (in or out): A camera move where the camera is moved toward the subject (truck in) or away from the subject (truck out).

Tweening: The automated process of "in-betweening" in Flash. By defining starting and ending keyframes, Flash can move the object in the starting frame to its final position in the ending frame, using the number of in-between frames specified. Can also apply to changing shapes in Flash.

VBI (Vertical Blanking Interval): The time during a broadcast signal when the scanning returns from the bottom of the screen to the top; in a broadcast situation, this interval or "gap" is used for coded information such as closed captioning.

VBR (Variable Bit-Rate Encoding): Allows for an adjustable data rate for MPEG or other video codecs based on the complexity of a scene, which allows for higher bit rates in difficult areas and lower bit rates in simpler ones.

Waveform: A visual representation of a sound that shows how the amplitude and frequency of the sound wave varies over time.

Widescreen: Video or film aspect ratios that are wider than a standard 4:3 image.

X-sheet: See dope sheet and exposure sheet.

Zoom: A camera move in which the camera lens is adjusted to make objects in the scene appear to move closer (zoom in) or move farther away (zoom out). The camera itself does not actually move.

Additional Resources for Video, Animation, and Postproduction

A clickable version of this appendix is available on the official book Web site at www.wiley.com/go/ftv.

CONTRIBUTOR WEB SITES

- Atomic Cartoons: www.atomiccartoons.com
- Bardel Entertainment: www.bardelentertainment.com
- Bullseye Art: www.bullseyeart.com
- Camp Chaos: www.campchaos.com
- Debreuil Digital Works: www.debreuil.com
- Flying Spot: www.flyingspot.com
- Honkworm: www.honkworm.com
- Mondo Media: www.mondomedia.com
- Sixty40: www.sixty40.com
- unit9: www.unit9.com

FLASH REFERENCE SITES

- The Official Macromedia Flash site: www.macromedia.com/flash/
- Flashkit — Flash Community site: www.flashkit.com
- We're-Here.com — Flash Community site: www.were-here.com

AUTHOR WEB SITES/FAVORITE LINKS

Janet Galore's recommendations:

- Janet's freelance site: www.t-minus.com
- *FishBar* history at Noah Tannen's site: www.noahtannen.com
- Animation World Network magazine: www.awn.com
- RES Magazine: www.res.com

Todd Kelsey's recommendations:

- Todd's production company: www.1950da.net
- Non-profit/cultural awareness: www.cftw.net
- Flash-based music videos: www.minivids.com
- Official mDVD site (Flash-based DVD delivery): www.microdvds.com
- Headquarters of Gerbil Liberation Front: www.gerbilfront.com

POSTPRODUCTION AND VIDEO EDITING

- Adobe Premiere, After Effects: www.adobe.com
- Avid Xpress DV, broadcast/film editing (etc.): www.avid.com.
- Final Cut Pro, DVD Studio Pro (etc.): www.apple.com
- Media Studio Pro (competitor to Premiere): www.ulead.com
- Sorenson Squeeze (quality video for the Web): www.sorenson.com

- Vegas Video, Sound Forge (etc.): www.sonicfoundry.com

OTHER APPLICATIONS MENTIONED IN THIS BOOK

- Final Draft: www.finaldraft.com
- Flash MX: www.macromedia.com
- Magpie Pro: www.thirdwishsoftware.com/magpiepro_faq.html
- ScriptMaker: www3.sympatico.ca/mbelli/sm.htm
- Softimage: www.softimage.com/
- Swish: www.swishzone.com/index_frame.html
- Swix/Flix: www.wildform.com
- Toonboom Studio: www.toonboomstudio.com
- USAnimation: www.usanimation.com
- De-Babelizer: www.equilibrium.com

DVD INFORMATION

- General DVD information: www.dvddemystified.com/dvdfaq.html
- Official site for *Macworld DVD Studio Pro Bible*: www.dvdspa.com
- Good discussion board: www.2-pop.com

DVD MANUFACTURING

- Full service competitive CD/DVD manufacturing, shaped discs, 3-inch discs (and so on): www.emvusa.com
- Full service DVD manufacturing: www.sanyo-verbatim.com

DVD AUTHORING

- Music video DVD production and Flash-based mDVD: www.1950da.net
- Video and DVD production services: www.dvd5.net

HARDWARE

- FireWire DVD Burners/DV-certified Hard Drives: www.all4dvd.com
- Macs: www.apple.com
- Desktop PCs: www.hp.com, www.dell.com
- Mac and PC video editing systems: www.promax.com
- Video boards: www.matrox.com

AUDIO

- ProTools: www.digidesign.com
- Sound Forge: www.sonicfoundry.com
- Logic Audio: www.emagic.com (Note: As of July 2002, Logic was purchased by Apple.)
- Nuendo (surround sound): www.steinberg.com
- Sonex room acoustics: www.mhtc.net/~lowey/
- Whisper Room prefabricated vocal recording booths: www.whisperroom.com/
- Pure Digital Audio: www.puredigitalaudio.org/home/index.shtml
- ProRec.com: www.prorec.com/
- Electronic Musician: www.electronicmusician.com/
- Home Recording.com: www.homerecording.com/
- Sweetwater Sound: www.sweetwater.com

SOUND EFFECTS AND MUSIC RESOURCES

Web sites for CD-ROM libraries as well as for royalty-free downloadable sound effects and music:

- Sound Ideas: www.sound-ideas.com/
- Sound Dogs: www.sounddogs.com/start.asp
- Hollywood Edge: www.hollywoodedge.com/
- CSS Music: www.cssmusic.com

STOCK FOOTAGE

- ArtBeats Digital Film Library: `www.artbeats.com`

VIDEO-TO-FILM TRANSFER

- How to Transfer Video to Film: `www.digieffects.com/frames/howtotransfervideotofilm.html`
- Film to Video Explained: `www.cs.tut.fi/~leopold/Ld/FilmToVideo/`
- Alpha Cine (transfer service): `www.alphacine.com/dfilm.htm`

FLASH AND DIGITAL MEDIA BOOKS

- *Flash MX Bible*, by Richard Reinhardt and Snow Dowd (Wiley)
- *Art of Flash Cartooning*, by John Kuramoto, Gary Leib, Daniel Gray (Sybex)
- *Streaming Media Bible*, by Steve Mack (Wiley)
- *Flash 5 Cartooning*, by Mark Clarkson (Wiley)
- *Flash Studio Secrets*, by Glenn Thomas (Wiley)
- *Macworld DVD Studio Pro Bible*, by Todd Kelsey and Chad Fahs (Wiley)
- *DVD Demystified*, by Jim Taylor (McGraw-Hill)

OTHER GOOD ANIMATION AND VIDEO PRODUCTION BOOKS

- *Cartoon Animation*, by Preston Blair (Walter Foster Publishing)
- *The Animator's Survival Kit*, by Richard Williams (Faber and Faber)
- *The Animation Book*, by Kit Laybourne (Three Rivers Press)
- *The Natural Way to Draw*, by Kimon Nicolaides (Houghton Mifflin Company)
- *Alternative Scriptwriting: Writing Beyond the Rules*, by Ken Dancyger and Jeff Rush (Focal Press)

- *Film Directing Shot by Shot*, by Stephen D. Katz (Michael Wiese Productions)
- *Television Production Handbook*, by Herbert Zettl (Wadsworth Publishing Company)

FLASH ANIMATION FESTIVALS AND SUBMISSION SITES

- I Want My Flash TV: Community site with Flash showcase: `www.iwantmyflashtv.com`
- RES Fest: Digital Film Festival: `www.resfest.com`
- Dmoz Directory of Animation Festivals: `dmoz.org/Arts/Animation/Festivals/`
- Vancouver Effects and Animation Festival: `www.veaf.com/`
- AtomShockwave.com: `www.atomshockwave.com`

ADDITIONAL RESOURCES

- Film Production Dictionary: `www.filmland.com/glossary/Dictionary.html`
- Electronic Cinematography: `www.gregssandbox.com/gtech/elecinema/elcineglossary.htm`
- Video Broadcast Standards: `www.alkenmrs.com/video/standards.html`
- Pull down Explained: `www.avdeals.com/classroom/Proscanexplained.htm`
- Flash to Video cheat sheet: `www.flickerlab.com/flashtovideo/`
- Digital Video Glossary at Adobe: `www.adobe.com/support/techguides/digitalvideo/dv_glossary/main.html`
- Official TechTV site: `www.techtv.com`

Appendix E

Contributor Profiles

We want to acknowledge the people who contributed their expertise, insights, and talent to the book.

ATOMIC CARTOONS

In February of 1999, veteran animation directors Trevor Bentley, Mauro Casalese, Olaf Miller, and Rob Davies founded Atomic Cartoons, in Vancouver, British Columbia. Atomic Cartoons has produced 26 episodes of *Milo's Bug Quest* for Sunwoo Entertainment, and the full-length Christmas specials *Grandma Got Run Over by a Reindeer* and *The Gaudins* for Phil Roman Entertainment. The studio has provided over 100 half-hours of pre-production for such clients as Warner Brothers, Nelvana, and Film Roman. The Chuck Jones series *Timberwolf* and the eye-popping demo for *Atomic Betty* are the latest in Atomic's arsenal (`www.atomiccartoons.com`).

TREVOR BENTLEY — ATOMIC CARTOONS

● E.1

Born and raised in the British Columbia Interior and formerly trained in fine arts and graphic design at Kwantlen College, Trevor Bentley (E.1) has worked within the animation industry for eleven years in a range of roles from designer, color stylist, to Director. Bentley landed his first animation gig when he joined the newly formed Studio B in Vancouver, B.C. He has worked on a broad range of shows for Warner Brothers, Los Angeles; Cartoon Network, Atlanta; and Nickelodeon, New York

251

before co-founding Atomic Cartoons. Presently, Bentley is heading up the Atomic Cartoons international co-production department (www.atomiccartoons.com).

MAURO CASALESE — ATOMIC CARTOONS

● E.2

Mauro Casalese (E.2) was born in Italy and raised in Ottawa, Ontario. Upon graduating from Sheridan College in Oakville, Ontario, Casalese worked in Dublin, Ireland as an animator on the popular kids show "Teenage Mutant Ninja Turtles." Upon returning to Canada, Casalese worked at several Canadian studios from Lacewood and Studio B, to Carbunkle Cartoons where he animated on the wildly popular "The Ren & Stimpy Show" and was a writer and director for "The Baby Huey Show." He went on to direct "The Woody Woodpecker Show" for Universal Studios in Hollywood before co-founding Atomic Cartoons in Vancouver, B.C. Casalese currently heads the Atomic Cartoons Web cartoon department (www.atomiccartoons.com).

ROB DAVIES — ATOMIC CARTOONS

● E.3

Born and raised in Vancouver, B.C., and formerly educated at Kwantlen College, Rob Davies (E.3) went on to attend the first animation program that Capilano College offered in 1991. Davies was hired straight out of Capilano College by Gordon Stanfield to work on BeetleJuice for Nelvana. Before winning a 2000 Daytime Emmy award, Davies was nominated for an Emmy for the 1999 "Pinky, Elmyra and the Brain" season. He has also won a Prism award in 1997 for the "Inherit the Wheeze" episode of "Pinky and the Brain." Davies is the President and CEO of Atomic Cartoons (www.atomiccartoons.com).

BULLSEYE ART

Founded in 1996, two-time Emmy nominated Bullseye Art designs award-winning creative for both the advertising and entertainment communities. Bullseye's client list includes such diverse names as Discovery Kids, MTV, Hachette Filipacchi, The Rosie O'Donnell Show, Sony Music, and VH1. No matter what the need or platform, Bullseye always delivers inspired, daring creative along with on-budget, on-time production.

BOB CESCA — CAMP CHAOS

● E.4

Bob Cesca (E.4) is the founder and President of Camp Chaos. One of the very first Web sites to offer regularly updated Flash-animated shows and games, Camp Chaos was officially launched in July of 1998 and became an incorporated animation and film production studio in January 1999. Camp Chaos creates cartoons offering an amusing alternative to traditional entertainment in a span of time short enough to view while your boss isn't looking. The Camp Chaos Suites & Casinos are located in the Pennsylvania-Dutchy outskirts of the Philadelphia metroplex, in the small hamlet of Wyomissing, Pennsylvania. Camp Chaos also has bases in Orlando, San Francisco, and Hollywood (`www.campchaos.com`).

RON CROWN — BARDEL ENTERTAINMENT

● E.5

Ron Crown (E.5) is Creative Director at Bardel Entertainment Inc., Vancouver B.C., where he develops and implements new animation techniques for broadcast productions. He recently completed the first four episodes of his own show, *The Mr. Dink Show*, currently with Atom Films for internet distribution and The Comedy Network for television broadcast. Crown won first place in the Flash Animation category at the Vancouver Effects and Animation festival. He trained at Sheridan College in Classical Animation. Bardel Entertainment's clients include DreamWorks SKG, Warner Bros., Columbia TriStar, Disney Interactive, Fox, and Nelvana. Their contracts include feature films, TV series and specials, interactive media, and the Internet (`www.bardelanmation.com/barani/portfolio MRDINKhtml`, `www.mrdink.com`, and `www.bardelanimation.com`).

SANDY DEBREUIL — DEBREUIL DIGITAL WORKS

● E.6

Debreuil Digital Works is co-owned by two brothers, Robin and Sandy Debreuil (E.6). Before joining forces, the Debreuil brothers had been involved in computer graphics independently for over ten years. They combined resources and experience to expand into Web-based graphic services, and in 1998 began diversifying into computer animation. After winning the 1999 Real Networks Flash Animation contest with "Reelin' Around," they began to work on animations for Web broadcast. They were one of the first companies to use Flash software to produce animations for TV commercial broadcasts. Sandy continues to produce animation for both the Web and television broadcast, while Robin has become a programming guru. Visit www.debreuil.com for more details and samples of their work.

JOHN EVERSHED — MONDO MEDIA

● E.7

John Evershed, (E.7) Mondo Media's CEO and executive producer, graduated from the University of Toronto in 1981 with a degree in English Literature. He has dedicated his career to combining art, technology, and advertising to create new and compelling entertainment experiences. In 1988, he co-founded Mondo Media with his partner Deirdre O'Malley. Mondo Media's list of strategic partners, clients, and distribution affiliates now includes industry leaders such as Yahoo!, BBC America, MTV, MSN, Warner Brothers, and AtomShockwave.com. Mr. Evershed is the executive producer of Mondo Media's Mondo Mini Shows including the award winning *The God and Devil Show*, *Like News*, and *Thugs on Film* (www.mondomedia.com).

CHAD FAHS

● E.8

Chad Fahs (E.8) is the co-author of *Macworld DVD Studio Pro Bible* and a forthcoming title on Adobe Premiere. In 1998 he began an Avid editing studio in Chicago, working with established artists and producers to create exciting video and interactive forms of art and entertainment. During this time, he consulted on streaming media projects, and became adept with the new variety of video applications, including Final Cut Pro, Premiere, and After Effects, while finding time to travel and collaborate with artists in Europe and Asia. Chad has also worked two years as a producer at one of the top Internet sites, training and working with clients from companies in the United States, Japan, and the United Kingdom. Currently, Chad writes, directs, and produces a variety of projects for a wide range of clients, including Apple and Adobe.

ERIK UTTER — FLYING SPOT

Erik Utter is Chief Engineer at Flying Spot, a Seattle-based broadcast design and postproduction company. The Flying Spot team has won national recognition for outstanding graphic design and editorial with multiple Prime-time and News/Documentary Emmy nominations and awards. Utilizing and interpreting the latest technology and trends, Erik provides technical consultation on some of the more complex postproduction projects and is also responsible for leading technology advances for the facility (www.flyingspot.com).

HONKWORM INTERNATIONAL

JOHAN LIEDGREN — HONKWORM INTERNATIONAL

● E.9

In 1997, Johan Liedgren (E.9) left his position as Director at Microsoft after seven years, where he managed contracts, distribution, reporting systems, and channel Internet migration. Originally from Sweden, he began his Microsoft career in Channel Development at Microsoft's Swedish subsidiary to continue at Microsoft European Headquarters in Paris, France. Before Microsoft, he spent six years as a management consultant with different companies working with competitive strategies, advertising, and investor relations. Johan studied philosophy and sociology at the University of Stockholm and served at the Swedish School of Navy Intelligence. Johan is currently CEO of Honkworm International, an online entertainment company, and an advisor/investor in several technology companies. Johan is also on the board of directors of Loudeye Technologies. Johan lives with his wife and two sons in Seattle, Washington (`www.honkworm.com`).

DAMIAN PAYNE — HONKWORM INTERNATIONAL

● E.10

Damian Payne (E10) joined Honkworm as a creative director and line producer in early 2000. Prior to this, Damian worked in film production as a First Assistant Director for features, television commercials, and music videos. Clients included Toyota, Honda, Buick, Budweiser, Boeing, Washington State Lottery, Washington Mutual, Microsoft, Sub Pop, and Sony. Damian studied screenwriting and fine art in London before moving to the States in 1993. He enjoys the company of a three-legged dog and a pouty blonde (`www.honkworm.com`).

DAN PEPPER — HONKWORM INTERNATIONAL

● E.11

Dan Pepper, (E.11) born in Seattle, began his career in media drawing storyboards with a green crayon on his parent's basement wall. After light corporal punishment, 16 birthdays, and four years of formal training in print production and graphic design, Dan went on to earn an undergraduate degree with an emphasis in Television Production and Direction from Oregon State University. In 1988, Dan cofounded Seattle Post, now known as Rocket Pictures, one of the Pacific Northwest's most prolific creative broadcast editorial shops. Dan later joined Honkworm International as Chief Operating Officer, working with clients such as Wongdoody, MTV, Fox Sports Network, Budweiser, Nike, Nokia, HBO, Starbucks, and Warner Brothers (`www.honkworm.com`).

CHRISTOPHER ANGUS MACRAE

● E.12

A Northwest native and Scotsman, Christopher Angus MacRae (E.12) grew up in New England, and was schooled at the University of Washington. Composer, sound engineer, and an accomplished musician, Christopher is able to play almost any instrument, notably drums, keyboards, bass, guitar, bagpipes, Theremin, and the kelp horn (harvested fresh from the kelp forests of Puget Sound). His work on several video game titles for Seattle-based Zombie Studios lead to his involvement with Honkworm in 1997. Christopher's voice talent, recording, and sound effects contributed to the success of Honkworm's *FishBar* series. Christopher makes music with Psilocybernaut, an electronic duo that has recorded with DJ Spooky. He currently operates a recording studio and label, Incisor Records, on Bainbridge Island, Washington (`www.subinfinity.com/psilo.html`).

BEN PIETOR, MARK SIMPSON, MATHEW TAYLOR, SCOTT COLLINS — SIXTY40

● E.13

Sixty40 (E.13) is where creativity meets TV, interactive, animation, and sound production. It is one of the new breed of design and production houses which offers all the elements of media creation under one roof. Sixty40 was started two years ago by four media specialists who shared the vision of a creative cross media production house, and has recently been busy producing work for Singleton Ogilvy & Mather, Pepsico beverages, News Limited newspapers, Warner Music Australia, ABC TV, EMI, and Fosters. The use of new technology not only allows Sixty40 to produce creative solutions faster and smarter; it also allows delivery of an idea over various media including broadcast, video, online, and print. Sixty40 is: Ben Pietor — TV and film; Mark Simpson — interactive and motion graphics; Mathew Taylor — animation and illustration; Scott Collins — music composition and sound design (`www.sixty40.com`).

TOM SACCHI — UNIT9 LTD.

● E.14

unit9 Ltd. is a 12-person digital production company with a strong creative and technology driven
ethic. Tom Sacchi (E.14) is one of unit9's founders —
he is the soothsayer and senior project manager. Tom
studied architecture in Florence, Italy. He led the way
to locate unit9 in London, and has managed most of
unit9's key projects. His broad knowledge and deep
experience of digital media makes him an invaluable
asset in managing and developing digital projects and
"cross channel" campaigns. The unit9 animation
team merges techniques and applications across digital media: pushing Flash to its limits to make 2D look
like 3D, and producing 3D that feels hand drawn and
organic. The team picked up a D&AD nomination
last year for the music video "Clinic" by The Second
Line, while also putting out the cross platform promo
for Mint Royale's "Show Me." Other work has
included style development work for PS2's The Third
Place, and an 8 minute short for the Sci-Fi channel
(www.unit9.com).

Index

Continued

Continued